DATE DUE

NO 16 '92			
FE 24 '98			
MR 10 '98			
MR 31 '98			
FE 8 '00			

Demco, Inc. 38-293

CASH FLOW PROBLEM SOLVER

Common Problems and Practical Solutions

BRYAN E. MILLING

SOURCEBOOKS TRADE
NAPERVILLE, ILLINOIS

Sourcebooks Trade
A Division of Sourcebooks, Inc.
P.O. Box 372
Naperville, Illinois, 60566
(708) 961-2161

Design and Production: Monica Paxson
Proofreading: Joyce Petersen

This publication is designed to provide accurate and authoritative information in regard to the subject matter covered. It is sold with the understanding that the publisher is not engaged in rendering legal, accounting, or other professional service. If legal advice or other expert assistance is required, the services of a competent professional person should be sought.

From a Declaration of Principles Jointly Adopted by a Committee of the American Bar Association and a Committee of Publishers and Associations

---

Library of Congress Cataloging-in-Publication Data

Milling, Bryan E.
    Cash flow problem solver : common problems and practical solutions
    / Bryan E. Milling
        p.   cm.
        ISBN 0-942061-28-4   -- ISBN 0-942061-27-6 (pbk.)
        I. Cash Management.   II. Title.

HG4028.C45M54   1991
658.15'246--dc20   91-29705
                                                        CIP

Printed and bound in the United States of America

10 9 8 7 6 5 4 3 2 1

Contents

Part III: Structural Management

Part IV: Leverage Management

Part V: Improving Your Cash Flow

Part VI: Positive Cash Flow Management

Introduction

Cash flow management is essential to the success of every business. In fact, it is often more important than the ability to manufacture a product or generate a sale. You can lose a customer without irreparable damage. But let a gap in your cash flow cause you to miss a payroll and you are out of business.

The *Cash Flow Problem Solver* is designed to help you avoid such crises. It identifies the fundamental principles of cash flow management and tells you how to apply those principles in your business. However, it isn't a textbook designed for professionals in finance and accounting. Instead, it is directed toward the business manager whose background is marketing or manufacturing or engineering—the typical entrepreneur.

Moreover, it takes a profit-oriented approach to cash flow management. That approach centers on some fundamental financial relationships:

How does a faster accounts receivable turnover rate benefit your bottom line?

How do idle assets affect your cash flow and profits?

How do you combat a crimp in your cash flow that causes you to lose valuable trade discounts?

The *Cash Flow Problem Solver* not only answers these questions but also provides realistic examples that illustrate the actual dollar cost of cash flow problems in a business, as well as the bottom-line benefits that can develop from effective cash flow management.

The emphasis on the bottom-line benefits of effective cash flow management is designed to hold your interest in a subject that many people find tedious.

However, the *Cash Flow Problem Solver* doesn't stop there. The ideas illustrated in the book are crystallized in a set of Cash Flow Concepts to encourage you to retain and utilize them. One Cash Flow Concept may identify a basic objective of accounts receivable management. Another will provide a signal to help you avoid a dangerous gap in your cash flow. Still another may suggest a financing method that will increase your earnings. These Cash Flow Concepts have evolved from my experience with more than 3,000 businesses encountered during my career in commercial finance and banking.

Your situation is unique, but your cash flow problems are common to every business. If you understand the basic concepts, you can adapt them to fit your special circumstances. Of course, not every concept will be useful to you, but if one idea serves as a reminder that helps you preserve the financial integrity of your business or increase your earnings, then your effort in reading this book will be worthwhile.

The first Cash Flow Concept emphasizes a critical fact:

Concept 1: Effective cash flow management is essential to the success of your business.

For your business to survive, you must have cash to pay expenses and retire other liabilities on schedule. In addition, cash provides a necessary buffer to help absorb an unforeseen business crisis or managerial mistake. You can weather a wildcat strike or a severe drop in sales if you have the necessary cash reserves. Without those reserves, the same setbacks can be disastrous.

Also, cash is essential for growth. In fact, no matter how profitable your business, it cannot grow without an expanding cash flow, either from retained earnings or from a combination of earnings and cash obtained from external financing. As you will see in Chapter 13, cash becomes the limiting factor in the growth of any business.

Finally, cash is essential for achieving the profit potential of your business. A dollar held in the form of accounts receivable or inventory cannot be reinvested profitably until you convert it back into cash. Receivables and inventory are necessary parts of the cash flow cycle, but cash makes the cycle revolve.

The *Cash Flow Problem Solver* uses maximum cash generation as the guiding principle of cash flow management. Your cash flow management effort should seek the most rapid conversion of your receivables and inventory into cash. Practical limits on the conversion rate exist in any circumstance. But the effort recognizes the crucial role that cash plays in achieving the basic business objectives.

To be consistent, we should discuss the efficient use of cash as an asset similar to accounts receivable and inventory. An overinvestment in cash imposes an opportunity cost on your business when you could employ that excess profitably elsewhere. Nevertheless, don't look for a chapter on the profitable investment of excess cash. Instead, the book will concentrate on the factors that disrupt a firm's cash flow and reduce its earnings.

After all, the lack of sufficient cash is always a problem. Seldom does excess cash lead to a serious business setback.

The *Cash Flow Problem Solver's* approach to cash flow management invites you to take control of your cash flow—to exercise *positive cash flow management*. Positive cash flow management reduces the disruptions and maintains the smooth, continuous cash flow essential to the growth and profitability of your business. Although the best management effort will not provide absolute control of your cash flow, you can solve or avoid many of the common cash flow problems. Moreover, positive cash flow management can benefit your bottom line.

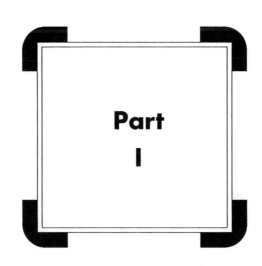

**Part
I**

The Cash
Flow
Process

Chapter 1

Cash Flow: A Practical View

The cash flow process in a business operates as a circular system of asset transformation. In simple form, the system looks like the schematic in Figure 1-1.

Figure 1-1
The Cash Flow Process

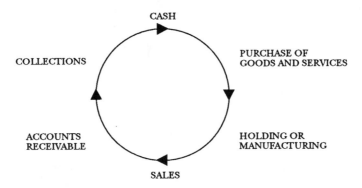

Any business begins with cash. The purchase of goods and services, perhaps coupled with a manufacturing process, transforms that asset into inventory. Each sale transforms inventory into accounts receivable. Then the collection process transforms accounts receivable back into cash. If the system works properly, the process repeats itself in a continuous cycle.

Of course, the system is more complex than the schematic suggests. Trade credit, external financing, and retained earnings increase the total resources revolving in the cycle. Conversely, debt reduction, dividends, and operating losses shrink those resources. The periodic purchase of fixed assets, which are not part of the day-to-day cash flow cycle, further complicates the picture. However, when the process works smoothly, each asset—cash, inventory, accounts receivable—moves continuously toward the next phase in the cycle.

The cash flow schematic is simplistic in another respect. It implies that the transformation process operates in a continuous, dynamic cycle. Unfortunately, the process seldom operates so smoothly. Instead, a firm's cash flow typically is erratic and subject to numerous disruptions. Cash Flow Concept No. 2 recognizes that fact:

Concept 2: The cash flow process is an erratic system of asset transformation.

For example, inventory sits as an idle asset until it is sold and delivered. Moreover, the seller must issue the proper invoices to transform sales into accounts receivable. A breakdown in any one of these tasks—the sale, the delivery, or the paperwork—interrupts the transformation process.

Similarly, until they are collected, accounts receivable serve only as evidence of the cash proceeds still due from sales. Failure to collect accounts as scheduled retards the transformation process. Since collection of receivables provides the major source of cash from operations, slow turning accounts receivable can threaten the survival of a business.

Even cash itself—the asset that fuels the system—contributes little until the business converts it into marketable inventory. The unavailability of product (because of a snowstorm that disrupts delivery of a vital component, or a strike at a supplier's facility) leaves cash as an idle asset that is no more productive than unsold inventory or uncollected accounts receivable. Indeed, cash flow management becomes a continuous effort to make the transformation process operate smoothly.

Unfortunately, even a conscientious management effort may not preclude cash flow problems. Many growing, profitable businesses encounter severe cash flow crises. If you find that statement surprising, then you probably harbor a common misconception about the actual operation of the cash flow through a business. That misconception underlies many of the cash flow problems discussed throughout the book. Neither a rising sales volume nor a profitable operation spontaneously produces a positive cash flow. The following discussion illustrates that fact.

The Illusion of Paper Profits

Dan A. Drake, a dynamic salesman with limited financial expertise, founded Drake Paper Company in 1987. Although profits were slim, the business grew to a $100,000 monthly sales volume by the latter part of 1990. In December of that year, Drake initiated an expansion program designed to produce a 50% increase in sales and place operations on a highly profitable basis.

The program produced immediate results. Sales increased from $100,000 in December to $150,000 in January 1991. As the firm's simplified income statement indicates, the higher volume generated $15,000 in earnings in the first month:

Drake Paper Company
Income Statement 1/1/91—1/31/91

Sales	$ 150,000
Cost of Sales	(105,000)
Operating Expenses	(30,000)
Earning	$ 15,000

Unfortunately, Drake was unable to enjoy his success. Despite the company's profitability, the rapid sales increase led to a *$25,000 cash flow deficit*. By the end of January, the firm was out of cash.

Before illustrating the factors that led to Drake's cash shortage, two facts about that deficit deserve emphasis.

First, the cash flow deficit was not the result of any extraordinary event. Rather, it developed naturally from the predictable relationships among the major elements in Drake's cash flow.

Second, the deficit came as a complete surprise to Dan Drake. He erroneously assumed that a profitable operation automatically produces a positive cash flow. He suffered from the "illusion of paper profits."

Drake forgot that the income statement is an accrual statement. It records sales when they occur, not thirty days later, when the business collects the accounts receivable that proceed from the sales.

Similarly, expenses accrue as incurred, although a company may pay those obligations in some subsequent period. Some expenses, such as depreciation and amortization of prepaid items, represent prior cash disbursements. These cloud the cash flow picture even further.

Accrual accounting remains essential for effective financial management. It enables a business to gauge its performance over a specific period by correctly matching revenues and expenses.

However, sales do not necessarily coincide with cash inflow. Nor do expenses (or cost of sales) coincide with cash disbursements.

In contrast, cash accounting registers the actual cash flow through a business. It recognizes the timing of the cash flow into a business from all sources, as well as the timing of the disbursements required to meet operating expenses and pay for purchases. A historical cash flow statement reflects actual past inflow and outflow. A projected statement, based on historical trends, predicts further cash flow.

Had Dan Drake recognized the significant difference between cash accounting and the illusory earnings implied by his income statement, the $25,000 deficit cash flow would not have come as a surprise. His cash flow statement for January (shown below) reflects the characteristics of Drake's cash flow:

1. Accounts receivable, which are the company's only source of cash, turn in thirty days; Drake collects 100% of the prior month's sales.
2. Drake purchased $105,000 in inventory in December to meet January's forecasted sales volume; to maintain its credit rating, the company has always paid for every purchase within thirty days.
3. Drake pays all operating expenses as incurred; none is accrued for payment in the following month.

Based on these characteristics, Drake's projected (and actual) cash flow for January developed as follows:

Drake Paper Company
Cash Flow Statement 1/1/91—1/31/91

Beginning Cash (in bank)	$ 10,000
Collections (December sales)	100,000
Operating Expenses	(30,000)
Payments (December purchases)	(105,000)
Cash Deficit	($25,000)

Thus an apparent $15,000 profit became a predictable $25,000 cash flow deficit. The $40,000 difference emphasizes the significant difference between accrual and cash accounting.

Actually, Drake didn't experience a deficit cash flow. Instead, he deferred payment to some suppliers, absorbing modest injury to his payment record. His cash flow problem was not disastrous; nevertheless, it could have been avoided. With the foresight provided by a projected cash flow statement, Drake could have filled the gap with external financing, additional investment, or perhaps by accelerating collection of his accounts receivable.

Drake's experience illustrates a primary tenet of cash flow management. You must differentiate between accrued sales and expenses and the cash flow associated with those transactions. Failure to do so can lead to the financial embarrassment of a sudden cash flow squeeze.

That important distinction deserves emphasis in Cash Flow Concept No. 3:

Concept 3: **Positive cash flow management requires a clear distinction between accrual accounting and cash flow accounting.**

Other accounting schedules add to the information provided by the basic income and cash flow statements. These are discussed as they apply to specific cases throughout the book. First, however, let's briefly review another financial statement that serves as a fundamental tool for cash flow management.

The Balance Sheet

The balance sheet is another accrual financial statement. It provides a snapshot of the financial structure of a business at a particular time. Drake Paper Company's experience illustrates how this financial tool can help identify a cash flow problem. That illustration centers on Drake's comparative 12/31/90 and 1/31/91 balance sheets in Table 1-1.

The earlier statement reflects the firm's financial structure as it appeared before the 50% sales increase. The latter statement shows how that increase altered Drake's financial structure. The comparison reiterates what we already know. By 1/31/91, the firm had depleted its cash.

Table 1-1
Comparative Balance Sheets

	12/31/90	1/31/91
Cash	$ 10,000	—
Accounts Receivable	100,000	$150,000
Inventory	105,000	105,000
Other Assets	20,000	20,000
Total Assets	$235,000	$275,000
Accounts Payable	$105,000	$130,000
Other Liabilities	20,000	20,000
Total Liabilities	$125,000	$150,000
Stockholder's Equity	$110,000	$125,000
Liabilities and Equity	$235,000	$275,000

We also now see how the effect of January's sales volume on the other elements in Drake's financial structure actually created the cash flow problem. Accounts receivable increased from $100,000 to $150,000 in one month. That asset expansion absorbed the firm's $15,000 profit and the $10,000 in beginning cash. The cash drain also forced the increase in liabilities reflected in accounts payable.

Note another fact suggested by the balance sheets. Based on the detrimental effects of the 50% jump in sales on Drake's cash flow and financial structure, further sales expansion becomes impossible. The growth in liabilities already has outpaced the firm's cash flow. Another sales increase would again be an accrued volume, not cash, and would exaggerate the fundamental problem. Indeed, a larger sales volume will lead to further deterioration in the firm's financial structure. Without external financing, accounts payable would fall so far past due that suppliers would refuse to extend additional credit consideration to the business.

Neither analysis of the income statement nor a review of the cash flow statement demonstrates the effect of sales, revenues, and cash flow on the firm's financial structure. In fact, a business may have a positive cash flow and a profitable operation over the short term, while its financial structure develops faults that portend future problems. In Drake's case, that came from an increase in accrued liabilities that outpaced the increase in cash.

Throughout the book, the value of the balance sheet will be illustrated in identifying and solving specific cash flow problems. Here, that potential is only suggested so that you will add the balance sheet to the income and cash flow statements as the fundamental tools for cash flow management.

Chapter 2

The Costs of Cash Flow Problems

Cash flow problems cost money. You may not be aware of the costs, or even of the problem. Nevertheless, the costs are real.

So, solving your cash flow problems does more than help avoid financial embarrassment. It also increases your earnings. Higher earnings follow naturally each time you avoid the potential cost of a cash flow problem. When you recognize these facts, the cash flow process becomes a profit center for you. And that perspective can lead to thousands of dollars in bottom-line benefits.

The Direct Cost of a Cash Flow Problem

Most business managers can calculate the direct cost of a cash flow problem. You will see numerous calculations as specific problems are discussed throughout the book. Here we will look at the direct cost of a cash flow problem incurred by Kamco, Inc., a small wholesaler of rubber tubing products.

Jerry Shipp founded Kamco in 1983. The company has been profitable since inception, and both sales and earnings increased steadily through 1989. However, earnings declined in 1990, despite an 11% rise in sales. As he reviewed his disappointing results in early 1991, Shipp centered his analysis on the financial data summarized in Table 2-1.

Shipp quickly recognized that Kamco's higher interest costs in 1990 led directly to the decline in earnings. However, he also recognized this expense as only a symptom of the real problem. Shipp correctly concluded that the higher interest costs came from the debt necessary to support an extraordinary rise in

Kamco, Inc.
Table 2-1
Comparative Financial Data

	1989	1990
Sales	$1,800,000	$2,000,000
Earnings before Interest Expense	90,000	100,000
Interest Expense*	(24,000)	(39,600)
Earnings after Interest Expense	$ 66,000	$ 60,400
Average Accounts Receivable	$ 200,000	$ 330,000
Average Bank Debt*	$ 200,000	$ 330,000

*Average interest rate is 12%.

Kamco's accounts receivable. In fact, receivables, bank debt, and interest costs all rose 65% in 1990. Retained earnings and trade credit supported the normal 11% expansion in the firm's other assets. (If the relationship between asset growth and the bottom side of the balance sheet—liabilities and stockholders' equity—is unfamiliar, see Chapter 12.)

Any excess investment in accounts receivable raises the need for a larger amount of borrowed money to avoid a cash flow deficit. In this instance, Shipp measured his overinvestment by comparing his average receivables in 1990 with the total appropriate, or "correct," for his rise in sales—an 11% increase over the 1989 average.

Average investment, 1990	$330,000
"Correct" Investment, 1990	222,000
Overinvestment	$108,000

Shipp's analysis proceeded on the assumption that Kamco's average investment in receivables in 1989 is at the proper level. While further analysis might disprove that assumption, Kamco's excess investment in accounts receivable in 1990 is certainly no less than $108,000. Moreover, the overinvestment led to a $12,960 reduction in the firm's earnings in 1990. That reduction—the direct cost of this cash flow problem—came from the extra bank debt, at 12% interest, required to carry the excess receivables. Indeed, had Shipp held his receivable investment in line with his sales growth, eliminating the need for extra debt, Kamco would have had a respectable increase in earnings in 1990 instead of the actual decline.

Note that Kamco did not suffer a cash flow crisis. The firm's borrowing power provided the cash necessary to meet all of its obligations satisfactorily. Of course, that didn't solve the cash flow problem—the overinvestment in accounts receivable. Instead, it served only as an expensive method for avoiding a crisis. So, Kamco's experience illustrates a cash flow problem can be expensive without becoming an emergency.

The Indirect Cost of a Cash Flow Problem

Kamco's experience shows you should not ignore a cash flow problem simply because it doesn't develop into a crisis. In other words, you should not ignore a cash flow problem merely because you don't suffer a direct, measurable expense. The cost of a cash flow problem may not appear as an expense at all, but rather as profits foregone.

Assume that Kamco has the same overinvestment in receivables, but that it carries the excess without the comparable increase in bank debts. Presumably, a strong equity base or lenient trade credit supports the overinvestment instead. Thus Kamco eliminates the $12,960 in extra interest costs and enjoys an increase in earnings.

Does that mean that the overinvestment in receivables has no effect on the company's bottom line? Indeed not! The overinvestment is still a cash flow problem, and that problem still hurts Kamco's earnings. Of course, the damage isn't visible in the form of higher interest costs. Instead, Kamco suffers an opportunity cost. Opportunity cost measures the indirect cost of a cash flow problem. It represents potential earnings lost.

In this instance, Kamco loses the potential earnings from $108,000 in cash. Eliminating the overinvestment in receivables would generate that much cash for profitable use elsewhere. The firm could profit from expanding inventory, reducing other bank debt, or merely from the interest earned on a corporate savings account. Those lost earnings, however calculated, measure the indirect cost of a cash flow problem. Of course, you won't find opportunity cost in an expense account, but the effect on your earnings is the same.

In later chapters, opportunity costs will measure the specific cost of several cash flow problems. Opportunity cost is measured in terms of the cost of borrowing. Thus if you have a 12% cost of borrowing, a $100,000 overinvestment in receivables leads to at least a $12,000 (annualized) opportunity cost.

While the specific rate varies with time and circumstance, borrowing cost serves as a conservative criterion for measuring opportunity cost. Indeed, you must earn more than your borrowing cost to justify incurring any debt at all. You should recognize your own opportunity cost in any circumstance. It must be equal to or larger than your cost of borrowing. It cannot be less.

That suggests the need to recognize the idea in:

Concept 4:   Make the cash flow process a profit center in your business.

That management effort can help every business increase its earnings.

Cash Capability

In the above examples, Kamco never suffers from a cash flow crisis. The firm had access to the cash necessary to meet all its obligations promptly. In financial terminology, Kamco had sufficient liquidity for its operations.

Liquidity is an important concept for cash flow management. It indicates that a firm has the capacity to meet its obligations on time. However, liquidity has other, broad accounting connotations which aren't necessary for our discussion. To avoid jargon, and to narrow the subject in order to concentrate on dollar flow, we measure liquidity in terms of *cash capability,* which measures the maximum cash available to a business at any particular time.

Cash capability measures the maximum cash available to support an increase in any other assets. It defines the practical limit on a firm's cash flow. Exceeding your cash capability leads to an unacceptable cash flow deficit or the failure to meet all obligations promptly. Exceeding your cash capability transforms a problem into a crisis.

Table 2-2 provides a practical view of cash capability. Firm A has $25,000 in cash and $100,000 in combined accounts receivable and inventory. The firm also has $25,000 in additional borrowing power from some external source, perhaps from a potential bank loan or additional supplier credit. Whatever the source, the $25,000 borrowing power, coupled with the $25,000 cash on hand, gives the firm $50,000 in cash capability. It has that much cash available from internal and external sources to invest in other assets.

Firm B, on the other hand, has exhausted its cash capability. The firm's higher investment in accounts receivable and inventory has absorbed all of its cash reserve and borrowing power. The business has reached the limit of its cash capability.

Cash capability is more than a catchy phrase. Because it defines the limits of the cash flow cycle, it is an estimate of your protection against a cash flow crisis. You may not have a perfectly balanced cycle. Few businesses do. But you can operate successfully so long as you don't exhaust your cash capability. And the

Table 2-2
Cash Capability

	Firm A	Firm B
Cash	$ 25,000	—
Accounts Receivable	50,000	$ 75,000
Inventory	50,000	75,000
Total Assets	$125,000	$150,000
Additional Borrowing Power	$ 25,000	—
Cash Capability	$ 50,000	$ 0

larger your cash capability, the less threat you suffer from any cash problem. The process that identifies that total deserves emphasis in Cash Flow Concept 5:

Concept 5: **A business can measure its cash capability as the sum of its cash reserves plus unutilized borrowing power.**

In any circumstance, a higher level of cash capability creates a larger buffer against cash flow problems.

At the same time, as Kamco, Inc.'s, experience illustrates, even a business with an adequate level of cash capability must exercise an attentive cash flow management effort to avoid the indirect costs of cash flow problems.

Part

II

Component Management

Chapter 3

Accounts Receivable in the Cash Flow Process

Accounts receivable represent the proceeds from a firm's sales. You trade your merchandise or service in exchange for your customer's promise to pay you in ten days or thirty days or perhaps even later. The payment of those receivables becomes the primary source of operating cash for your business. Too many broken promises to pay can leave your business without the funds to meet payroll, retire expenses, or service debt requirements.

Of course, most business managers are aware of this. But not all can translate this awareness into successful, efficient cash flow management. This chapter illustrates the relationship between accounts receivable and the cash flow process.

Collection Period and the Cash Flow Process

Assuming a constant sales volume, a single concept—average collection period—defines the relationship between accounts receivable and the cash flow process. The average collection period measures the length of time your average sales dollar remains in the form of an accounts receivable.

Of course, the average collection period alone doesn't determine the size of a firm's investment in receivables. Sales volume also has a direct influence. The larger the sales volume, the larger the investment in receivables. However, holding sales constant helps emphasize the critical relationship between accounts receivable and the cash flow process.

The Production Lumber, Inc. (PLI), demonstrates the relationship. PLI operates as a wholesale lumber broker. The company purchases lumber in carload lots from west coast mills and ships it directly to its customers. PLI never takes possession of the lumber and consequently carries no inventory. Thus the firm has a simple financial structure.

In fact, as indicated in PLI's 9/30/90 balance sheet (Table 3-1), PLI's only assets are cash and accounts receivable. Accounts payable make up the only liabilities.

Table 3-1 reflects the following characteristics about the company's business:

1. PLI generates an average sales volume of $5,000 a day, or $150,000 per month.
2. All sales are made on thirty day terms, and all customers pay within those terms.
3. Purchases average 85% of monthly sales volume; all suppliers require payment in ten days.

These characteristics leave PLI with an investment in receivables that holds constant at $150,000. Of course, that investment converts to cash at the rate of $5,000 a day, reflecting the thirty day collection period for PLI's receivables.

Table 3-1
Production Lumber, Inc.

9/30/90 Balance Sheet		Cash Flow 9/1/90-9/30/90	
Cash	$ 10,000	Beginning Cash	$ 10,000
Accounts Receivable	150,000	Collections (prior month's sales)	150,000
Total Assets	$160,000	Total Cash Available	$160,000
Accounts Payable	$ 42,500	Payment for Purchases	$127,500
Stockholders' Equity	117,500	Expenses	32,500
Liabilities & Equity	$160,000	Ending Cash	$ 10,000

Table 3-1, Column 2, shows that PLI's thirty day collection period satisfies the firm's present cash flow requirements. Although the constant $10,000 beginning and ending monthly cash balance shows that the firm is operating only at a break-even level—neither making nor losing money—the thirty day collection period meets the cash flow requirements for PLI's normal operations.

Now, assume that over the next six months PLI produces the same $150,000 monthly sales volume. However, during that period, the average collection period stretches from thirty to sixty days. The company still has $5,000 a day in sales, but the average sales dollar remains as a receivable for sixty days.

Table 3-2 summarizes the effect that this longer collection period has on PLI's financial structure and cash flow.

Table 3-2
Production Lumber, Inc.

3/31/91 Balance Sheet		Cash Flow 3/1/91-3/31/91	
Cash	—	Beginning Cash	—
Accounts Receivable	$300,000	Collections	$150,000
Total Assets	$300,000	Total Cash Available	$150,000
Accounts Payable	$182,500	Payment for Purchases	$127,500
Stockholders' Equity	117,500	Expenses	22,500
Liabilities & Equity	$300,000	Ending Cash	—

Accounts receivable total $300,000. The firm has no beginning and ending monthly cash balance, and supplier credit stretches well beyond the normal industry allowance of ten days. Yet nothing has changed in PLI's operation except the collection period. The firm still has $150,000 in monthly cash collections. But that cash is not sufficient to pay for the purchases required for the two-month sales volume. Indeed, receivables now convert to cash at only half the rate at which PLI generates sales. The inevitable result is a cash flow crisis.

That fact earns recognition in:

Concept 6: **The average collection period defines the relationship between accounts receivable and the cash flow process.**

The longer the collection period, the higher the investment in accounts receivable.

Calculating Collection Period

Using Cash Flow Concept No. 6 requires two tasks. First, you must calculate the average collection period for your accounts receivable. Then you must relate that period, and changes in that period, to your cash flow.

To calculate the average collection period for your business:

1. Divide annual sales by 360 to determine your average daily sales volume.
2. Divide that figure into the present balance of your accounts receivable.

For example, if a business has $2 million in annual sales and $200,000 in accounts receivable, the calculation becomes:

1. Sales per day $= \dfrac{\$2,000,000}{360} = \$5,555$

2. Average Collection Period $= \dfrac{\$2,000,000}{\$5,555} = 36$ days

Each sales dollar rests in the form of a receivable for 36 days.

Calculating collection period over the previous twelve months usually provides sufficient accuracy for the cash flow management effort. However, if you have had a recent fluctuation in sales, you should use a daily sales figure that reflects that fact. It can make a significant difference.

For example, assume that $600,000 of the above sales volume came in the most recent quarter. To reflect that, the calculation then becomes:

1. Sales per day $= \dfrac{\$600,000}{90 \text{ days}} = \$6,666$

2. Average Collection Period $= \dfrac{\$200,000}{\$6,666} = 30$ days

The average collection period becomes significantly shorter. Naturally, that difference would influence any management decision affecting your investment in accounts receivable.

Cash Flow and Collection Period

To use the collection period in your cash flow management effort, you must recognize how a change in the collection period affects your cash flow. To repeat the basic relationship, the longer the collection period, the larger the investment in accounts receivable. However, positive cash flow management requires a more precise perspective. That perspective comes in Tables 3-3 and 3-4.

Table 3-3 details the effect different collection periods have on investment in accounts receivable over a range of daily sales from $1,000 to $5,000 a day. Use this table to measure the impact changes in collection period have on your cash flow.

To illustrate, let's determine the cash generation potential from a modest reduction in collection period. Assume that your sales average $2,000 a day and your average collection period is forty-five days, and you reduce your collection period to forty days. From Table 3-3, you can see that the shorter collection period reduces your investment in receivables from $90,000 to $80,000. That reduction generates $10,000 in cash that you can invest profitably elsewhere, or you can add it to your cash reserves.

Table 3-4 simplifies the analytic process. It relates the number of days you reduce your average collection period to the cash that reduction generates. For example, if you have $2,000 a day in sales, you will generate $6,000 in cash from a three-day reduction in the average collection period. Viewed from another perspective, the lower collection period reduces your cash requirements by $6,000. This can provide a simple solution to many minor cash flow problems.

In any event, remember the basic concept. Reducing the average collection period improves your cash flow as it converts accounts receivable into cash more rapidly.

The average collection period calculation provides a fundamental tool for positive cash flow management. Chapter 4 helps you apply that tool as a criterion for component management.

Table 3-3
Effect of Collection Period on Investment in Accounts Receivable

Average Collection Period (days)	Sales per Day				
	$ 1,000	$ 2,000	$ 3,000	$ 4,000	$ 5,000
	Investment in Accounts Receivable				
30	$30,000	$ 60,000	$ 90,000	$120,000	$150,000
35	35,000	70,000	105,000	140,000	175,000
40	40,000	80,000	120,000	160,000	200,000
45	45,000	90,000	135,000	180,000	225,000
50	50,000	100,000	150,000	200,000	250,000
55	55,000	110,000	165,000	220,000	275,000
60	60,000	120,000	180,000	240,000	300,000

Table 3-4

Effect of a Reduction in

Average Collection Period on Cash Flow

Reduction in Average Collection Period (days)			Sales per Day		
	$ 1,000	$ 2,000	$ 3,000	$ 4,000	$ 5,000
			Cash Generated		
1	$ 1,000	$ 2,000	$ 3,000	$ 4,000	$ 5,000
3	3,000	6,000	9,000	12,000	15,000
5	5,000	10,000	15,000	20,000	25,000
7	7,000	14,000	21,000	28,000	35,000
10	10,000	20,000	30,000	40,000	50,000

Chapter 4

Component Analysis: Accounts Receivable

The collection period calculation measures how long it takes to convert your investment in accounts receivable into cash. But you must proceed beyond that calculation to determine your proper collection period and identify any component problems that might cause an overinvestment in accounts receivable. This chapter reviews the fundamental tools for component analysis.

Comparative Analysis: Average Collection Period

The correct collection period translates into the proper investment in accounts receivable. That becomes the natural target for your component management effort. That effort can begin with a comparison of your present average collection period with previous collection periods.

For example, assume that you have calculated your average collection period as illustrated in Chapter 3 and found that your average sales dollar rests in the form of a receivable for fifty-three days. Using the collection period calculated at the end of the latest full year of operations as a point of comparison, you have the following figures:

	Current	Prior
Average Collection Period (days)	53	42
Average A/R Investment (per $1,000 in daily sales)	$53,000	$42,000

Measured against your previous standard, you see an eleven day increase in your average collection period. That produces an $11,000 dent in your cash capability for each $1,000 in daily sales.

However, using prior experience as the sole standard for comparison leaves a gap in your analysis. That assumes the previous average collection period is appropriate.

But you can't rely on this assumption. Your average collection period last year does not necessarily define what is appropriate for your business now or in the future.

Consequently, you need another way to estimate the correct collection period for your business. You can do that by looking at comparable competitor standards. Mutual customers, credit terms, and credit policies should lead to common average collection periods. Unless warranted by special circumstances, your collection period should approximate your competitors'.

Many business managers are unaware of the availability of their competitors' financial data for comparative analysis. Of course, few closed corporations release financial information directly to competitors. But, while preserving anonymity, many firms provide that data to industry publications, which collate and publish comparative financial data regularly.

Assume that you find your fifty-three day average collection period compares unfavorably with a forty day average for your industry. This increases the probability that you have an over-investment in accounts receivable.

Alternatively, assume that the longer collection period approximates the industry average. Measured against competitive standards, this year's fifty-three day collection period apparently is correct for your business.

That suggests a longer average collection period may stand as a competitive necessity. That holds true even though the business inevitably sacrifices some cash capability. That emphasizes the value of comparing your average collection period against both internal and external standards.

If comparative data from industry sources prove elusive, use the data provided by Dun and Bradstreet or Robert Morris Associates. These firms collect and publish a variety of financial data categorized by industry and sales volume. Most businesses will find representative data drawn from a number of similar firms. Whatever the source of your data, don't overlook the value of comparative analysis.

Comparative Analysis: The Receivables/Sales Ratio

Comparative analysis of your collection period, either against internal or external data, may not identify a recent buildup in accounts receivable. Indeed, an expanding investment can become a problem before it results in a significant increase in your average collection period, particularly when measured over the previous twelve months. Consequently, you also should look at your monthly "accounts receivable to sales" ratio. That measures the relationship between your investment in receivables and your sales volume. This might reveal a component problem before it seriously impairs your cash flow or earnings.

The analytic process is straightforward. At the end of each month, divide your current investment in accounts receivable by the sales generated during that month. For example, assume that on June 30, 1991, your investment in receivables totaled $150,000. During that month, you generated $100,000 in sales. The calculation becomes:

$$\frac{\text{Accounts Receivable}}{\text{Sales}} = \frac{\$150,000}{\$100,000} = 1.5$$

Standing alone, the ratio tells you only that your receivables at the end of June were 150% of sales for that month. But the ratio gains potential as a problem spotter when you compare it to calculations from previous months. A change in the ratio can serve as a harbinger of an impending change in the prevailing trend of your cash flow.

To illustrate, assume that your sales for July 1991 increase to $110,000. At the end of the month, your investment in accounts receivable totals $190,000. A higher sales volume naturally leads to a larger investment in accounts receivable. But repeating the calculation, you find:

$$\frac{\text{Accounts Receivable}}{\text{Sales}} = \frac{\$190,000}{\$110,000} = 1.7$$

The higher ratio of receivables to sales means that your investment in accounts receivable grew more rapidly than sales. This change in the relationship between your investment in receivables and your sales volume often shows the first sign of a potential component problem.

Of course, you might dispense with the actual calculation each month and rely on an estimate of the relationship between your sales volume and your investment in accounts receivable. However, actually going through the calculation each month helps reduce the potential errors inherent in such estimates. That simple calculation, when compared with the calculations from previous months, can draw attention to a component problem long before it develops into a crisis.

If your business is seasonal and a major portion of your sales occur in a particular part of the year, adjust your receivables to sales ratio analysis accordingly. Compare your current monthly ratio against that for the same month of the previous year. This will prevent the distortions that inevitably arise from seasonal fluctuations in sales and collections.

That provides another approach to the benefits that can come from this component management tool. That earns recognition in:

Concept 7:   Use comparative analysis to identify the correct collection period for your business.

While comparative analysis contributes to your component management effort, it has some natural limitations. As the first step in problem recognition, it enables you to identify a potential overinvestment (or underinvestment) in accounts receivable. But you must proceed further to find the specific cause of any deviation from the norm.

Moreover, comparative analysis does not account for the unique characteristics of a business that can justify a collection period or a receivables to sales ratio that differs significantly from the standards. For example, if you boost sales with the aid of a more lenient credit policy, your collection period naturally will exceed that of your more conservative competitors. Alternatively, if you are undercapitalized, you may need a short collection period to generate the cash necessary for survival. Your averages will fall below the industry norms.

The Aged Analysis of Accounts Receivable

Another tool for component analysis also enables you to spot problems in their early stages. In this instance it also helps you identify the specific source of the problems.

Table 4-1 demonstrates the potential of this tool. With an aging analysis drawn from a firm that sells on net thirty day terms, the firm expects payment thirty days from the date of the sale. The analysis is normally constructed as of the last day of the month.

1. Column 1 includes the debt due from each customer.
2. Column 2 summarizes the accounts due from sales made during the month just ended, that is, current accounts not yet due and payable.
3. Column 3 isolates those receivables still due from sales made in the previous month; those amounts are 1 to 30 days past due.

Table 4-1
Sample Aged Analysis of Accounts Receivable

Customer	Total A/R	Current	1-30 Past Due	31-60 Past Due	Over 60 Past Due
Page Distributing	$ 12,000	$ 2,000	$ 4,000	$4,000	$2,000
Jones Manufacturing	27,000	27,000	—	—	—
Sales, Inc.	9,000	9,000	—	—	—
Houston Wire	15,000	—	15,000	—	—
American Wholesale	17,000	10,000	4,000	3,000	—
Woodwork, Inc.	3,000	—	3,000	—	—
MFI	5,000	5,000	—	—	—
Continental Supply	12,000	12,000	—	—	—
Total	$100,000	$65,000	$26,000	$7,000	$2,000

4. Column 4 identifies amounts that remain unpaid from sales made two months previously; those receivables are 31 to 60 days past due.
5. Column 5 pinpoints any account more than 60 days past due.

Design your aging analysis to suit your own circumstance. For example, a grocery wholesaler typically sells on seven day terms. Consequently, she uses a weekly aging analysis that separates accounts due according to her own special terms. Similarly, a firm allowing sixty days for payment would adjust the format in Table 4-1. Regardless of the specific form, however, observe the benefits that you can derive from an aged analysis of your accounts receivable.

First, the analysis identifies the specific accounts within the total that make up an overinvestment. Referring to Table 4-1, you can easily see the receivables that lengthen the firm's average collection period beyond thirty days.

Also, the aging analysis can provide a picture of any recent change in the makeup of a firm's receivables. Table 4-1 reflects a typical mix of current and past due accounts. Certainly every business carries some customers that do not pay promptly, but if the pattern of past-due accounts changes (by comparison with aging analysis from previous months), you will see the deviation almost immediately. An aging analysis allows you to spot the early development of a potential accounts receivable problem.

The accounts in the third column (indicating payments are one to thirty days past due) may not portend a problem. But as you see an increase in such accounts from one month to the next, you should recognize an undesirable trend. Unless you respond to that trend, it will lead to a longer average collection period and a higher, more costly investment in accounts receivable.

That adds to the reasons for recognizing the contribution an aging analysis makes to component management in:

Concept 8: Complete component analysis requires a monthly aging of your accounts receivable.

The absence of that cash flow management tool leaves a manager at a disadvantage.

Chapter 5

Component Management: Credit Terms

Credit terms set a time limit on each customer's promise to pay for a purchase. When he purchases your product or service, the customer understands that you expect payment within a designated length of time. You agree to "carry" the customer's account for the designated period.

If every customer pays in accordance with the designated terms, then those terms determine your collection period. However, that perfect coincidence rarely occurs. Almost every business has customers who take longer to pay. But your designated credit terms still exert a significant influence on your customer payment habits and the cash flow in your business. This chapter discusses that influence.

Credit Terms and the Cash Flow Process

Our initial look at the relationship between your credit terms and the cash flow process ignores the influence those terms exert on your sales volume. That look centers on the Hillsboro Ceramics Company, a manufacturer of high grade industrial ceramics for sale to the pharmaceutical industry. Hillsboro occupies a unique position. Demand for its products exceeds supply. Consequently, the company sells all its $5,000 daily production on a continuous basis. Taking advantage of this demand/supply relationship, Hillsboro presently has the shortest credit terms possible. The company requires cash payment at the time of purchase. Yet it still sells 100% of its production.

At the same time, management recognizes the volatility of the marketplace. It wants to retain customers when competition increases or demand subsides. Consequently, it decides to offer "reasonable" terms for payment and absorb the cost associated with carrying an investment in accounts receivable in exchange for a loyal customer base in the future.

Before adopting this policy, John Thompson, Hillsboro's controller, analyzed the effects the primary alternative credit terms would have on the firm's cash flow and earnings. Thompson's analysis began with the following assumptions:

1. Regardless of the terms offered, Hillsboro will maintain the same $5,000 average daily sales volume; production already equals capacity.
2. The company will incur a 12% per annum cost—financial or opportunity— from carrying an investment in accounts receivable.
3. All customers will pay strictly in accordance with whatever terms the firm designates.

Table 5-1 illustrates the investment in receivables (and the cost of carrying that investment) that will result from allowing ten, thirty, or sixty days for payment. In this instance, we assume that the carrying costs translate directly into a reduction in Hillsboro's earnings. The results of Thompson's analysis show that longer credit terms lead to a higher investment in accounts receivable. Thus they have a more detrimental effect on earnings.

Table 5-1
Effect of Credit Terms on
Investment in Accounts Receivable

Credit Terms	Investment in Accounts Receivable	Carrying Costs at 12% per Year
Net 10 Days	$ 50,000	$ 6,000
Net 30 Days	150,000	18,000
Net 60 Days	300,000	36,000

Allowing ten days for payment reduces Hillsboro's annual earnings by $6,000, compared to its profits from making all sales for cash. This reduction comes from the cost of carrying the $50,000 average investment in receivables that naturally accrues from ten day credit terms. Increasing those terms to thirty days reduces earnings by $18,000, while sixty day terms assess a $36,000 penalty on Hillsboro's bottom line.

It is also important to note how the alternative credit terms affect Hillsboro's cash flow. The ten day terms absorb $50,000 of the firm's cash capability. Hillsboro must reduce its cash reserves that much, or it must have a like amount of borrowing power. Longer terms naturally increase that drain. Indeed, allowing sixty days for payment absorbs $300,000 of Hillsboro's cash capability. This is a substantial consideration, even for a large firm.

Using Thompson's analysis, Hillsboro's management decided to absorb the least expense possible in their effort to build customer loyalty. They selected ten day credit terms as the standard corporate policy.

Few firms occupy Hillsboro's enviable position. Demand seldom exceeds supply on a continuous basis. At the same time, if you can exercise some liberty in selecting your credit terms, recognize how that decision will affect your cash flow and earnings. We set that management precept in:

Concept 9: Credit terms directly influence the cash flow and earnings in a business.

Don't exaggerate the significance of the influence credit terms have on your cash flow and require cash payment for all purchases. The cost of carrying a reasonable investment in accounts receivable is a normal business expense. In fact, you often will find that your credit terms have a greater effect on earnings than your prices.

For example, Hillsboro might increase its prices by 10% to offset the cost of carrying the investment in receivables that comes with its new credit terms. The price increase would probably be viewed by Hillsboro's customers as a negligible price to pay for more liberal credit terms.

Credit terms also exert another influence. They also affect a firm's sales volume. So, a manager should recognize that influence when he selects the credit terms for his business. The following section considers that influence.

Credit Terms, Sales Volume, and Cash Capability

Most businesses have a large number of competitors who offer similar products and services. Credit terms inevitably become an important part of that competition. A business might lengthen its credit terms because it will increase sales. Other competitive factors remaining equal, longer credit terms allow customers to retain their cash longer without violating the terms. Longer credit terms increase their cash capability.

The firm that offers longer selling terms suffers an opportunity cost, because longer terms lead naturally to a larger, more costly investment in accounts receivable. So the decision to offer more liberal terms requires a fair estimate of the trade off between the cost of a larger investment in accounts receivable and the bottom-line benefits of a higher sales volume.

We use the ABC Distributing Company to illustrate one approach to analyzing that trade off. ABC is a regional distributor of small electric motors. Operating in a highly competitive market, the firm can gain no significant advantage from price structure, product quality, or service capability. So, ABC's management explored the potential bottom-line benefits that might come from allowing longer terms for payment. The analysis began with a review of the relevant factors in the firm's current operations:

1. ABC now generates $50,000 per month in sales; in line with industry practice, all sales are made on thirty day terms. Since all customers observe those terms, ABC carries a $50,000 investment in accounts receivable.
2. ABC earns a 20% gross margin on sales; that is, after covering product and sales costs, twenty cents out of each dollar remains to cover the firm's fixed costs of $7,500 per month. In addition, that gross margin must cover ABC's 1% monthly cost of carrying its investment in accounts receivable.
3. After covering the above costs, ABC's present sales volume nets $2,000 in monthly earnings.

Marketing surveys suggest that ABC indeed can increase sales by offering longer credit terms. In fact, each thirty day increase in ABC's designated payment terms will lead to a $10,000 increase in monthly sales. Table 5-2 considers the effects the higher volume will have on the firm's earnings and its investment in accounts receivable.

Table 5-2
Effect of Longer Credit Terms on Sales, Cash Flow, and Earnings

	Credit Terms (days)		
	30	60	90
Sales Volume (monthly)	$50,000	$ 60,000	$ 70,000
Average A/R	50,000	120,000	210,000
Gross Margin (20% of sales)	10,000	12,000	14,000
Fixed Costs	(7,500)	(7,500)	(7,500)
A/R Carrying Cost (1% per month)	(500)	(1,200)	(2,100)
Net Monthly Earnings	$ 2,000	$ 3,300	$ 4,400

First, note that the analysis assumes that all of ABC's customers will observe the longer terms allowed for payment. This is a valid assumption, since no business should pay sooner than necessary. Nevertheless, each projected increase in credit terms leads to higher earnings, even after considering the cost of carrying a larger investment in accounts receivable. The $10,000 sales increase that comes from lengthening payment terms from thirty to sixty days ultimately translates into a $1,300 rise in earnings. This becomes an annual $15,600 bottom-line benefit. Then, increasing its credit terms from sixty to ninety days adds another $10,000 to ABC's monthly volume, and it provides another $1,100 increase in monthly earnings.

Of course, longer credit terms absorb a firm's cash capability. Increasing ABC's payment terms from thirty to sixty days raised its investment in receivables from $50,000 to $120,000. That increase uses $70,000 of ABC's cash capability. The firm must draw that amount from its cash reserves or borrowing power to carry the increase in assets.

This analysis ignores another cost inevitably associated with longer credit terms. Longer credit terms increase the loss a business suffers from bad-debt write-offs. The new customers you gain with more lenient terms tend to be financially weaker, perhaps unable to comply with the shorter time allowed for payment by your competitors. Note that the expense exists, and that the example overstates ABC's real increase in profits.

Also note that even if you possess unlimited cash capability the potential gains from longer credit terms aren't infinite. At some point, the cost of carrying a gigantic investment in receivables will offset the incremental gains from higher sales. But within practical limits the potential gains from extended selling terms can be significant. Remember this as:

Concept 10: Longer credit terms can increase earnings.

Finally, we must add one additional qualification. If you operate in a highly competitive environment, you may realize only temporary gains from extending your payment terms. Competitors may emulate your actions as soon as they recognize your gains. In such instances, your sales may soon return to a lower level, while the extended payment period remains constant. You end up with the same sales volume, but with a higher investment in accounts receivable. A short term gain turns into a long term reduction in earnings. Consider that potential result before you lengthen your selling terms.

Cash Discounts in the Cash Flow Process

Many businesses allow discounts off the original sales price if a customer pays for a purchase within a short, specified time after shipment. For example, a business might allow a 1% or 2% discount if a customer pays for a purchase within ten days. The firm requires full payment if the buyer takes thirty days to pay.

Before you decide to offer cash discounts, you must estimate the resulting costs and benefits. First, recognize the potential benefits.

When a customer pays in accordance with the discount terms, it shortens your average collection period and accelerates your cash flow. That reduces your investment in receivables, as well as the costs associated with carrying that investment.

However, allowing discounts for early payment also exerts some detrimental effects on your bottom line. The basic circumstances of the ABC Distributing Company illustrate how to weigh those negative effects against the benefits. We will consider the effect on ABC's cash flow and earnings from offering any one of three alternative selling terms to its customers:

1. Net 30 days
2. 1% 10, net 30 days
3. 2% 10, net 30 days

We assume that ABC's sales will remain a constant $50,000 a month regardless of the selling terms offered. However, customer payment habits will vary in response to the different terms. Naturally, if ABC offers no discounts, all customers will take the full thirty days to pay. At the other extreme, every customer will pay within ten days in exchange for a 2% discount. This incentive for early payment is too large for any customer to ignore.

Mixed results come from offering a 1% discount for payment in ten days. Projections indicate that only half of the firm's customers will take advantage of the smaller discount. The other half will pay the full price in thirty days.

Table 5-3 summarizes the effects these alternative selling terms have on ABC's cash flow and earnings. The summary again assumes that the firm incurs a 12% annual cost from carrying its investment in accounts receivable. This cost, added to any discounts allowed, measures the total expenses associated with each of the alternative selling terms.

Note that ABC suffers the least cost when it offers no discounts for early payment. While that policy leads to a $50,000 investment in receivables, the firm's annual cost of carrying that investment totals $6,000.

Table 5-3
ABC Distributing
Effects of Cash Discounts on Cash Flow and Earnings

Selling Terms	% Taking Discounts	Average A/R	Annual Carrying Cost (12%)	Annual Cost Discounts Allowed	Effect on Earnings
Net 30 Days	N/A	$50,000	$6,000	—	($6,000)
1% 10, Net 30 Days	50%	33,333	3,999	3,000	(6,999)
2% 10, Net 30 Days	100%	16,666	1,999	12,000	(13,999)

Now, note how allowing discounts for early payments affects earnings. Offering a 1% discount reduces ABC's earnings by $6,999, compared to the $6,000 reduction effected by the net thirty day terms. The savings gained from reducing the size of the firm's investment in receivables are more than offset by the cost of the discounts.

Allowing 2% discounts is even more expensive. Not only is the discount larger but every customer takes it. Indeed, that policy leads to a $13,999 reduction in ABC's earnings.

Observe Table 5-3 from a different perspective, the relationship between ABC's payment terms and its investment in accounts receivable. If no discounts are included in the selling terms, ABC must carry the $50,000 investment in accounts receivable. It must commit that much cash capability to its investment in that single asset.

While that investment level is the most profitable, a limited cash capability may force ABC to offer discounts. A 1% discount reduces the drain on that capacity to $33,333 while the 2% discount further reduces the investment in receivables to $16,666. We summarize the trade-offs illustrated in Table 5-3 in:

Concept 11: Trade discounts help a firm's cash flow at the expense of its earnings.

Of course, if you can reinvest the accelerated cash flow rapidly and profitably, the earnings you lose from today's discounts may ultimately increase your profits. But that doesn't eliminate the implications of Cash Flow Concept No. 11.

A Financial View of Trade Discounts

The 2% discount for early payment is irresistible to ABC Distributing's customers. But only half of the same customers will take advantage of a 1% discount allowed for payments made ten days after a purchase. Yet both discounts reduce net purchase costs. Recognizing the financial view of cash discounts explains that apparent contradiction.

When you allow a discount for payment in ten days instead of thirty, you actually pay your customer for the use of his funds for the twenty days you otherwise would have to wait for full payment. Consequently, we can view cash discounts a business allows for early payments as an interest charge a business pays for borrowed funds. Figure 5-1 illustrates this with a look at a $1,000 sale made on 2% 10, net 30 day credit terms.

Figure 5-1
A Financial View of Cash Discounts

(Assume a $1,000 sale made on 2% 10, Net 30 Day credit terms)

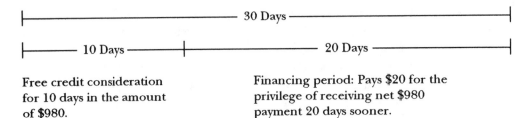

If the buyer doesn't pay for the purchase by the tenth day, he must pay the full $1,000 list price for the purchase. In that event, the purchaser typically will delay payment until the end of the thirty day credit term. However, the seller allows a 2% discount if the purchaser remits payment on the tenth day. That allowance becomes the interest charge the seller pays to obtain $980 of the purchaser's funds twenty days before the required due date. The twenty day term marks the length of the financing period.

The cost of allowing a $20 discount for early payment may not appear significant, but that allowance pays for relatively short term financing. To complete our financial view, we should translate the cost of the discount allowed into an annualized interest rate. The proper management perspective develops only when you annualize that cost.

One approach to developing that perspective begins by determining the total number of financing periods that accumulate from a firm's selling terms during a standard 360 day business year. Referring to Figure 5-1, the seller's twenty day financing period occurs eighteen times over the course of the year (360 / 20). The approximate annualized interest rate appears when you multiply the number of credit periods in a year by the percentage cost a business incurs from allowing a single discount.

For example, the business allowing a 1% discount for payment in ten days incurs an annualized 18% interest charge for the privilege of gaining that payment twenty days earlier than the limit set by the full thirty day credit period. The cumulative cost of the 1% discounts a business allows can leave a significant dent in its earnings.

The same calculation process indicates that a business that allows a 2% discount for payment in ten days incurs a 36% annualized charge to gain early customer remittances. Certainly every businessman will find that rate exorbitant.

The above calculation process can be used to determine the approximate annual interest rate a business incurs from allowing any discount for early customer payment. Merely identify the number of credit terms within a year. Then multiply that total by the percentage cost of each discount allowed. The final answer will not be precise, but it will be sufficient to enter into the decision process that determines whether or not a business should allow discounts for early customer payments.

At the same time, we should review the calculation process that provides a more accurate measure of the annualized interest charge a business incurs from allowing discounts for early payments:

$$\begin{matrix} \text{Annualized interest} \\ \text{cost of allowing} \\ \text{a cash discount} \end{matrix} = \frac{\text{Discount percent}}{(100 - \text{discount percent})} \times \frac{365}{(\text{Credit limit} - \text{discount period})}$$

Using the 2% 10, net 30-day credit terms, we find:

$$\text{Annualized interest cost} = \frac{2\%}{(100\% - 2\%)} \times \frac{365}{(30 - 10)}$$

$$= \frac{2\%}{98\%} \times \frac{365}{20} = 37.2\%$$

A business actually incurs an annualized 37.2% interest charge from allowing a 2% discount for payment ten days after a purchase instead of full payment in thirty days. The same formula can be used to determine the cost of allowing any discount included in a firm's credit terms. Table 5-4 displays the cost of allowing the more common discounts a business may consider offering for early payment. It also helps explain the different response customers have to a 1% versus a 2% cash discount allowed for payments made in ten days instead of thirty. Indeed, the cost a customer pays for missing a discount is the same as a business incurs from allowing it.

Table 5-4
The Annualized Interest Cost from
Allowing Cash Discounts for Early Payment

Credit Terms	Annualized Percentage Cost
1/10, Net 30	18.4%
2/10, Net 30	37.2
3/10, Net 30	56.4
1/10, Net 60	7.4
2/10, Net 60	14.9
3/10, Net 60	22.6

A customer will take a 2% discount, even if it leaves him in a cash flow bind, because losing that discount is equivalent to paying a 37.2% annual borrowing cost. A customer also suffers a cost when he misses a 1% discount, but the penalty is less severe. A customer is more likely to pass up the smaller discount as an alternative to straining his cash capability.

The perceptive reader has by now surmised that a business can profit by eliminating discounts from its selling terms. This holds true even if the business has to use its borrowing power to carry the resulting higher investment in accounts receivable.

However, that should not prompt any rash action. Other factors also deserve fair consideration.

For example, industry custom may dictate your selling terms. If your customers expect cash discounts for early payment, eliminating those discounts will drive them to your competitors. In such instances, discounts become a normal business expense recognized in your price structure.

Don't overlook the effect that eliminating discounts will have on your cash flow. This decision can lead to an increase in receivables that may impose a significant drain on your cash capability. The increase may absorb the cash reserves and borrowing power that may be essential for the firm's survival. Exchanging cash discounts for survival will always remain a fair trade.

Chapter 6

Component Management: Credit Policy

Rarely does every customer pay in accordance with a seller's designated terms. In some instances, clerical error or honest oversight may delay payment. In other instances, customers may defer payment to protest some real or imagined problem with a product or service. In other circumstances, customers who fail to pay within a firm's designated terms simply suffer from their own cash flow problems. They lack the capability to generate or borrow the cash to honor their obligations promptly.

You could refuse to sell to anyone who failed to pay within your designated terms, but that restriction might prove to be expensive. Many businesses increase their earnings from sales to slow paying customers.

At the same time, too many slow paying customers can create a cash flow problem. That calls for a well designed credit policy that satisfies your earnings objectives while still operating within the limits of your cash capability.

This chapter will focus on the impact a change in a firm's credit policy has on its sales, cash flow, and earnings. It also introduces the concept of cash insurance, which employs an insurance policy to protect a business against the cash drain caused by uncollectible accounts receivable. That protection reduces the risk a business normally accepts when it carries a significant investment in receivables.

Credit Policy and Cash Flow

Chem-Etch operates as a regional manufacturer of printed circuit boards for sales to the electronics industry. In one sense, the firm enjoys an enviable position. It sells the maximum plant capacity of $3,000 daily for a monthly volume of $90,000.

However, the company attained that position only after a struggle to achieve industry acceptance for its products. To earn that acceptance, Chem-Etch adopted a credit policy that encouraged sales at the expense of its cash capability. In fact, it willingly sold to customers who clearly lacked the financial ability to pay in accordance with the thirty day selling terms.

While that policy helped push up the firm's sales volume, it finally led to a cash flow problem. By 9/30/90, Chem-Etch's average collection period reached 75 days. That left the firm with a $225,000 investment in accounts receivable. On the same day, as illustrated in Table 6-1, the firm reached the natural limit set by its cash capability. Chem-Etch was out of cash, a common experience among young, growing businesses. Such businesses often make sales volume a singular objective and presume that that justifies a liberal credit policy.

Table 6-1
Effect of Credit Policy on Cash Flow
Chem-Etch, Inc.

	9/30/90	12/31/90	3/31/91
Daily Sales	$ 3,000	$ 3,000	$ 3,000
Collection Period (days)	75	60	45
A/R Investment	225,000	180,000	135,000
Cash	—	45,000	90,000
A/R Carrying Cost (at 10% a year)	22,500	18,000	13,500
Reduction in Carrying Cost	—	4,500	9,000

Naturally, Chem-Etch's cash flow problem put an end to that policy. Since the firm was operating at capacity (and turning down new orders daily), the need to induce sales with such a liberal policy no longer existed. Consequently, the company adopted a more restrictive credit policy that soon reduced its average collection period to sixty days, still thirty days beyond the firm's designated terms.

Table 6-1 illustrates the predictable effect of that more restrictive policy. By 12/31/90 Chem-Etch's investment in accounts receivable dropped to $180,000, providing the company with a healthy $45,000 cash reserve.

In addition to relieving the cash flow bind, the more restrictive credit policy provided Chem-Etch with another benefit. It reduced the costs associated with carrying an investment in accounts receivable. The new policy gave the firm a $4,500 (annualized) bottom-line benefit.

When the more restrictive policy had no effect on sales, Chem-Etch tightened the credit reins again and set a forty-five day payment period as an objective. Over the following three months, the firm's receivables dropped to $135,000, its cash reserves rose to $90,000, and Chem-Etch began to feel the benefits of a $9,000 reduction in annual carrying costs.

We recognize the relationship illustrated by Chem-Etch's experience in:

Concept 12: Credit policy has a direct effect on the cash flow and earnings in a business.

The following section takes a closer look at that effect.

Credit Policy and Sales Volume

Your credit policy affects sales volume in the same manner as your designated selling terms. A liberal credit policy contributes to higher sales, while a more restrictive policy tends to reduce sales. This should come as no surprise. After all, whatever your designated selling terms, your credit policy defines your *implied terms*.

Your implied terms reflect the average time you actually allow customers to pay for their purchases. For example, assume that you designate thirty days as your standard selling terms, but your credit policy approves sales to customers who habitually pay in sixty days. Inevitably, you will attract customers precluded from buying elsewhere because of more restrictive credit requirements. The longer implied terms encourage an increase in sales.

To understand the relationship between implied terms and your cash flow and earnings, look again at Table 5-2 in Chapter 5. The same principles apply to both implied and designated selling terms. Increasing those terms from ten to either thirty or sixty days will increase your sales volume. Also, the earnings on that additional volume typically will outpace the rising costs of carrying a larger investment in accounts receivable. In either instance, longer terms increase both sales and profits at the expense of your cash capability.

You can't control your implied terms precisely, but you should recognize the relationship between your sales volume and the implied terms set by your credit policy.

Credit Policy Rules

A tighter credit policy reduces the length of your implied selling terms and shortens your average collection period. A tighter policy also accelerates collections and reduces your investment in accounts receivable. It improves your cash flow.

However, a more restrictive credit policy tends to reduce sales. As you tighten your credit standards, prospective customers must show more financial strength and have a better payment history to qualify for credit consideration. Those who fail to meet your standards must buy elsewhere. That reduces the number of prospective customers available to you, and inevitably it reduces your sales volume.

If the demand for your products or services exceeds your present capacity, a tighter credit policy may not affect your sales. Normally, however, when you consider tightening your credit reins, you should weigh the benefits of a better cash flow against the lower earnings from a reduced sales volume.

Obviously you get the opposite effect from loosening your credit reins. A more liberal credit policy leads to a longer average collection period and a larger investment in accounts receivable. That simultaneously absorbs some of your cash capability and hurts your cash flow. A less restrictive policy, which lengthens the implied term allowed for payment, also encourages a boost in sales because it expands the pool of potential customers.

Moreover, as suggested in Table 5-2, those longer implied terms ultimately can increase your earnings. You gain that benefit so long as the profits on the higher volume offset the rising costs that come from carrying a larger investment in accounts receivable.

Practical limits exist on the benefits you can derive from a more lenient credit policy. And you should recognize those limits before you open your credit lines to any customer who walks in the door.

In any event, never make payment within your designated terms a moral issue. It is less important that a customer pays within a certain term than it is that you realize the maximum bottom-line benefits from his purchase. Many business managers lose sales and earnings because they refuse to allow customers to delay payments beyond the designated due dates. So long as your designated terms don't strain your cash capability, profits take precedence over prompt payment.

The Limits on a Liberal Credit Policy

Longer selling terms, whether designated or implied, can increase your earnings. You gain that benefit when the profit margin on sales induced by those terms exceeds the cost of carrying a larger investment in accounts receivable. That potential was illustrated with the case of ABC Distributing Company in Chapter 5.

However, higher earnings from a more liberal credit policy are not automatic. The profit potential from changing your credit policy depends on some key factors not emphasized in ABC's experience.

The profit margin you realize from each additional sales dollar stands as the key factor that determines the benefits that might flow from a more liberal credit policy. In the case of ABC, a healthy 10% margin on new sales easily offset the modest 1% per month cost of carrying the firm's investment in accounts receivable. Obviously, a business that operates with a narrower margin will not enjoy the same benefits. Nor will the business that suffers an unusually high cost from carrying its investment in receivables realize similar gains. Those costs often rise more rapidly than a firm's investment in receivables.

Another factor not considered in ABC's experience—bad-debt write-offs—also exerts a significant influence on the profits you generate with a more liberal credit policy. Although every business suffers some loss from customers who ultimately fail to pay for their purchases, the business that adopts a less restrictive credit policy inevitably will watch that rate rise.

A number of the customers you attract with your liberal policy lack the capacity to pay within normal industry terms. They have cash flow problems. Moreover, as you increase the time you allow a customer to pay for a purchase, you increase the chances that his problems will develop into your disaster. That inevitably contributes to a higher bad-debt expense.

Below, you will see how that higher expense can offset the benefits of a higher sales volume. In fact, a small increase in bad-debt experience (as a percentage of total sales) can make a big dent in your earnings. You can't predict the size of the dent accurately, but you can be certain that it will appear. Thus it becomes a factor in your estimate of the benefits from a more liberal credit policy.

Don't forget that when you allow longer terms for payment, you must have the cash capability to absorb the resulting increase in your accounts receivable. In fact, if a more liberal credit policy would stretch that capability, you might be more comfortable with lower earnings from your present credit policy. You won't earn as much, but you will reduce the risk of having a cash flow problem.

Let's look at an example that recognizes the limits on the benefits that can be derived from a more liberal credit policy. That example moves us closer to a real business environment, and it serves as a model for analyzing your own situation.

The East Texas Service Corporation (ETSC) is a direct competitor of the ABC Distributing Company. Recognizing the sales increase garnered by ABC's longer selling terms, ETSC decided to adopt a similar policy but with two important differences.

First, rather than extending its selling terms, ETSC adopted a more liberal credit policy, gradually lengthening its implied terms. That approach presumably encouraged the firm's existing customers to pay in accordance with the designated thirty day terms, while it still allowed sales to businesses that lacked that capability. Also, ETSC's analysis included a fair assessment of the effect longer implied terms would have on the firm's bad-debt expense. Recognizing these differences, the firm's analysis was based on the following assumptions:

1. Each ten day increase in average collection period that ETSC allows will increase sales by $300 per day, or $108,000 per year.
2. ETSC earns 9% on sales before deducting any loss from bad debts, or the cost of carrying the firm's investment in accounts receivable.
3. The company incurs a 12% annual cost from carrying its average investment in receivables.
4. The firm's present thirty day terms result in bad-debt write-offs that amount to 1% of ETSC's annual sales volume.
5. Estimates indicate that each ten day increase in the average collection period will increase that loss rate by one quarter of 1%. For example, a forty day collection period will increase the loss from bad debts to 1.25% of total sales.

Table 6-2 summarizes the results of ETSC's analysis. As anticipated, the sales gained by increasing the firm's average collection period from thirty to forty days lead to higher earnings. While the $2,520 gain is modest, it does represent earnings foregone with a more restrictive credit policy.

By allowing the average collection period to increase to fifty days, ETSC gains an additional $1,260 in earnings, and total profits rise to $56,700 per year. But that marks the limit on the company's gains from a more liberal credit policy. Indeed, increasing the collection period from fifty to sixty days provides no addition to earnings, despite another $108,000 increase in sales. Any further increase in collection period allowed by even more liberal credit guidelines actually reduces earnings.

Let's review the facts that limited the benefits ETSC derives from lengthening its implied terms. The firm's profit margin (before deducting carrying costs and bad-debt expenses) is a full percentage point below that enjoyed at ABC Distributing Company. This small difference becomes significant when applied to the total sales volume in a business. Indeed, it translates into a $10,000 reduction in earnings on each $1 million in sales volume.

In addition, ETSC incurs a higher cost from carrying its investment in accounts receivable. That difference becomes significant when measured against a large investment carried for a full year.

Table 6-2
Limits on a Liberal Credit Policy
East Texas Service Corporation
Implied Terms (days)

	30	40	50	60	70
Daily Sales	$ 2,100	$ 2,400	$ 2,700	$ 3,000	$ 3,300
Annual Sales	756,000	864,000	972,000	1,080,000	1,188,000
Average A/R	63,000	96,000	135,000	180,000	231,000
EBCC at 9%	68,040	77,760	87,480	97,200	106,920
ARCC at 12%	(7,560)	(11,520)	(16,200)	(21,600)	(27,720)
Bad Debts (as a percent of annual sales)	(7,560) (1%)	(10,800) (1.25%)	(14,580) (1.5%)	(18,900) (1.75%)	(23,760) (2%)
Net Earnings	$ 52,920	$ 55,440	$ 56,700	$ 56,700	$ 55,440

Finally, the rising bad-debt expense naturally associated with a more liberal credit policy completes the detrimental effect on the gains anticipated from the higher sales volume. As implied terms increase, so do bad debts. No realistic analysis can ignore that fact.

How these factors affect your business depends on your special circumstance. Also, you must decide if your cash capability will allow you to carry the incremental accounts receivable. Then you can determine whether longer implied terms can be profitable for you.

Credit Policy and Sales Price

We've seen that a business inevitably incurs an increase in carrying costs and bad-debt losses whenever it uses a liberal credit policy to induce a higher sales volume. Carrying costs increase as a longer average collection period leads to a larger investment in accounts receivable. At the same time, a business absorbs higher losses from bad debts. In both instances, the more liberal the credit policy, the larger the increase in costs. That can limit the benefits a business can derive from a more liberal credit policy.

However, a business with sufficient cash capability can adopt another policy that overcomes that limit. It can adjust prices. Even a modest price adjustment can offset the higher costs associated with a more liberal credit policy.

To illustrate the potential of that policy, let's examine the results that come from a two-tiered price structure tied to customer payment habits. In this instance, assume that a supplier sets a $10 per unit price for customers who observe his designated thirty day terms for payment. Customers who take sixty days to pay must absorb a 10% premium. Product costs in either instance hold constant at $7 per unit. Table 6-3 compares the results that come from selling 1,000-unit lots to both kinds of customers.

Table 6-3
Credit Policy and Sales Price

	30 Days Payment Price ($10.00)	60 Days Payment Price ($11.00)
Units	1,000	1,000
Monthly Sales Volume	$10,000	$11,000
Average A/R Investment	10,000	22,000

Gross Earnings Calculation

Sales	$10,000	$11,000
Product Costs at $7 per Unit	(7,000)	(7,000)
Monthly A/R Carrying Cost (1% per month)	(100)	(220)
Bad-Debt Losses	(100)	(220)
Gross Earnings	$ 2,800	$ 3,560

Column 1 measures the gross earnings from sales to customers who observe the thirty-day payment terms. Deductions for accounts receivable carrying costs and a bad-debt reserve leave the supplier with $2,800 in gross earnings. Of course, the business has to cover operating expenses out of that margin. But the gross margin calculation is sufficient for comparison here.

Now, examine Column 2, which shows the results that come from the 10% price adjustment applied to the same unit volume of sales to customers who take sixty days to pay.

The firm suffers two cost increases from that policy. The seller's investment in receivables rises. The $11,000 monthly volume translates into a $22,000 higher average investment in receivables. Also, bad-debt losses increase from 1% to 2% of the monthly sales volume. That naturally follows from sales to slow paying customers.

However, the 10% price differential easily offsets both the higher accounts receivable carrying costs and the increase in losses from bad debts. And the price adjustment produces a $760 net increment in earnings. That measures the benefit the seller derives from contributing her cash capability to a slow-paying customer for an extra thirty days.

In fact, even a 5% price differential would produce a slight increase in earnings for the supplier. This emphasizes that only a small differential can easily offset the cost that comes from selling to slow-paying customers. Of course, you must have the cash capability to carry the investment in receivables that results from those sales. But if you have the capability, adjusting your prices upward can increase your earnings.

This potential earns recognition in:

**Concept 13:   An upward price adjustment
can offset the cost of selling to
slow paying customers.**

The customer who pays slowly seldom complains about a modest price differential. She is more interested in liberal credit consideration that eases the strain on her own cash flow. Typically, she is willing to pay for that consideration.

Credit Insurance

Despite its long, successful history as a cash management tool, credit insurance remains an obscure concept to many business managers. Indeed, the business manager who insures her buildings, equipment, and vehicles against common perils often overlooks protecting an asset that is often more critical for the survival of her business—her accounts receivable.

A vehicle theft or a warehouse fire obviously can disrupt a business. But the inability to collect a large receivable can cut off the cash flow critical for survival. The value of credit protection will become apparent as we review the basic concept and operation of credit insurance. Not only can that protection prevent a cash flow crisis but it can also lead to higher earnings.

The Indemnification Principle

A business that adopts a more liberal credit policy to increase sales accepts the risk—indeed, the inevitability—of higher bad-debt write-offs. Certainly, you can offset those losses by adopting a complementary policy that adjusts prices upward to slow paying customers. But that still does not remove the risk.

In fact, you must recognize that bad-debt losses seldom occur in a systematic proportion to sales. You may accurately project an average loss rate over an extended period, but each loss actually occurs on an individual, random basis.

For example, a business might realistically anticipate $100,000 in total bad-debt losses for the next ten years. However, the precise timing of the write-offs belies prediction. The business might lose $10,000 each year for ten years, or it might suffer a $100,000 loss in one year, but none in the other nine. A $10,000 loss from bad debts might not impose a serious strain on your cash flow. However, taking $100,000 from uncollectible accounts in one year can threaten your firm's survival.

Recognizing this fact, credit insurance indemnifies a business against the catastrophic loss in cash that might occur when a large receivable becomes uncollectible because of (1) debtor bankruptcy, (2) debtor composition (reorganization of debt by creditors), or (3) any other proceeding that reflects a debtor's insolvency. In such events, the insurance company replaces much of the cash flow that otherwise would be lost in a bad-debt write-off. The insurance policy sets the terms of the basic reimbursement.

The Credit Insurance Policy

The credit insurance policy establishes the principles of the relationship between a business and a credit insurance company. The contract, or policy, identifies the specific risks that will shift from the business to the insurer.

Usually, a policy provides coverage for losses suffered from any of a firm's accounts receivable that become uncollectible. However, that coverage is subject to two practical limits.

First, the insurance company applies a deductible amount to each loss. For example, if a $10,000 account proves uncollectible under terms of the policy, the business might receive a $7,500 cash reimbursement from the insurer and absorb the $2,500 loss. The terms of the contract set the specific deductible amount.

The deductible provision encourages the business to maintain prudent credit and collection policies. That interest might wane if the firm received 100% protection against any loss. Credit insurance protects against catastrophe, not recklessness.

Second, the insurance company limits the maximum coverage for each debtor. Typically, those limits are tied to ratings established by national credit-rating agencies, such as Dun and Bradstreet. For example, a company with a D &

B rating of BB1 might automatically qualify for a maximum $25,000 in coverage under terms of the credit insurance policy. A business with a higher rating qualifies for more coverage. One with a lower rating receives less.

In the absence of ratings, special endorsements specify the amount of risk acceptable to the insurer. A covered business can extend credit consideration in excess of the coverage limits, but it must accept the full risk of loss associated with that excess.

The cost for credit insurance remains modest. While premiums vary, the coverage may cost 1/4% to 1/2% of annual sales. That may be a small price to pay for survival. Moreover, credit insurance can encourage management policies that pay the cost of the coverage and increase earnings.

Confident Credit Policy

A business can use a more liberal credit policy to encourage a higher sales volume that increases earnings. Credit insurance contributes an element of confidence to the businessperson who adopts that policy.

Of course, credit insurance doesn't provide the cash capability to carry the increased investment in receivables that results from that policy. A business must obtain that capability from other sources.

At the same time, credit insurance can give a business manager confidence that she suffers a reduced risk from an erroneous credit decision. She can concentrate on sales rather than credit and collections. That benefit earns emphasis in:

Concept 14: Credit insurance provides protection against the cash drain caused by uncollectible accounts receivable.

Credit insurance doesn't cover imprudence, but it adds an element of confidence to a more liberal credit policy. The loss from a mistake will be tangible, but it won't be terminal. *

Don't overlook the value of credit insurance. If your business has the cash capability, you can enjoy higher profits without the threat of uncollectible accounts. Indeed, such protection may ensure the profitability of a more liberal credit policy.

Chapter 7

Inventory in the Cash Flow Process

To meet customer demand as it arises, most businesses invest in some quantity of merchandise. That merchandise investment measures the size of a company's inventory. Since a business typically pays for its inventory at the time of purchase or within thirty days thereafter, the size of its investment in inventory exerts an important influence on its cash flow. This chapter illustrates that influence.

Inventory and Accounts Receivable

Inventory has the same relationship to the cash flow process as accounts receivable. But some important differences between the two components make inventory management more challenging.

For example, accounts receivable are self-liquidating assets. Once a sale is made, a receivable converts naturally into cash when collected.

Inventory is a less accommodating asset. Indeed, you have to push it through the cash flow cycle. It sits idle until you generate the sale that converts it into cash or accounts receivable.

Apart from the purchase cost, it usually is more expensive to carry an investment in inventory than in accounts receivable. Of course, the financial or opportunity cost of carrying either investment is the same. Additionally, an investment in receivables requires a reasonable expenditure for a credit and collection effort. But these costs seldom match the expenses associated with carrying inventory.

First, you must warehouse your stock. You must buy or lease a facility that enables you to store and maintain your investment in a salable condition. And the larger your total inventory, the larger your warehouse expense.

An investment in inventory also requires unavoidable handling costs, such as personnel, equipment, and processing. You incur those costs each time you take delivery of a new purchase or generate a sale. Naturally, your handling costs increase proportionately with your sales volume. Moreover, you must insure your inventory against the threat of fire, theft, and other perils. The larger and more perishable your inventory, the higher your insurance expense. While you also can insure accounts receivable against losses from bad debts, the costs are not nearly comparable to those associated with your physical inventory.

Finally, many inventory items have a limited shelf life. For several reasons, that investment can lose value while a business holds inventory for sale.

For example, a grocer must discard unsold vegetables after only a day or two. A chemical distributor suffers the same fate with some compounds that lose potency a week or a month after production.

Even nonperishable inventory can lose value while it sits in your warehouse. In some instances, it may become obsolete, made unsalable by technological innovation or merely by a change in customer preference. Even a minor improvement in a competitor's product can transform your leading source of revenue into a back shelf item.

In other instances, competitive price pressure can reduce the value of your investment. Your inventory inevitably loses some salability whenever your competitors lower prices to attract sales. While you can view that as an opportunity cost—you end up with a smaller profit margin rather than higher expense—the effect on your earnings is the same.

The cost of carrying inventory should be kept in perspective. You should measure the actual or potential costs of carrying inventory against the benefits you stand to gain from that investment. You can recognize that gain best by comparing it with your investment in receivables.

Accounts receivable, once generated from sales, become sterile assets. They contribute nothing until they are converted into cash through collection. In contrast, any item in your inventory can produce additional profits for your business, and it can contribute a much larger return than any other investment you normally make.

For example, if you generate a $10 sale from an item that costs $7, you gain a $3 contribution to your operating costs and profits. That gain represents a 42% return on your investment. Should you repeat that sale, or turn that inventory item, four times a year, the cumulative annual return on your investment becomes

168%. This potential return justifies the higher carrying costs inevitably associated with your investment in inventory. Of course, the potential profits from any inventory shouldn't encourage you to carry a quantity that could exhaust your cash capability. But you should balance the potential profits against the cost of carrying that investment.

You should also recognize one important similarity between accounts receivable and inventory. You can't reduce your investment in either asset below some minimum level without hurting your sales and profits. If you shorten your designated or implied selling terms too much, you will lose sales to your more liberal competitors. You will reduce your investment in accounts receivable, but chances are good that you also will reduce your earnings. Lower revenue generally translates into lower profits.

You suffer a similar fate when you try to lower your investment in inventory too far. That is, you begin to lose sales to your better stocked competitors. You suffer stock-out costs whenever you do not have an item on hand to meet customer demand.

Stock-out cost is another opportunity cost. But it is more difficult to measure than one resulting from an overinvestment in accounts receivable or inventory.

As a minimum measure of the expense, you can estimate your stock-out cost in terms of a customer's dissatisfaction that arises from having to wait for a particular item. That dissatisfaction naturally makes him more susceptible to your competitors.

At the next level, the stock-out cost increases when your customer actually does buy the product elsewhere. If you regain his business in the future, the potential profit from the single lost sale measures your stock-out or opportunity cost.

You incur the maximum opportunity cost should you ultimately lose all of the customer's future business to a better stocked competitor. Consequently, when you determine your proper investment in inventory, you must weigh the stock-out costs that come from having too little inventory against the costs of carrying a larger investment.

The Average Investment Period

Similar to the collection period calculation in Chapter 3, average investment period measures the length of time each dollar invested in inventory remains in that form before a sale converts it into cash or into an account receivable. So, it provides the conceptual foundation for managing a firm's investment in inventory.

The data to illustrate this concept come from the case of Tire Distributors, Inc., a wholesaler located in a large southwestern state. In summary form, TDI generated the following results in its fiscal year ending 8/31/90:

Sales	$ 2,400,000
Cost of Goods Sold	(1,920,000)
Operating Cost	(390,000)
Earnings	$ 90,000

However, TDI's profitable operation did not preclude a cash flow problem. Table 7-1 presents a picture of the problem that gives you a look at the firm's 8/31/90 balance sheet. That financial statement reflects the following facts about the company's operation:

1. TDI's $300,000 investment in accounts receivable comes from a forty-five day collection period and a $200,000 monthly sales volume.
2. At 8/31/90 TDI was carrying a $480,000 investment in inventory.
3. The company presently purchases $160,000 per month from its suppliers, an amount equal to TDI's monthly cost of sales.
4. The firm's suppliers allow a 2% discount for payment within ten days after a purchase, while the full purchase price is due in thirty days.

It is easy to see that with purchases of $160,000 per month and accounts payable of $240,000 per month, TDI is violating its suppliers' payment requirements. Even with the aid of a $250,000 bank loan, the firm is paying suppliers forty-five days after purchase, rather than within the expected thirty days.

Table 7-1
Tire Distributors, Inc.
8/31/90 Balance Sheet

Cash	$ 10,000
Accounts Receivable	300,000
Inventory	480,000
Total Assets	$790,000
Accounts Payable	$240,000
Bank Loan	250,000
Total Liabilities	$490,000
Stockholder's Equity	300,000
Liabilities and Equity	$790,000

In spite of their designated terms, at 8/31/90 TDI's suppliers obviously tolerated the firm's payment practices. Indeed, the suppliers apparently were seeking sales more avidly than prompt payment. At the same time, TDI's payment practices cost the firm dearly. In fact, the inability to pay for purchases within ten days cost TDI $3,200 in lost discounts each month ($160,000 x 2%). And that doesn't consider the financial or opportunity cost associated with a potential over-investment in inventory.

Recognizing the expensive cost of a cash flow problem, TDI's management searched for a way to take advantage of the lost discounts. As a first step in that search, management found that the firm needed $187,000 in cash to take supplier discounts. This total comes from the difference between TDI's actual accounts payable at 8/31/90 and the amount that would be due if the company took all available discounts. Thus if TDI took all discounts on $160,000 in monthly purchases, accounts payable could not exceed the average purchase amount for any ten day period. That becomes one-third of $160,000, or $53,333. Based on the $240,000 in accounts payable due, TDI needed $187,000.

Management then began to look for a source for the cash necessary to take the supplier discounts. Immediately, that search ran into two roadblocks.

First, TDI's banker refused to increase its loan above the $250,000 total outstanding at 8/31/90. The required $187,000 increase would exceed even a liberal banker's limit.

Second, management analyzed the potential benefits that might come from a reduction in TDI's average collection period. However, it found that since the existing forty-five day collection period approximated the industry average, any significant reduction imposed by shorter selling terms or a tighter credit policy would injure sales. Generating cash by reducing the firm's investment in accounts receivable was not a realistic alternative.

TDI's management examined the one remaining potential solution to its problem. The cash might come from a reduction in the firm's investment in inventory. That analysis began with the calculation of the average investment period.

That calculation involves a two step process:

1. Divide cost of goods sold by 360 to obtain the average daily cost of goods sold.
2. Divide that total into the firm's present investment in inventory to find the average investment period.

TDI's calculation becomes:

1. $$\text{Average Daily Cost of Goods Sold} = \frac{\$1,920,000}{360} = \$5,333$$

2. Average Investment Period $= \dfrac{\$480,000}{\$5,333} = 90$ Days

At 8/31/90, the average dollar TDI invested in inventory remained in that form for ninety days.

We illustrate how TDI uses that information to solve its cash flow problem below. Here, simply recognize that average investment period is analogous to average collection period. Reducing the length of either period releases cash a business can reemploy elsewhere.

Using Average Investment Period

Average investment period relates your daily cost of goods sold to your total investment in inventory. It measures the average number of days' sales you maintain in stock. To use that information, you must recognize how a change in that investment period affects your cash flow.

TDI's experience illustrates those effects. The average investment period calculation indicated that the firm had inventory sufficient for ninety days' sales at 8/31/90. That calculation averages the investment periods for all of the items that make up the firm's total inventory. For example, TDI's inventory of some tire sizes was sufficient for only sixty days' sales, while other sizes on hand would satisfy normal customer demand for six months or more.

Additional research into supplier shipping habits indicated that TDI seldom had to wait more than thirty days for delivery of any order placed with any supplier. Indeed, most suppliers shipped major orders in even less time.

Combining these facts led to a solution of TDI's cash flow problem. Management correctly concluded that it was unnecessary to maintain inventory on hand sufficient for ninety days' sales, when any item in that inventory could be restocked in thirty days or less.

Thus TDI's management decided to reduce the average investment period from ninety to fifty days. This objective would leave the firm with inventory adequate to service most customer requirements promptly, and it would still carry inventory necessary for twenty days' sales beyond the normal restocking period. That cushion was designed to satisfy extraordinary customer demand or unavoidable delays in shipping by suppliers.

Significantly, the lower investment in inventory generated $213,320 in cash for TDI. Inventory dropped from $480,000 to $266,680. Table 7-2 illustrates the effect the lower investment had on the firm's financial structure. Note two important facts about that structure.

First, the cash enabled TDI to reduce accounts payable to the level necessary to earn the firm the 2% discounts allowed for payment within ten days. TDI's monthly bottom-line benefit from that result translates into a $38,400 annual increase in earnings. That's significant in any business league.

Second, the reduction in inventory also added more than $26,000 to the firm's cash reserves. As the lower investment improved earnings, it also enhanced TDI's cash position.

Table 7-2
Tire Distributors, Inc.
12/31/90 Balance Sheet

Cash	$ 36,653
Accounts Receivable	300,000
Inventory	266,680
Total Assets	$603,333
Accounts Payable	$ 53,333
Bank Loan	250,000
Total Liabilities	$303,333
Stockholders' Equity	300,000
Liabilities and Equity	$603,333

You can easily estimate the potential cash you can generate from a reduction in inventory. Merely measure your average investment period against that actually required to satisfy the real needs of your business. Interrelate your sales projections with each supplier's ability to deliver his products on time. You may find, as in TDI's circumstance, that you can reduce your inventory substantially without hurting your sales volume. Of course, you won't reduce your inventory to a level that would increase your stock-out costs. But recognize that excess inventory is not only costly to carry but also absorbs your limited cash capability. Eliminating any excess inventory improves your cash flow and increases your earnings.

Cash Flow Concept No. 15 provides the foundation for managing a firm's investment in inventory:

Concept 15: Average investment period defines the relationship between your inventory and the cash flow process.

Table 7-3 illustrates the direct relationship between average investment period and cash flow. If your cost of goods sold averages $2,000 per day, then a ten day reduction in average investment period contributes $20,000 to your cash flow. If you can effect that reduction without an increase in stock-out costs, you will generate that much cash from profitable reinvestment elsewhere.

Table 7-3
Effect of Investment Period on Average Total Inventory

Average Investment Period Days	Cost of Goods Sold per Day				
	$ 1,000	$ 2,000	$ 3,000	$ 4,000	$ 5,000
	Total Inventory				
30	30,000	60,000	90,000	120,000	150,000
35	35,000	70,000	105,000	140,000	175,000
40	40,000	80,000	120,000	160,000	200,000
45	45,000	90,000	135,000	180,000	225,000
50	50,000	100,000	150,000	200,000	250,000
55	55,000	110,000	165,000	220,000	275,000
60	60,000	120,000	180,000	240,000	300,000

Also recognize that reducing your investment in inventory provides a larger bottom-line benefit than a comparable reduction in accounts receivable. After all, not only do you reduce the financial (or opportunity) cost of carrying an excess investment but you reduce the physical carrying costs. The total benefit can be substantial.

Chapter 8

Component Analysis: Inventory

The financial formula introduced in Chapter 7 provides useful insight into the relationship between inventory and the cash flow process. However, you must proceed beyond those basic calculations to identify any overinvestment in inventory, as well as to isolate the underlying problem that precipitates that overinvestment. This chapter facilitates those objectives by reviewing the basic tools for analyzing inventory in the cash flow process.

Comparative Analysis: Average Investment Period

Component management emphasizes the most efficient, profitable investment in accounts receivable and inventory in the cash flow process. The emphasis recognizes that you can have a cash flow adequate for normal operations but still carry an excess investment in either component. Comparative analysis of a firm's average investment period can help identify an excess investment in inventory.

So, if your current average investment period exceeds that experienced by your business in prior periods, you may have an overinvestment in inventory. Further analysis might contradict that view, but any discrepancy from past performance invites a deeper look.

Similarly, if your investment period is longer than that of your competitors (perhaps using comparative data available from Dun and Bradstreet or Robert Morris Associates), an excess investment in inventory may be exerting a subtle, detrimental effect on your bottom line.

Remember also that a significant difference in either instance doesn't prove the existence of a component problem. A special sale or an extraordinary purchase opportunity may justify a temporary overinvestment in inventory measured by normal standards. But deviations from the norm do call for explanation.

This reaffirms the important benefit you derive from comparative analysis. It draws attention to the extraordinary, the problem that needs to be corrected, or the circumstance that at least deserves explanation. Regarding inventory, that translates into:

Concept 16: **Comparative analysis helps identify the correct average investment period for your inventory.**

The correct investment period translates into the proper investment level in inventory. That becomes the target for your component management effort.

Comparative Analysis: The Inventory/Sales Ratio

Continuing the analogy with the comparative analysis of your accounts receivable, you can use a regular examination of your inventory to sales ratio to identify a potential overinvestment in inventory. The ratio compares your investment in inventory to your monthly sales total.

For example, if your inventory at the end of last month totaled $300,000, and sales for the same month reached $150,000, the calculation becomes:

$$\frac{\text{Inventory}}{\text{Sales}} = \frac{\$300,000}{\$150,000} = 2$$

Your investment in inventory was twice your sales volume for the month. The ratio provides a straightforward summary of the relationship between those two critical elements.

Now, assume that your normal operation requires an investment in inventory that doubles your monthly sales volume. The ratio then becomes the standard against which you compare the results of your operations every month.

If any monthly calculation results in a higher inventory to sales ratio—that is, above 2 to 1—you can assume that you have a potential component problem. Of course, the ratio rises in response to both an increase in inventory and a drop in sales. So, the immediate problem may not lie in faulty component management. Indeed, it may be a problem associated with your sales effort or perhaps with a general decline in the economy.

Alternatively, should the ratio between inventory and sales fall below 2 to 1, or whatever standard is appropriate for your business, then you may deserve a compliment for managing your inventory efficiently. After all, that result comes from either a higher sales volume relative to your investment in inventory or a lower inventory level relative to sales. Over the short term, either circumstance is desirable.

You also should recognize the other possible implication of a lower inventory to sales ratio. As you increase sales relative to any investment in inventory, you also increase the risk of incurring stock-out costs. The benefits from a better cash flow may be offset by the opportunity costs associated with lost sales.

In any instance, the inventory/sales ratio serves the same function as any other tool for comparative analysis—to draw attention to a potential over-investment in inventory. But you must look further to locate the specific source of that problem.

Turnover Analysis

A periodic count of every item in stock remains the first fundamental principle of sound inventory management. The physical count serves two primary objectives.

First, it enables you to verify the accuracy of your accounting procedures that keep track of your investment in inventory. As you verify the exact amount of each item in stock, you confirm the value of your investment.

Second, and even more important, the physical count provides the basic data necessary to perform a turnover analysis of your inventory. Turnover analysis then becomes a fundamental tool that enables you to control your investment in inventory.

Average investment period still defines the relationship between your inventory and the cash flow process. However, there is a limitation inherent in the information provided by that calculation. As the term implies, it defines an "average" relationship. That presumes that every item you stock turns at exactly the same rate. Thus a sixty day average investment period asserts that each product that makes up your total investment in inventory moves from purchase to resale in exactly two months. It also implies that your stock of every item in inventory is sufficient for two months' sales.

Those are valid assumptions if your inventory includes only one product. However, most businesses carry a wide variety of different products. Inevitably, some products turn more rapidly than others.

Whatever your average investment period, when you consider specific items within your inventory, you may have an overinvestment in some, the correct investment in others, and insufficient investment in still others. Consequently, complete component analysis requires that you go beyond the average investment period calculation and examine your investment in each product that you carry. You must perform turnover analysis.

Turnover analysis measures the amount of your investment in each item in stock against the amount actually required, based on your recent sales experience. To illustrate this, we return to the case of Tire Distributors, Inc., discussed in Chapter 7.

TDI solved its cash flow problem by reducing its average investment in inventory from a level appropriate for ninety days' sales to a level still sufficient for fifty days' sales. Of course, that reduction didn't occur spontaneously. Instead, the firm used turnover analysis to identify the specific tire sizes that made up the overinvestment in inventory.

The analysis proceeded on three assumptions:

1. TDI had no need to stock a quantity of any tire above that necessary to satisfy two months' sales.
2. TDI measured that standard by looking at the actual sales activity over the previous sixty days for each tire in stock.
3. As a starting point for analysis, TDI conducted a physical count of its inventory, which included a breakdown of the number of each tire size in stock.

Let's review some of the relevant results of TDI's analysis illustrated in Table 8-1.

TDI found 420 tires, Stock No. 100, on hand at 8/31/90. But only 140 had been sold during the last sixty days. The stock on hand of that single tire was sufficient for normal demand for the next six months. TDI could carry one third the inventory of that item without the serious risk of incurring any stock-out costs.

Analysis of Stock No. 101 showed that the amount in stock was exactly right for sixty days' sales. TDI's investment in that item was appropriate for its sales volume.

Now, look at the results of Stock No. 102. Although the firm sold 540 units over the previous two month period, only 270 were on hand for sale at 8/31/90. Perhaps TDI was awaiting delivery of 270 units to bring that stock item up to the proper 540 level to meet normal demand. If not, the firm was confronting the possibility of stock-out costs because of a deficient inventory of a rapidly selling tire.

TDI's investments in Stock Nos. 103 and 104 also were excessive. Those items became candidates for the firm's reduction program. We find the same result

Table 8-1
Inventory Item Analysis
Tire Distributors, Inc., @ 8/31/90

Tire Stock Number	Number in Stock	Number Sold Last 60 Days	Days Sale in Inventory	Action
100	420	140	180	Reduce
101	300	300	60	Satisfactory
102	270	540	30	Increase
103	850	170	300	Reduce
104	90	30	180	Reduce
105	63	9	420	Eliminate

from Stock No. 105. However, that item, a relatively small part of TDI's total inventory, produced sales of only 9 units over the sample sales period. This suggests probable obsolescence, and management should eliminate the item altogether from the investment in inventory.

Of course, TDI may carry that item to meet the sporadic demands of a customer who buys a significant number of other tire sizes. If not, that item becomes excess inventory. It doesn't generate enough sales to justify carrying it at all.

Now, let's review the primary benefits of inventory item analysis.

Item analysis enables you to identify the specific items in stock that make up an overinvestment in inventory. Eliminating that excess reduces the size of your average investment in inventory and improves your cash flow. It also serves as an early warning problem spotter, analogous to the aging analysis of accounts receivable. So, remember:

Concept 17: Item analysis identifies the specific source of an overinvestment in inventory.

An overinvestment in inventory seldom develops suddenly. Instead, the buildup occurs slowly. One item moves more slowly than average, then another. As you identify these slower moving products on a regular basis, you can make the appropriate adjustments before the cumulative effects hurt your cash flow or earnings. Of course, your response might be to lower your inventory level or increase your sales effort for those particular items. In either circumstance, item analysis provides the signal for action. Used properly, this problem spotter can add significant earnings to your bottom line.

Chapter 9

Component Management: Quantity Control

Effective quantity control is the key to successful inventory management. You want to maintain an inventory level adequate for anticipated sales requirements while avoiding an overinvestment that exerts a detrimental effect on your cash flow and earnings. This chapter introduces some cash flow concepts that help achieve those objectives.

The Elements of Inventory Investment

The proper investment in inventory generates the maximum earnings for a business without stretching the limit of its cash capability. Of course, no business maintains that investment continuously. But that objective serves as the normal target of the quantity control effort.

The stock necessary to satisfy normal day to day sales requirements makes up the core of that target. For example, assume that an office supply firm sells an average of 10 boxes of carbon paper per day, or 300 boxes per month. If the firm buys carbon paper only once a month, then each order should call for no fewer than 300 boxes. This is the minimum to satisfy normal sales requirements.

Since customer demand fluctuates over any short term period, sales of any particular item can exceed normal requirements. So an investment in inventory properly includes some *safety stock*.

Safety stock describes that part of a firm's inventory that satisfies a modest, unanticipated increase in customer demand. It provides a measure of protection against stock-out costs. For example, the office supply firm might begin each month with an inventory of 330 boxes of carbon paper. While that total exceeds normal requirements, the 30 extra boxes provide a cushion to satisfy an unanticipated increase in demand. Note that the cost of carrying the safety stock should be less than the opportunity cost incurred from the loss of those potential sales.

Safety stock also helps to offset shortages that might result from erratic supplier shipments. An unforeseen strike, snowstorm, or material shortage can delay shipment of any order. Safety stock helps defer the potential decrease in sales caused by such disruptions.

Growth stock stands as the final element in a firm's target investment in inventory. That stock satisfies the demand created by a projected increase in sales volume. Certainly no effort to increase sales makes sense unless you carry the stock necessary to supply the higher volume.

Assume that the office supply firm adds a salesman in an effort to expand its market. At the same time, the firm must increase its inventory of carbon paper, as well as all other items, to satisfy the anticipated increase in sales. If the higher volume does not follow, the firm will find itself with a temporary overinvestment in inventory. But that is a necessary risk inherent in any push to increase sales. Cash Flow Concept No. 18 adds up the elements that enter into a firm's target inventory investment:

Concept 18: Normal stock plus safety stock plus growth stock equals the target investment in inventory.

Of course, the investment in inventory must be properly allocated among the different products that make up that total. And the total should not exceed the firm's cash capability.

Estimating Inventory Requirements

A realistic sales projection is a necessary precedent in estimating inventory requirements. Ideally, that forecast will proceed from a knowledgeable assessment of the projected economic environment, and the anticipated influence that environment will have on a firm's market. Recognizing the constraints set by competition, a business then should forecast its annual unit sales volume based on Cash Flow Concept No. 18. And the annual unit projection should be dispersed across the operating periods—quarters, months, or weeks—that are most appropriate for setting purchase requirements.

Every sales forecast contains a margin of error. Unpredictable fluctuations in customer demand remain inevitable. However, that does not eliminate the contribution a sales forecast makes to the inventory management effort. Even a casual forecast provides some basis for controlling a firm's investment in inventory. The business proceeding without a sales forecast lacks the management premise necessary for that control.

We will examine one approach that relates a firm's inventory requirements to a particular sales projection. The approach centers on the experience of Atlas Belts, Inc., a small distributor of power transmission belts.

Atlas presently generates $200,000 per month in sales. However, over the next twelve months, the firm expects that volume to increase steadily to $400,000 per month. Specifically, the firm expects the following sales for the next four quarters:

| | Quarters | | | |
	1	2	3	4
Projected Sales	$750,000	$900,000	$1,050,000	$1,200,000
Monthly Average	250,000	300,000	350,000	400,000

Beginning with these projections, Atlas developed its inventory requirements for each quarter based on its operational characteristics:

1. Product costs average 75% of sales.
2. Unacceptable stock-out costs are incurred whenever inventory drops below the level necessary to satisfy two months' sales volume.
3. Inventory necessary for projected sales must be on hand at the beginning of each month.

Atlas can project its inventory requirements first by multiplying the anticipated monthly volume by 75%, the average cost of sales. Multiplying that total by two provides the inventory level necessary to satisfy the projected sales volume while avoiding stock-out costs.

For example, the inventory necessary to begin the firm's first quarter comes from the calculation:

Projected Monthly Sales		Cost of Sales				Two Months' Requirements
$250,000	x	75%	x	2	=	$375,000

The calculation provides an estimate of the company's total inventory requirements. The firm must complement the estimate with item analysis, perhaps coupled with specific product sales projections, to achieve the correct inventory mix. Atlas must also relate the estimated inventory requirements to its cash capability.

Projected Inventory and the Cash Flow Process

Estimating the inventory requirements necessary to achieve any projected sales volume is an essential step in cash flow management. However, if the inventory requirements exceed the limits set by your cash capability, you must reduce your ambitions or risk the embarrassment of a cash flow problem.

The eventual results of the projections developed by Atlas Belts indicated a cash flow deficit. That result, summarized in Table 9-1, reflects additional facts about the firm's operations:

1. Atlas will begin the projected year with a $62,500 cash reserve, as indicated in the first column in Table 9-1.
2. The firm's credit and collection policies produce a constant thirty day average collection period from its accounts receivable.
3. All of the firm's suppliers require payment for all purchases within thirty days. While they offer no discounts for early payment, suppliers quickly eliminate slow-paying customers from credit considerations.
4. Atlas earns 5% from all sales.
5. Atlas anticipates no increase in the $200,000 bank loan outstanding at the beginning of the projected year.

Table 9-1
Projected Quarterly Balance Sheets
Atlas Belt, Inc.

	1	2	3	4
Cash	$ 62,500	$ 12,500	($ 30,000)	($ 65,000)
Accounts Receivable	200,000	250,000	300,000	350,000
Inventory	375,000	450,000	525,000	600,000
Total Assets	$637,500	$712,500	$795,000	$885,000
Accounts Payable	$187,500	$225,000	$262,500	$300,000
Bank Loan	200,000	200,000	200,000	200,000
Total Liabilities	$387,500	$425,000	$462,500	$500,000
Stockholders' Equity	250,000	287,500	332,500	385,000
Liabilities & Equity	$637,500	$712,500	$795,000	$885,000

Now observe what happens to the firm's cash position as it hypothetically achieves the sales projected for the first three quarters during the upcoming year.

To meet supplier requirements Atlas must maintain accounts payable on a thirty day basis. But the increase in receivables and inventory naturally associated with the higher sales volume absorbs the firm's cash reserves. In fact, by the end of the third quarter, the projections indicate an unavoidable and unacceptable deficit cash position. The cash flow problem develops despite the firm's profitable operations and efficient accounts receivable management. That suggests the benefit from:

Concept 19: Estimated inventory requirements must recognize the limits set by the cash capability in a business.

Atlas either must reduce its projected sales volume for the upcoming year or obtain additional cash from another source to supplement its cash reserves. Otherwise, the inventory requirement would exceed the firm's cash capability and result in a serious cash flow problem.

Managing for Profits

Relating inventory requirements to cash capability is an important element of positive cash flow management. However, if you have adequate cash capability, you may find it profitable to change your management emphasis. Instead of seeking the most efficient cash flow, you can direct your management efforts toward producing the largest bottom-line benefits for your business.

Although seeking maximum profits is a natural business objective, even the most profitable investment in inventory often exceeds the limits set by a firm's cash capability. The experience of Atlas Belts proved that.

We presume here that cash capability doesn't stand as an obstacle to profitability. In that happy event, the component management effort changes its orientation and seeks the most profitable inventory investment level. To find that level, you must achieve the proper balance between two contradictory categories of costs.

Acquisition Costs

Every business manager recognizes the direct cost of acquiring inventory, the purchase price of the merchandise. However, many overlook other acquisition costs which increase the actual costs of any particular order.

A business can measure its acquisition costs (apart from the inventory purchase price) as the total of the following:

1. The administrative costs that arise from scheduling, entering, and receiving an order.
2. The labor costs associated with receiving, inspecting, and shelving each order.
3. The cost of accounting and paying for an order.

Two facts concerning these costs become relevant here.

First, the administrative, accounting, and labor costs associated with any order are more significant than many business managers realize. The cumulative acquisition costs from numerous orders can exert a significant downward effect on your earnings.

Second, those cumulative acquisition costs hold relatively constant regardless of the size of the order involved. Apart from the cost of the merchandise, it costs little more to order and receive 1,000 units for stock than it does 100 units.

Thus you can reasonably conclude that as you increase the size of each order, you reduce the total number of orders you enter each year. And as you reduce the number of purchase orders, you reduce your annual cumulative acquisition costs.

To illustrate how reducing these costs can benefit the bottom line in a business, we will use the experience of the Southwest Light Company, a regional bulb distributor. For the upcoming year, Southwest projects sales of 24,000 packages of its standard 100 watt bulbs. Beginning with that projection, the firm analyzed its acquisition costs based on three assumptions:

1. Southwest's supplier of 100 watt bulbs requires a minimum order of 4,000 units; however, Southwest can order any amount above that minimum.
2. The company has the warehouse capacity to store the 24,000 units required for the full year's projected sales.
3. Southwest's cumulative acquisition costs total $600 for each order entered.

In this instance, we also assume that Southwest's unit purchase price remains constant regardless of the size of the order entered with its supplier.

Table 9-2 illustrates the anticipated results of the firm's analysis. As Southwest reduces the number of orders entered during the year—by increasing the size of each order—it reduces its annual acquisition costs. In fact, by including the total annual requirement for 24,000 units in one order, Southwest reduces its acquisition costs for the year to only $600. That is $3,000 less than the costs the firm would incur by purchasing the same stock in six minimum order lots.

Table 9-2
Annual Acquisition-Cost Analysis
Southwest Light Company

Order Size (units)	4,000	6,000	8,000	12,000	24,000
Number of Orders	6	4	3	2	1
Annual Acquisition Costs ($600 per order)	$3,600	$2,400	$1,800	$ 1,200	$ 600

The cost relationships associated with acquisition costs receive recognition in:

Concept 20: **Inventory acquisition costs rise as a business increases the number of orders entered per year.**

Using a single order to obtain your total annual requirement for every item you stock reduces acquisition cost to a minimum. Of course, as acquisition costs drop, your average investment in inventory increases. So, another cost consideration enters into inventory management analysis.

Carrying Costs

The cost a business incurs from carrying inventory remains directly related to the size of its average investment. Naturally, the financial or opportunity costs rise in proportion to the size of that investment. Other carrying costs also increase, although the proportions are less precise.

As you increase your investment in inventory, you increase your warehouse costs. You need more space to store more inventory. As your investment grows, you also will see rising insurance and maintenance costs, as well as an increase in the expenses that come from deterioration or obsolescence.

It is easy to surmise the cumulative increase in carrying costs easily can offset the gain you realize from reducing your acquisition costs to a minimum by reducing the number of orders entered during the year. A two-step analysis supports this assertion. That analysis proceeds from the following assumptions:

1. A business sells its stock at a constant, predictable rate.
2. A business receives each new order on the same day that it sells the last item from the previous order.

3. However determined, all orders for each item are exactly the same size.
4. A business has no need to carry any safety stock.

Beginning with these assumptions, we can calculate the average investment for each item a business stocks, using the following order quantity:

$$\text{Average Inventory} = \frac{\text{Size of Each Order}}{2}$$

While the calculation may not provide a precise average, it is sufficiently precise for most business circumstances.

Table 9-3 uses the calculation to estimate Southwest Light's average investment in inventory that would result using the order sizes in Table 9-2. Predictably, Southwest's average investment in 100 watt bulbs increases as it reduces the number of orders entered per year.

Table 9-3 also measures the annual carrying costs that the firm can anticipate from the alternative ordering frequencies. The analysis first translates the investment into financial terms, using $1.50 per unit as a constant purchase cost. Then it assumes that carrying costs average 15% of the average investment. Presumably, the 15% cost includes Southwest's financial or opportunity costs, as well as the warehouse, maintenance, insurance, and any other costs that are necessary to support an investment in inventory.

Table 9-3
Average Investment Analysis
Southwest Light Company

Order Size (units)	4,000	6,000	8,000	12,000	24,000
Average Units in Stock	2,000	3,000	4,000	6,000	12,000
Average Investment at $1.50 per Unit	$3,000	$4,500	$6,000	$9,000	$18,000
Carrying Cost at 15% of Average Investment	$ 450	$ 675	$ 900	$1,350	$ 2,700

Note what happens to Southwest Light's annual inventory carrying costs as it reduces the number of times it orders 100 watt bulbs in a year. As the number of orders decreases, the average investment in inventory rises rapidly. So, too, do the associated carrying costs. If Southwest enters only one order for the year, those carrying costs rise to $2,700.

That logical relationship earns emphasis in:

Concept 21:   Annual inventory carrying costs rise as the average size of that investment increases.

Thus, as you reduce acquisition costs by ordering less frequently, you see a rise in the cost of carrying your inventory.

Achieving the Most Profitable Balance

You achieve the maximum bottom-line benefits when your average investment in inventory minimizes the total of your acquisition and carrying costs. You can identify that investment level in one of two ways.

You can perform a tabular comparison of the costs that come from various acquisition alternatives. Table 9-4 illustrates that approach, again using the Southwest Light Company data. The table totals the acquisition and carrying costs for each purchase quantity considered. The minimum total identifies the order size—and ultimately the average investment—that is most profitable (least costly) for the firm.

Table 9-4
Total Inventory Cost Analysis
Southwest Light Company

Order Size (units)	4,000	6,000	8,000	12,000	24,000
Annual Procurement Costs	$3,600	$2,400	$1,800	$1,200	$ 600
Annual Carrying Costs	450	675	900	1,350	2,700
Total Costs	$4,050	$3,075	$2,700	$2,550	$3,300

Southwest incurs the least cost by ordering 12,000 units twice a year. That represents the most economic ordering quantity for 100 watt light bulbs. We crystallize the principle underlying this analysis in:

Concept 22:   Profitable inventory management purchases major inventory items in the most economic quantities.

As an alternative to the tabular analysis, you can use the Economic Ordering Quantity (EOQ) formula.

The EOQ Calculation

A tabular analysis can become tedious and time consuming. Fortunately, you can identify the most economic ordering quantity for an item with the aid of an electronic calculator and the standard financial formula:

$$EOQ = \sqrt{\frac{2SO}{CP}}$$

where

S = Anticipated annual unit sales

O = Fixed costs per order

C = Annual inventory carrying cost, expressed as a percentage of the product's purchase price

P = The unit purchase price for the product

To illustrate the calculation process, we use the data from Southwest Light:

S = 24,000 units

O = $600

C = 15%

P = $1.50

The calculation becomes:

$$EOQ = \sqrt{\frac{2 \times 24,000 \times \$600}{(15\%)(\$1.50)}} = \sqrt{128,000,000} = 11,313 \text{ units}$$

Southwest Light's most profitable order quantity is 11,313 units, rather than the 12,000 units indicated in the tabular comparison. (As a practical matter, the difference would not produce a significant effect on the firm's bottom line.)

So, if you can isolate your anticipated sales volume, acquisition costs, and carrying costs, you can use the EOQ formula to determine the most profitable purchase quantities for the major items that make up your investment in inventory.

Achieving the objective set forth in Cash Flow Concept No. 22 leads naturally to the most profitable investment in inventory for your business.

Quantity Discounts in EOQ Analysis

We assumed that Southwest Light's purchase price for 100 watt bulbs held constant regardless of the number of units included in any order. Presumably, the firm paid $1.50 per unit for a 4,000-unit order or a 24,000-unit order.

This isn't a realistic assumption. Many businesses allow discounts off the list unit price for larger quantity purchases. Justification for quantity discounts proceeds from the same logic that underlies the EOQ analysis. It costs little more to ship a larger order than a small order. Thus a business reduces its total shipping costs by filling fewer, larger orders.

Selling in larger quantities also provides other savings for a business. Typically the firm will carry a lower average investment in stock and enjoy a higher inventory turnover rate. That translates directly into lower carrying cost.

The cumulative benefits from these reduced costs easily become significant enough to justify quantity discounts to encourage larger orders. Should they become available, you must alter your EOQ analysis to weigh the effect those discounts might have on your most profitable ordering quantity.

Table 9-5 demonstrates one approach to that analysis. Let's now assume that larger quantity purchases earn Southwest Light Co. quantity discounts.

Table 9-5
Effect of Quantity Discounts on EOQ Analysis
Southwest Light Company

Order Size	4,000	8,000	12,000	24,000
Cost (per unit)	$1.50	$1.40	$1.30	$1.20
Annual Cost (24,000 units)	$36,000	$33,600	$31,200	$28,800
Annual Procurement Cost	3,600	1,800	1,200	600
Annual Carrying Cost	450	900	1,350	2,700
Total Annual Costs	$40,050	$36,300	$33,750	$32,100

The supplier's pricing structure begins with a $1.50 unit price for quantities ordered in lots fewer than 8,000. At 8,000 units, the price drops to $1.40, at 12,000 to $1.30, and finally to a low of $1.20 for 24,000 units. Notice how the discounts affect Southwest Light's EOQ analysis. Despite higher carrying costs, the firm's most profitable ordering quantity rises from 12,000 to 24,000 units. The quantity discounts offset the higher carrying costs and contribute to Southwest Light's earnings. The potential benefits from quantity discounts are significant.

Remember this as:

Concept 23: EOQ analysis should include consideration of any available quantity discounts.

You should take advantage of every bit of profit potential that can come from your component management effort. But although EOQ analysis can become a valuable component management tool, you also should consider some inherent limitations as you weigh the benefits that the analysis offers.

First, remind yourself of the natural limits set by the cash capability in your business. You can't enjoy the benefits of large quantity purchases if they lead to cash flow crises. Certainly a limited cash capability restricts your purchase options, whatever profit potential you lose.

Also, EOQ analysis ignores inflation as an element in inventory management. Anticipatory purchasing to beat impending price increases has become an important concern in practical inventory management. As prices rise more rapidly, you may find profitable justification to buy as much as your cash capability will allow, regardless of the decision criteria that come from your EOQ analysis.

Of course, neither qualification negates the value of EOQ analysis. In any circumstance, the analysis should become a key element in your component management effort.

The Re-order Point

Determining the economic ordering quantity for a product remains a futile exercise unless a business also identifies the proper time to place each order with its supplier. To identify the re-order point for a product:

Reorder Point $=$ Order Lead Time (in days) $\times$ Average Daily Sales Rate $+$ Safety Stock

Figure 9-1 illustrates the interrelationship between the economic ordering quantity and re-order point for a product. The illustration develops from several assumptions:

1. A business averages five unit sales of the product daily.
2. The economic ordering quantity for the product is 100 units.

3. The business carries a twenty-five unit safety stock.
4. The firm's supplier normally makes delivery ten days after receiving each order.

As indicated in Figure 9-1, as soon as the firm's inventory level reaches seventy-five units—ten days' normal sales plus the twenty-five unit safety stock—the firm should reorder an amount equal to the product's economic ordering quantity, or 100 units. Presumably, the order will be received when the firm's inventory of the product drops to the twenty-five unit safety stock level. The safety stock provides the inventory necessary to absorb an unforeseen jump in sales or delay in delivery.

Figure 9-1
The Reorder Point

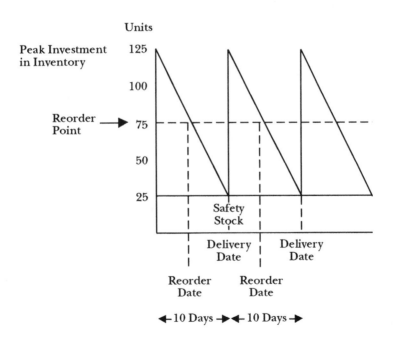

Chapter 10

Component Management: Accounting Methods

Inventory is a unique component in the cash flow cycle. In fact, it is the only component that changes in value according to the accounting principle you employ to keep track of it. The principles you use to value your inventory affect both the earnings and cash flow in your business. This chapter illustrates the major alternative accounting principles and the influence each has on a firm's earnings and cash flow.

Earnings as Cash Flow

Until now, we have concentrated on factors that affect the day-to-day cash flow cycle. We alter that approach here and note the relationship between earnings and the cash flow process.

To illustrate this relationship, we use the unusual circumstance of Autry Sports, Inc., a wholesale sporting goods operation. Autry recently completed two consecutive fiscal year ends with exactly the same investment in accounts receivable and inventory. The firm maintained the same total accounts payable to suppliers while incurring no other debt. However, in the interim bounded by the two fiscal year end statements, Autry Sports generated $100,000 in earnings. Table 10-1 demonstrates how those results affected the firm's financial structure.

Since all other assets and liabilities remained constant, the earnings translated directly into a $100,000 increase in Autry's cash balance. As each dollar in earnings increased the firm's net worth, it also expanded its cash reserves.

Table 10-1
Comparative Fiscal Year-End Balance Sheets
Autry Sports, Inc.

	7/31/89	7/31/90
Cash	$ 50,000	$150,000
Accounts Receivable	200,000	200,000
Inventory	300,000	300,000
Total Assets	$550,000	$650,000
Accounts Payable	$150,000	$150,000
Stockholders' Equity	400,000	500,000
Liabilities and Equity	$550,000	$650,000

Autry's experience suggests a different definition of cash flow in a business. It describes the cash a business generates from operations in the course of a year, or the annual cash flow.

Here we isolate the contribution that comes from earnings. That contribution easily can become an important management consideration. After all, earnings make up another source of cash that can be used to increase assets or decrease liabilities. Or, from Autry's example, you can use that contribution to increase your cash reserves. We recognize that contribution in:

Concept 24: Earnings represent an addition to the cash flow in a business.

Of course, the cash from earnings flows into a business incrementally throughout the year. But viewing it on an annual basis provides a better perspective for understanding the concept.

Note that throughout most of the book we ignore the income tax obligations that naturally arise in a profitable operation. In most instances, tax considerations have no effect on the major cash flow concepts that we discuss.

However, the following discussion makes an exception to illustrate the effects the two major inventory accounting methods have on the cash flow that proceeds from earnings.

FIFO Versus LIFO Inventory Accounting

A business can value its fiscal year-end inventory in accordance with one of two major accounting principles.

FIFO accounting, or first in first out, proceeds on the logical assumption that a business sells its inventory in the order it is acquired. Presumably, the first item purchased from a supplier becomes the first product sold to a customer. All subsequent purchases are then sold sequentially. At the end of the fiscal year, FIFO accounting values the ending inventory, or unsold stock still on hand, using the actual dollar cost of the items most recently acquired.

LIFO accounting, or last in first out, assumes that a business sells its inventory in the reverse order in which it was acquired. Presumably, the business sells its latest purchase from a supplier before any like item already in stock. Then, at year's end, the business values its unsold inventory using the costs from the earliest purchases.

We will use the case of Odd Ball Bearing Company to illustrate these principles. Then, we will measure the effect each alternative has on Odd Ball's earnings and cash flow.

Odd Ball Bearing Company, a wholesale distributor of industrial bearings, recently completed its first year in business. Table 10-2 summarizes the firm's inventory activity during that year. The summary measures the movement of inventory in terms of the number of units, or boxes of bearings, purchased and sold, as well as the actual dollar costs associated with those units.

Odd Ball began operations with 1,500 units in stock, each having an average price of $2.00. Consequently, the firm's opening day inventory carried a value of $3,000.

During the first six months in business, Odd Ball purchased 7,500 additional units for inventory. However, persistent inflation in the bearing business increased the average cost per unit during that period to $3.00. The 3,750 units purchased in the third quarter cost $3.50 each, while the average price rose to $4.50 per unit for the last 3,750 units purchased during that year.

Measured in terms of actual dollar cost, Odd Ball's purchases for inventory in its first year of operation totaled $55,500. This is the total cost of the actual inventory on hand at the end of the year, coupled with what was sold during the year.

Using the information in Table 10-2, Odd Ball's accountant calculated the fiscal year end value in accordance with each of the two major accounting alternatives. Using FIFO accounting for the 5,250 units on hand at the end of the fiscal year, the accountant calculated the following inventory value:

3,750 units	x	$4.50	=	$16,875
1,500 units	x	$3.50	=	$ 5,250
Ending Inventory Value				
(5,250 units)			=	$22,125

Table 10-2
Annual Inventory Activity
Odd Ball Bearing Company

	Units	Cost per Unit	Actual Cost
Beginning Inventory	1,500	$2.00	$ 3,000
Purchases:			
1st Quarter	3,500	$3.00	$10,500
2nd Quarter	4,000	3.00	12,000
3rd Quarter	3,750	3.50	13,125
4th Quarter	3,750	4.50	16,875
Total Inventory Available for Sale	16,500	—	$55,500
Ending Inventory	5,250	—	*

* Varies according to which accounting principle is used.

Presumably, all 3,750 units purchased during Odd Ball's fourth quarter remain unsold at year's end. Also, 1,500 units acquired during the third quarter remain in stock. Using the prices for the actual purchases within each quarter results in a $22,150 FIFO value for Odd Ball's fiscal year end inventory.

The accountant then valued the firm's inventory using LIFO accounting. This method leads to the following valuation for the 5,250 units Odd Ball had on hand at the end of its fiscal year:

1,500 units	x	$2.00	=	$ 3,000
3,750 units	x	$3.00	=	$11,250
Ending Inventory Value (5,250 units)			=	$14,250

LIFO accounting assumes that the firm's year end inventory includes the original 1,500 units on hand when the year began, plus the first 3,750 units acquired during the first six months of operation. The logic of LIFO asserts that all sales came from the stock purchased after the first 5,250 units. That logic leads to a $14,250 final value for Odd Ball's year end inventory, $7,875 less than that measured by FIFO accounting.

Now let's see how the alternative inventory values affect Odd Ball's cash flow.

Inventory Valuation and Cash Flow from Earnings

The FIFO and LIFO accounting principles exert different influences on a firm's earnings calculation. Actual sales remain the same and actual inventory purchase costs do not change. However, different ending inventory values lead to different earnings results. That affects a firm's income tax obligation, which influences its annual cash flow.

A two-step process illustrates the difference which results from the two accounting principles. First, we examine the effect the different year-end inventory values have on the cost-of-goods-sold total used to calculate earnings. Then we look at the effect that calculation has on a firm's income tax obligation.

Table 10-3 summarizes the first step in that process with the comparative cost-of-goods-sold calculations that come from FIFO and LIFO inventory valuations.

Both alternatives begin with Odd Ball's opening day $3,000 inventory. To total both calculations add the actual purchase price of the inventory acquired during the year to obtain the total cost of the inventory available for sale. To determine the cost of goods sold, each calculation subtracts the alternative ending inventory values from the total inventory available for sale. We already know that LIFO accounting produces a lower ending inventory value than does FIFO accounting. Here that difference leads to a $7,875 higher cost-of-goods-sold total.

Table 10-3
Comparative Effects of FIFO and LIFO
Accounting on the Cost-of-Goods-Sold Calculation
Odd Ball Bearing Company

Beginning Inventory	$ 3,000	$ 3,000
Purchases (actual cost)	52,500	52,500
Total Inventory Available for Sale	$ 55,500	$ 55,500
Less: Ending Inventory	(22,125)	(14,250)
Cost of Goods Sold	$ 33,375	$ 41,250

Up to this point, neither accounting alternative has had any effect on Odd Ball's daily or annual cash flow. Sales revenue remains constant in either circumstance, and the actual purchase costs for the firm's inventory remain the same. The only difference comes from the different methods of valuing the inventory Odd Ball had on hand at the end of the fiscal year.

Table 10-4 illustrates where that difference becomes relevant. It compares Odd Ball's earnings calculations using the cost-of-goods-sold totals derived from the alternative accounting principles.

FIFO accounting, with the lower cost-of-goods-sold total, leads to pretax earnings $7,875 above those calculated using the LIFO accounting data. Up to this point, neither alternative has had an effect on Odd Ball's cash flow. However, the next step in the calculation applies a 40% tax rate to the firm's pretax earnings. Now the difference tells.

Table 10-4
Effect of FIFO and LIFO Accounting on Earnings
Odd Ball Bearing Company

Sales	$ 60,000	$ 60,000
Cost of Goods Sold	(33,375)	(41,250)
Operating Expenses	(10,000)	(10,000)
Pre-tax Earnings	$ 16,625	$ 8,750
Taxes at 40%	(6,650)	(3,500)
After-tax Earnings	$ 9,975	$ 5,250

FIFO accounting leaves Odd Ball with a $6,650 tax obligation, compared to the $3,500 liability that comes from LIFO accounting. Viewed from another perspective, FIFO accounting increases the firm's cash income tax obligation (local, state, and federal) $3,150 above that calculated with the LIFO method. This difference becomes more explicit by comparing the annual cash flows that come from the two accounting alternatives.

Comparative Cash Flows

To emphasize the different results that come from FIFO and LIFO accounting, we will review the actual annual cash flow that Odd Ball Bearing will experience in either circumstance. This review relies on the following simplified assumptions:

1. Odd Ball offers no credit terms; all sales are made in exchange for cash at the time of purchase.
2. The firm pays cash for all purchases and operating expenses; Odd Ball defers no obligation in the form of accounts payable or accrued liabilities.

3. The company has cash reserves sufficient to handle all business on a cash basis.

Table 10-5 compares the annual cash required to fund Odd Ball's operation, using both accounting alternatives. We ignore cash flow into the business from sales in this illustration, presuming that it is an element of the cash flow "sufficient" for operations. Confirming our earlier analysis, LIFO accounting reduces the cash expenditures required for Odd Ball's first year in business by $3,150.

To keep both principles in perspective, remember:

Concept 25: LIFO inventory accounting usually leads to a better annual cash flow than FIFO accounting.

The difference in cash flow in Odd Ball's circumstance may not be particularly exciting, but Odd Ball is a very small business. Increase its volume from $60,000 to $600,000 for the year and the cash benefit from LIFO accounting rises proportionately to $37,200.

Table 10-5
Effects of FIFO and LIFO Accounting on Cash Flow
Odd Ball Bearing Company

	FIFO	LIFO
Beginning Inventory	$ 3,000	$ 3,000
Purchases	52,500	52,500
Operating Expenses	10,000	10,000
Taxes	6,650	3,500
Total Cash Requirements	$72,150	$69,000

Now, let's see how that cash flow affects Odd Ball's financial structure.

Inventory Valuation and Financial Structure

Let's look at the different effects LIFO and FIFO accounting have on the financial structure of a business—the balance sheet. To amplify the effects LIFO and FIFO have on the balance sheet, we add Odd Ball's opening day balance sheet, as illustrated in Table 10-6, Column 1.

On opening day, the company had only $3,000 in inventory and $25,000 in cash. This is a simple but healthy financial structure for almost any new business. But now examine the comparative financial structures that exist at the end of Odd Ball's first year using the two accounting principles.

Table 10-6
Effect of FIFO and LIFO Accounting on Balance Sheets

	Beginning Balance Sheet	End of Year FIFO	End of Year LIFO
Cash	$25,000	$15,850	$19,000
Inventory	3,000	22,125	14,250
Total Assets	$28,000	$37,975	$33,250
Stockholders' Equity	$28,000	$37,975	$33,250

As one might suspect, LIFO accounting leaves the firm with $3,150 more cash on hand than FIFO accounting. This benefit accrues despite the lower earnings that apparently result from the LIFO calculation. Of course, the year-end balance sheet also reflects the lower inventory valuation that comes from LIFO accounting. That difference translates ultimately into a lower total for the stockholders' equity account than with FIFO accounting.

The positive effect that LIFO accounting exerts on Odd Ball's cash flow is, psychologically at least, partially offset by an understatement in the firm's inventory value and a lower net worth. The lower net worth can become an argument against LIFO accounting. At the same time, recognize the difference reflects the accounting principles, not the actual value. Concentrate on the additional cash a business can gain with the aid of LIFO accounting.

The Logic and Limits of LIFO Accounting

Because a business sells most of its inventory sequentially as purchased, it is impossible to justify LIFO accounting in physical terms. Nevertheless, LIFO accounting, which assumes a business sells its inventory in reverse of the order acquired, is more logical than one might suspect. And it is easy to justify in the modern economic environment.

That logic argues that a business should relate its current sales to its current costs. In an inflationary environment, where prices rise persistently, using the most recent costs for the cost-of-goods-sold calculation makes more sense than the use of older, lower costs that are no longer realistic. While LIFO accounting lowers a firm's apparent earnings, it also provides a valuable cash contribution to help offset the higher cost of replacement inventory. In fact, LIFO accounting represents a valuable weapon against inflation.

Along with this logic, you also should recognize the limits on LIFO accounting. First, the principle exerts a positive influence on cash flow only in an inflationary environment. In the event that your industry experiences a year of declining prices, LIFO accounting will lead to higher earnings and a smaller annual cash flow than FIFO accounting.

The modern economic environment leaves little hope of declining prices. Price trends will proceed steadily upward. Should we move into a deflationary era, LIFO accounting would have a detrimental impact on your cash flow.

LIFO accounting also understates the true financial strength of a business because it lowers the inventory valuation, earnings, and net worth. To the extent that the lower values lead to a critical view of creditworthiness, LIFO accounting becomes detrimental to a business. In any event, those limitations don't negate the cash benefits you can derive from LIFO accounting.

Part
III

Structural
Management

Chapter 11

Financial Structure and the Cash Flow Process

Even the most proficient component management effort does not preclude cash flow problems. A satisfactory cash flow requires financially sound interrelationships among all of the elements that appear on your balance sheet. At the same time, the cash flow cycle ultimately becomes the controlling factor in that interrelationship.

This chapter examines the minimum cash investment required for a business, exclusive of any potential assistance from creditors. Few enterprises prosper without financial assistance, but the restriction illustrates a fundamental tenet of structural management.

Then, we build on that conceptual foundation to illustrate the position creditors hold in your financial structure. Creditors provide a valuable addition to your cash capability. In fact, that contribution may provide the boost you need to achieve a profitable sales volume.

Requirements of the Cash Flow Cycle

The natural cash flow cycle converts cash into inventory, then inventory into accounts receivable, which convert back into cash. Efficient management of your receivables and inventory improves cash flow and contributes to higher earnings. However, whether your sales volume is large or small, your financial structure must provide the necessary cash capability.

We use the Bayline Bolt Corporation to illustrate this concept. Bayline, a bolt wholesaler, was founded recently by Glen Mayes, a salesman with many years of experience in the industry.

Before beginning operations, Mayes projected his initial cash requirements based on the following assumptions:

1. Bayline would generate $1,000 per day, or $30,000 per month, in sales from inception.
2. The forty-five day collection period standard in the industry will translate that volume into a $45,000 average investment in accounts receivable.
3. Achieving that sales objective will require a $48,000 average investment in inventory; a smaller investment will lead to excessive stock-out problems.
4. Bayline's cost of goods sold will be 80% of its sales, resulting in a 20% gross profit margin, exclusive of operating expenses.
5. Bayline's monthly operating costs, exclusive of inventory purchases, will average $6,000.
6. Presumably, the initial sales volume will provide break-even operating results; the firm will neither make nor lose money.

Mayes's projections also recognized a common constraint that is confronted by many new business ventures. He could not count on trade credit consideration; all suppliers would require cash payment for all purchases upon delivery.

Beginning with these assumptions, Mayes found that the cash flow cycle set by the anticipated operating characteristics determined the cash investment required to initiate operations. The investment had to be sufficient to support the anticipated investment in accounts receivable and inventory, plus provide the $7,000 Mayes believed was the minimum necessary for operating cash. The cumulative cash investment had to fund all of the components in the cash flow cycle.

Table 11-1 demonstrates that requirement with a look at three of Bayline's balance sheets.

Prior to initiating operations, Mayes invested $100,000 in cash in the business. The firm has at this point no other assets or liabilities. Since Bayline lacks any external credit consideration, the $100,000 also represents the firm's total cash capability.

By opening day, Bayline had purchased (for cash) the $48,000 in inventory necessary to achieve the $1,000 daily sales volume. After opening day, the firm purchased inventory on a daily basis (again for cash) to replace what was sold. Remember, Bayline had to maintain that minimum investment to achieve the projected sales volume.

Table 11-1
Relationship Between Financial Structure
and the Cash Flow Cycle
Bayline Bolt Corporation

	Comparative Balance Sheets		
	Prior to Opening	Opening	45 Days After
Cash	$100,000	$ 52,000	$ 7,000
Accounts Receivable	—	—	45,000
Inventory	—	48,000	48,000
Total Assets	$100,000	$100,000	$100,000
Liabilities	—	—	—
Stockholders' Equity	$100,000	$100,000	$100,000

Forty-five days after beginning operations, while maintaining the $48,000 investment in inventory, Bayline has a $45,000 investment in accounts receivable. Of course, the remainder of Mayes's original investment rests in his operating account.

Column 3 reflects the financial structure that evolves naturally from Bayline's cash expenditures during the first forty-five days in business. To summarize those expenditures:

Beginning Cash	$100,000
Initial Inventory Purchase	(48,000)
Replacement Inventory Purchases	
(80% of selling price)	(36,000)
Operating Expenses	
(45 days at $6,000 per month)	(9,000)
Cash Reserve	$ 7,000

Note two important implications suggested by Bayline's cash flow and financial structure. First, the gross profit on sales (accrued in the form of 20% of the firm's investment in receivables) exactly offsets the $9,000 in operating expenses. As anticipated, the $1,000 daily sales volume does result in a break-even operation. Second, with the $1,000 daily sales volume and the other operating characteristics, Bayline's investment in accounts receivable and inventory cannot be less than $93,000.

A lower inventory level would preclude the daily sales volume necessary to prevent a loss. So, too, would any attempt to reduce the firm's average collection period below the industry average. Enforcing a shorter period would steer customers toward Bayline's more lenient competitors. The cash flow cycle set by the firm's operating characteristics dictates the initial investment and the resulting financial structure necessary to conduct a break-even sales volume. Any investment less than $100,000 would lead to unavoidable losses. We emphasize this in:

Concept 26: A balanced financial structure provides the cash capability necessary to support the natural cash flow cycle.

Figure 11-1 provides a conceptual view that should help clarify the relationship. Note two additional facts about Bayline's circumstance forty-five days after opening.

Figure 11-1
Financial Structure and Cash Flow Cycle

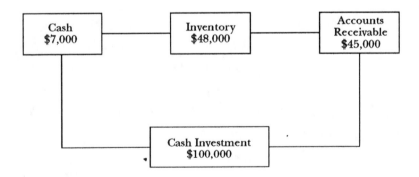

First, so long as Bayline continues to generate $1,000 a day in sales, the financial structure will remain unchanged. Each day's new sales will be exactly offset by an equal collection of accounts receivable from previous sales. Similarly, operating expenses will continue to equal Bayline's gross profit margin from those sales.

Second, without additional cash capability, Bayline cannot increase sales to a profitable level. Any increase in sales would require a pro-rata increase in accounts receivable and inventory that would quickly exhaust the firm's minimal cash reserves. That would lead to a cash flow problem.

For example, assume Mayes decided to increase Bayline's daily sales volume to $1,250 a day, or $37,500 a month, without increasing the cash investment.

Table 11-2 shows the effects of the higher sales volume on Bayline's financial structure. Based on the original operating assumptions, that volume would require a $60,000 investment in inventory—an amount sufficient for sixty days' sales—and a $56,250 investment in accounts receivable.

Table 11-2
Effect of Higher Volume on Financial Structure
Bayline Bolt Corporation

Cash	($16,250)
Accounts Receivable	56,250
Inventory	60,000
Total Assets	$100,000
Stockholders' Equity	$100,000

Naturally, Bayline would never reach the $16,250 deficit cash position. The firm's suppliers, still requiring cash payment on delivery, would cease shipments as soon as the firm exhausted its cash capability. The higher volume would produce an unacceptable, unbalanced financial structure.

The Creditor's Contribution to Cash Capability

Glen Mayes quickly recognized that he could not increase his sales volume above the break-even level without expanding his cash capability. Lacking the resources to increase his cash investment in Bayline, Mayes pursued a logical alternative. He negotiated more reasonable payment terms from his suppliers.

Bayline's suppliers agreed to allow thirty day payment terms for all purchases. This was a reasonable response to a customer who paid cash for $24,000 in purchases each month for several months in a row. Taking advantage of the cash capability supplied by more liberal payment terms, Mayes quickly pushed Bayline's sales up to $1,250 per day. This volume produced two significant changes in the firm's financial circumstances.

First, the higher volume made Bayline a profitable operation. Since Mayes held fixed costs constant, the firm began generating the following monthly earnings:

Sales	$ 37,500
Costs of Sales	(30,000)
Fixed Costs	(6,000)
Monthly Earnings	$ 1,500

Second, Bayline generated the higher volume without straining its cash capability. Table 11-3 reflects the creditor's contribution to Bayline's financial structure. (To simplify the illustration, we ignore the profits that come from Bayline's higher volume.) The $24,000 in supplier credit enables Bayline to carry the higher investment in inventory and accounts receivable that came with the sales increase. Figure 11-2 provides a conceptual view of the contribution the $24,000 in credit consideration made to Bayline's cash flow and financial structure.

Table 11-3
Creditor's Contribution to the Cash Flow Cycle
Bayline Bolt Corporation

Cash	$ 7,750
Accounts Receivable	56,250
Inventory	60,000
Total Assets	$124,000
Accounts Payable	$ 24,000
Stockholders' Equity	100,000
Liabilities and Equity	$124,000

Bayline's experience demonstrates that credit consideration enables a business to increase the total asset investment revolving in its cash flow cycle. The benefit from that effort is summarized in Cash Flow Concept No. 27:

Concept 27: Credit consideration increases the cash capability in a business.

Figure 11-2
Creditors' Contribution to the Cash Flow Cycle

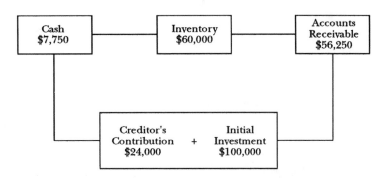

Note that a business gains the benefit regardless of the source of the credit consideration. For example, had Mayes obtained a $24,000 bank loan while continuing to pay cash for all purchases, the financial results would have been the same. Of course, borrowing costs would have lowered earnings slightly.

Chapter 12

Structural Management: A Matter of Balance

A fundamental accounting principle should underlie the management of your firm's financial structure. Your assets must equal your liabilities plus stockholders' equity. This chapter demonstrates how you can use this principle to anticipate the effects of any financial decision on the cash flow process in your business.

The Balance Sheet Equation

Managing your financial structure and cash flow centers on a basic accounting equation:

$$\text{Total Assets} = \text{Total Liabilities} + \text{Stockholders' Equity}$$

Many business managers overlook this fundamental requirement in their cash flow management. Often they commit themselves to expanding assets without estimating the effects this expansion will have on their firms' financial structure and the cash flow process. Yet, as suggested by the equation, a $50,000 increase in liabilities or stockholders' equity (or some combination of the two) must accompany a $50,000 increase in total assets. Moreover, both increases in the balance sheet accounts must observe the demands set by the cash flow cycle.

Cash Capability and Financial Structure

Cash capability describes the total resources a firm has available to finance an increase in the assets revolving in the cash flow cycle. The total cash capability in a business is measured as the sum of its cash reserves plus any unused credit consideration.

However, employing cash capability as a management concept can be complicated. When you commit some portion of that capability, you must recognize how that decision affects your financial structure and cash flow cycle. You must also anticipate both the immediate and future effects of those decisions. Failure to estimate carefully the results of any major decision can lead to a cash flow crisis.

Table 12-1 illustrates this potential problem with a view of the comparative balance sheets of a small wholesaler, Priority Products, Inc.

Column 1 represents PPI's financial structure, with a $100,000 monthly sales volume. That financial statement reflects the characteristics of the firm's operations:

1. All customers observe PPI's thirty day selling terms; the firm collects $100,000 in cash each month from the previous month's sales.
2. PPI purchases $75,000 per month from its suppliers on thirty day terms; a strict management policy requires payment in strict accordance with those terms.
3. Fixed cash expenses average $25,000 per month.

These characteristics leave PPI with a break-even operation. Income equals expenses, and cash collected each month equals cash expended.

Table 12-1
Structural Management and Cash Capability
Priority Products, Inc.

	1	2	3
Cash	$ 25,000	$ 25,000	—
Accounts Receivable	100,000	100,000	$125,000
Inventory	100,000	125,000	125,000
Total Assets	$225,000	$250,000	$250,000
Liabilities	$ 75,000	$100,000	$100,000
Stockholders' Equity	150,000	150,000	150,000
Liabilities and Equity	$225,000	$250,000	$250,000

Now, consider the results of PPI's decision to increase sales above the break-even level.

We will assume that the firm already has $50,000 in additional cash capability to finance an increase in sales. In addition to the $25,000 in cash reserves, PPI has $25,000 in unused credit consideration. Recognizing this, PPI's management decides to increase the firm's investment in inventory from $100,000 to $125,000. Projections suggest that the higher investment will help increase sales to $125,000 per month and lead to profitable operations.

The increase in inventory must use $25,000 of PPI's cash capability. Either an increase in liabilities or a decrease in cash reserves must supply the funds for the new inventory. Of course, some combination of cash reserves and liabilities that total $25,000 also would provide the cash capability necessary for the inventory. However, assume that management can exercise only one alternative.

Column 2 recognizes management's logical option to use the creditors' consideration to finance the expansion in inventory. Thus, PPI's inventory, total assets, and liabilities all rise by $25,000. The financial structure remains balanced. However, the changes indicated in the financial structure represent only the initial effects of the decision to increase inventory. Positive cash flow management also requires considering the future alterations in that structure if the sales projections prove to be accurate.

Column 3 visualizes that future when PPI achieves the higher sales volume of $125,000 per month, while it also maintains the increased investment in inventory. We see that the successful sales effort leads PPI directly into a cash flow problem. As sales increased, so did the firm's investment in accounts receivable. As that rise absorbed the rest of the firm's cash capability, cash reserves dropped to zero. PPI is out of cash.

PPI's experience illustrates a critical concept. Any decision to increase your investment in any asset other than cash absorbs some of your cash capability. It effects a change in your financial structure represented by an increase in liabilities or a decrease in cash. In any instance, you must have sufficient capability to absorb the increase or decrease. The critical relationship can be stated succinctly in:

Concept 28:   A balance sheet must balance.

The cash flow cycle imposes demands that must be met by the cash capability held in your financial structure. So, you must look beyond the present and anticipate the future consequences of your decision.

When any doubts exist about the potential effects of any decision on your financial structure, turn to Cash Flow Concept No. 28. Then measure the effects your decision has on your financial structure and cash flow cycle. That foresight may preclude a cash flow problem.

Losses: A Drain on Cash Capability

In the case of Priority Products, we assumed the equity account was constant in order to orient our primary concern—day-to-day cash flow management. Now, adopting a slightly different perspective, let's examine the effects profits and losses have on the financial structure and cash capability in a business.

Return to Priority Product's initial balance sheet (now in Table 12-2). We will now presume PPI holds its investment in accounts receivable and inventory constant from one year to the next. Assume PPI suffers a $25,000 loss for the year following the date of the initial balance sheet. That loss translates into an equal reduction in PPI's equity account. The equity drops from $150,000 to $125,000.

Table 12-2
Effect of a Loss on Financial Structure
Priority Products, Inc.

	1	2	3
Cash	$ 25,000	$ 25,000	—
Accounts Receivable	100,000	100,000	$100,000
Inventory	100,000	100,000	100,000
Total Assets	$225,000	$225,000	$200,000
Liabilities	$ 75,000	$100,000	$ 75,000
Stockholders' Equity	150,000	125,000	125,000
Liabilities and Equity	$225,000	$225,000	$200,000

Of course, no account in a firm's financial structure can change independently. The balance sheet always balances. Since we are holding PPI's investment in accounts receivable and inventory constant, we can anticipate the potential effects of the loss on the other elements in the firm's financial structure.

As one extreme, PPI's total liabilities might increase by $25,000, as shown in Table 12-2, Column 2. Any increase in liabilities absorbs an equivalent amount of cash capability. At the other extreme, PPI might hold its liabilities constant at the expense of its cash reserves. But that policy, reflected in Column 3, leaves the business in a desperate cash position. Indeed, those reserves dwindle down to nothing.

PPI's management logically would seek some reasonable balance between the two extremes. Also, the loss could be offset by additional cash investments by stockholders, or perhaps by negotiating larger lines of credit. However, none of these options changes the point of the illustration. You should foresee the inevitable penalty that a loss exacts on a firm's cash capability. We summarize that effect in:

Concept 29: **An operating loss drains an equivalent amount of cash capability from a business.**

Now, let's examine the positive side of the picture.

Profits: A Contribution to Cash Capability

An operating profit has an opposite effect from a loss. Table 12-3 helps illustrate that logical fact.

Again we proceed from PPI's initial balance sheet and assume that accounts receivable and inventory remain constant. We also assume that PPI generates $25,000 in earnings during the one year period following the initial balance sheet.

Table 12-3
Effect of a Profit on Financial Structure
Priority Products, Inc.

	1	2	3
Cash	$ 25,000	$ 25,000	$ 50,000
Accounts Receivable	100,000	100,000	100,000
Inventory	100,000	100,000	100,000
Total Assets	$225,000	$225,000	$250,000
Liabilities	$ 75,000	$ 50,000	$ 75,000
Stockholders' Equity	150,000	175,000	175,000
Liabilities and Equity	$225,000	$225,000	$250,000

Note the effects those profits have on the firm's financial structure. Of course, PPI's equity account increases by an amount equal to the earnings. Profits translate directly into an increase in the net worth of a business. But as that occurs, other changes also must occur in the firm's financial structure.

Considering the extremes, the $25,000 increase in equity must be matched by either a matching reduction in total liabilities or by an equivalent increase in cash. Table 12-3, Columns 2 and 3, illustrates these results.

The positive cash flow manager might select some balance between the two extremes. However, the earnings contribute $25,000 to PPI's cash capability as they reduce liabilities or increase cash reserves. That becomes:

Concept 30: Earnings provide an equivalent increase in cash capability in a business.

Our illustration centered on the cumulative effects of a full year's operations profits and losses. Of course, profits and losses typically occur incrementally throughout the year. In PPI's experience, for example, we can assume that the $25,000 in earnings increased the firm's equity and cash capability at an average rate of about $2,100 per month. From this you should be able to anticipate the potential benefits held in earnings. You can do that because most businesses accrue profits in the form of uncollected accounts receivable. The actual cash flows into the business only when customers pay.

Similarly, you can anticipate the detrimental effects of a loss. An operating loss usually appears first in the form of accrued expenses or accounts payable. A loss this month doesn't drain cash from the business until next month. Of course, the only way you can anticipate either result is to prepare an income statement and balance sheet promptly at the end of each month. That information will help you offset the effects of a loss or take advantage of the cash capability that will flow in from a profit.

Chapter 13

Structural Management: Financial Forecasting

In Chapter 1 the Drake Paper Company's experience demonstrated the crucial difference between accrual and cash flow accounting. Drake's rapid increase in sales produced higher earnings but left the firm with a cash flow problem. The earnings rested in the form of uncollected accounts receivable, while payments to suppliers and operating expenses exhausted Drake's cash reserves.

Based on the discussion in Chapters 11 and 12, you now can view Drake's problem as a structural one. Since a balance sheet must balance, an increase in liabilities or stockholders' equity must match any expansion in assets associated with a rising sales volume.

Moreover, Drake's experience is a common occurrence among growing businesses. Success often leads to cash flow problems. Even a business that expands at a relatively modest rate can outpace its cash capability.

This makes financial forecasting an essential task for the business manager practicing positive cash flow management. Neither the amount nor the source of the funds necessary to support any increase in assets should come as a surprise. This chapter illustrates the inevitable financing needs that arise in a growing business, along with the process that helps you to forecast those needs.

The Growth Syndrome

Most business managers seek growth as a natural business objective. They press constantly to increase sales this month over last month and this year over last year. This pressure comes from two primary sources.

First, the desire for growth is an instinctive drive. Failure to satisfy that drive, however measured, ultimately leads to frustration. In the business environment, that drive translates into a constant push for higher sales. In addition, the expansion rate in a business becomes a measure of relative achievement. Presumably, a 20% growth rate represents a larger achievement than a 10% growth rate. Thus growth rate stands as a gauge for comparison among business managers.

Second, the desire for growth is a natural financial requirement. The business that doesn't grow stagnates financially, even though it may operate profitably. Any year inflation outpaces earnings increases, a business inevitably falls behind. The higher earnings that accompany increasing sales become a financial requirement. These effects act as natural spurs that encourage business expansion.

The Structural Limits on Growth

Chapters 11 and 12 emphasized that a firm's cash flow cycle dictates the financial structure and cash capability necessary to avoid a cash flow problem. We examine the same concept here from a different perspective, one that helps define how rapidly a business can grow without using borrowed funds.

To illustrate, we will use the Energy Window Company, a manufacturer of thermal glass windows. Since the firm's product improves insulation, demand is now sufficient to allow Energy Window to double its present $200,000 monthly sales volume.

However, before yielding to that demand by increasing production, Herb Elliot, Energy Window's controller, measured the effect rapid growth would have on the firm's financial structure. He found that the realistic limit on that prospective growth rate fell well below 100%.

Elliot's analysis began with a review of Energy Window's relevant characteristics:

1. A sixty day average collection period translates the present volume into a $400,000 investment in accounts receivable; that collection period is consistent with the industry average.

2. Material costs average 75% of sales, or $150,000 per month; experience indicates that the firm must maintain an inventory sufficient for two months' sales on hand in order to achieve any projected volume.

3. Suppliers typically allow thirty days for payment. Company policy requires strict observance of those terms; consequently, accounts payable cannot exceed one month's purchases or 50% of the inventory in stock.

4. The firm maintains a minimum $50,000 cash balance (to satisfy bank requirements).

5. Any increase in sales requires a proportionate increase in cash, accounts receivable, and inventory.

These characteristics translate into the financial structure in Table 13-1.

However, note a prominent element that has not been mentioned. Energy Window presently has a $350,000 bank loan. In fact, the loan provides the cash capability essential for the business to generate its present $200,000 monthly volume while paying suppliers for all purchases within the prescribed thirty day terms. The presence of the bank loan also explains the need for the $50,000 minimum cash balance. Those funds meet the bank's compensating balance requirements for the loan.

Table 13-1
Energy Window Company

Cash	$ 50,000
Accounts Receivable	400,000
Inventory	300,000
Total Assets	$750,000
Accounts Payable	$150,000
Bank Loan	350,000
Total Liabilities	$500,000
Stockholders' Equity	250,000
Liabilities and Equity	$750,000

The need for the bank loan also suggests the critical constraint that imposes the natural limit on Energy Window's growth rate. While observing the firm's operating requirements, the growth rate cannot outpace the financing available to support the increase in assets that naturally accompanies higher sales.

The problem is even more complex than it first appears, since the need for financing typically expands more rapidly than the sales volume in a growing business. Lenders may set the brake on growth sooner than you might imagine.

To prove these assertions, let's review Elliot's original analysis, which now proceeds in two logical steps.

First, Elliot identified the financing required to support the increase in Energy Window's assets anticipated from various growth rates. Second, he identified the upper limit on the available financing. Table 13-2 summarizes the first phase in that analysis. It projects the anticipated increase in assets and corresponding demands for financing that will come from growth rates ranging from 10% to 50%.

To simplify the illustration, we temporarily ignore the contribution earnings make toward balancing the firm's rising assets. As we will see, that contribution is real, but it does not affect the principal point. That is, the growth rate in a business is limited by the external financing available to support the accompanying increase in assets.

Now, look at the critical points in Table 13-2. Note that a modest 10% increase in sales leads to a $75,000 increase in assets. While an increase in supplier debt—accounts payable—provides $15,000 in support, Energy Window needs an additional $60,000 in financing to carry the higher asset investment. (We assume here that accounts payable automatically expand at the same rate as sales.)

As the projected growth rate increases, the need for additional financing rises rapidly. Indeed, a 50% expansion rate calls for a $300,000 increase in bank (or other) financing. Also note that the 50% increase in sales requires an 85% increase in new external financing. Proportionate debt requirements outpace the expansion in assets.

Armed with these projections, Elliot then proceeded to the second step in his analysis. He identified the bank's lending limits applicable to Energy Window's circumstance. Unfortunately, by normal bank credit standards, the firm's financial structure does not justify the additional $300,000 in credit consideration necessary to support a 50% growth rate. The financing required to fund a 30% or 40% expansion rate also is out of the question. Without that financial assistance, Energy Window must hold its growth rate below those levels.

Actually, we can't specify the exact amount of financial aid available from Energy Window's bank. The final determination requires more precise credit analysis. Nevertheless, Elliot's analysis demonstrates the critical point emphasized in:

Concept 31:   A firm's financial structure limits its growth rate.

Table 13-2
Growth Financing Requirements
Energy Window Company

Growth Rate	10%	20%	30%	40%	50%
Total Asset Increase	$75,000	$150,000	$225,000	$300,000	$375,000
Less: Accounts Payable Increase	(15,000)	(30,000)	(45,000)	(60,000)	(75,000)
Additional Financing Required	$60,000	$120,000	$180,000	$240,000	$300,000
Increase in Necessary Financing in Proportion to Bank Loan	17%	34%	51%	68%	85%

A growth rate that exceeds the limits set by a firm's financial structure creates cash flow problems.

The Financial Forecasting Process

The process that anticipates a firm's financing requirements proceeds through five straightforward steps:

1. Express any projected sales increase as a percentage of the current operating period's—the current year, quarter, or month.
2. Multiply the firm's existing investment in current assets by the percentage sales increase anticipated during the upcoming operating period. This identifies the total asset expansion the business should expect.
3. Multiply the firm's accounts payable and accrued liabilities by the anticipated percentage increase in sales. This identifies the financial support for the asset expansion that will come from the spontaneous increase in liabilities.
4. Identify the increase in retained earnings the business expects during the upcoming operating period. This will equal the firm's anticipated net earnings, less any dividend payments to stockholders.
5. Subtracting the totals found in steps 3 and 4 from that found in step 2 identifies the firm's net new financing requirements.

Another look at the Energy Window Company illustrates the financial forecasting process.

In this instance, we assume that management has arbitrarily decided to push Energy Window's monthly average sales volume up to $320,000. This represents a 60% increase over the $200,000 monthly average produced during the firm's fiscal year ending 8/31/91.

In addition, we will move Energy Window a step closer to the real world and assume that the firm will produce $300,000 in earnings from its $3,840,000 total sales volume ($320,000 x 12) for the year ending 8/31/92. Half of those earnings will flow from the business in the form of dividend payments to stockholders. So Energy Window will retain $150,000 out of its total earnings to help support its expected expansion in assets. Now we can proceed with the financial forecasting process.

First, multiplying the firm's $750,000 in assets on 8/31/91 by 60% indicates that Energy Window should anticipate a $450,000 increase in its total asset investment during 1992. The business will need an increase in liabilities and stockholders' equity (in any combination) that matches the asset expansion.

Energy Window can expect a 60%, or $90,000, increase in its accounts payable. Presumably, the firm's trade credit lines will expand at the same rate as its sales. Certainly that will hold true so long as Energy Window maintains the ability to pay its suppliers promptly. A business that accrues some liabilities—salaries, wages, taxes—would include them in the calculation process, along with its accounts payable.

The spontaneous increase in accounts payable will provide $90,000 in support for Energy Window's anticipated increase in assets. As noted, another $150,000 in support will come from earnings retained in the business. These totals can be interrelated to forecast Energy Window's financing requirements for 1992:

Anticipated asset expansion	$450,000
Less	
Anticipated spontaneous increase in liabilities	(90,000)
Less	
Addition to retained earnings	(150,000)
Net new financing requirements	$210,000

Energy Window needs $210,000 in additional financing to maintain a balanced financial structure during the upcoming year. In the absence of that financing, whatever the source, the mandated 60% increase in sales will create a severe cash flow problem. Energy Window will quickly exhaust its cash reserves and lose the ability to honor supplier payment terms. The need for financial forecasting can be emphasized in:

Concept 32: Financial forecasting helps anticipate a firm's financing requirements.

This foresight can help a business avoid cash flow problems.

In any event, recognize the critical contribution the financial forecasting process makes to a business. The process enables a business to foresee the need for new financing. This need does not appear as a surprise that can precipitate a financial crisis. Instead, a business gains the time necessary to arrange for the new financing or, as discussed below, effect actions that may reduce the need for financing.

Offsetting the Financial Limits on Growth

No business manager wants to impose limits on the growth rate in his business. So, we should touch on an important concept that can help you overcome, at least partially, any limits on the growth financing available from external lenders. Indeed, managing your accounts receivable and inventory more efficiently generates cash that you can devote to the demands of an increasing sales volume.

To illustrate, let's take another look at the Energy Window Company. We previously assumed that Energy Window's sixty day average collection period would remain constant as sales increased. Thus the firm's investment in receivables would expand as rapidly as sales.

However, Herb Elliot, seeking to overcome the firm's financing limits, connected two important facts. First, he recognized that the market demand for Energy Window's products provided the major impetus in the drive for expansion. In fact, the lack of adequate financing stands as the only obstacle to a 100% increase in sales. Second, that same demand gave the firm the flexibility to impose shorter payment terms or a more stringent credit policy without hurting sales. Effecting either policy would lower the company's average collection period and improve its cash flow.

These facts encouraged Elliot to cast a new projection estimating the growth potential from the cash that would flow from reducing Energy Window's average collection period from sixty to forty-five days.

As the first step, Elliot considered the potential benefits from enforcing the shorter collection period on the firm's present $200,000 monthly sales volume. He found that the new policy would lower the investment in receivables from $400,000 to $300,000. That reduction provides $100,000 in cash for investment elsewhere. That offers the potential for substantial increase in cash capability even if the company does not press for a higher sales volume.

But Energy Window does want to expand sales. So, Elliot proceeded with the second step in the analysis to project the financing requirements associated with a higher sales volume. However, he altered three of this working assumptions:

1. Energy Window would quickly develop and maintain a forty-five day average collection period.
2. The first $100,000 increase in assets from any sales increase would absorb the cash initially generated by the lower collection period at 8/31/91.
3. The firm's asset base from its present $200,000 monthly sales volume becomes $650,000 after the reduction in accounts receivable.

Table 13-3 summarizes the results of Elliot's analysis.

Table 13-3
Effect of Lower Average Collection Period
on Growth Financing Requirements
Energy Window Company

Growth Rate	10%	20%	30%	40%	50%
Total Asset Increase	$ 65,000	$130,000	$195,000	$260,000	$325,000
Less: Accounts Payable Increase	(15,000)	(30,000)	(45,000)	(60,000)	(75,000)
Less: The cash capability originally generated by reducing the collection period from 60 to 45 days	(100,000)	(100,000)	(100,000)	(100,000)	(100,000)
Financing Requirements	($50,000)	—	$50,000	$100,000	$150,000

The $100,000 in cash that came from the reduction in Energy's receivables at 8/31/91, coupled with the spontaneous increase in accounts payable, provides internal financing for the company's first 20% increase in sales. The business can generate that increase without any other external financing. At the same time, the lower initial asset base reduces the total asset growth that comes with any alternative increase in sales (although the growth rate remains the same). Thus a 50% increase in sales requires $150,000 in new bank financing, only half of that called for in the previous projection. And in the firm's new financial position, gained with the aid of a shorter collection period, Energy Window's bank is more likely to provide the smaller amount of new funds necessary to achieve the 50% rate of expansion. Thus, better receivables management offsets a major portion of the limits set by any external financing source.

Remember this as:

Concept 33: Better component management facilitates growth in a business.

Of course, better component management remains a desirable management objective in any instance. But it can make a critical contribution to the financing needs in a rapidly growing business.

Chapter 14

Structural Management: Fixed Assets and Depreciation

Maintaining a focus on the day-to-day cash flow process excludes a consideration of the impact an investment in fixed assets has on the cash flow process. This impact can be significant, and the significance increases as fixed assets become a larger element in a firm's financial structure. This chapter illustrates those facts and reviews the important concepts that should orient management of a firm's investment in fixed assets.

The Initial Investment

A new investment in fixed assets permanently absorbs some of your cash capability. You must commit cash reserves, perhaps coupled with external financing, sufficient to make up the purchase price of the assets. You easily can measure that direct requirement, but the total cash capability required for a new fixed asset investment usually exceeds the direct acquisition cost. Failure to anticipate these additional requirements can lead to a cash flow problem.

To illustrate, let's look at a proposed $200,000 fixed asset acquisition by the Growth Company. The assets will facilitate an increase in production and provide the potential for a $30,000 monthly increase in sales. As a direct requirement, the Growth Company needs $200,000 in cash capability to complete the acquisition.

However, that does not measure the total cash capability necessary to fund the new investment. The Growth Company also should anticipate the cash capability required to support a larger investment in accounts receivable and inventory.

For example, assume that the company maintains an investment in inventory equal to two months' sales volume and a forty-five day average collection period. If the company completes the fixed asset acquisition and achieves the projected increase in sales, the investment in the two major components in the cash flow cycle will rise as follows:

Inventory (2 times projected sales increase)	=	$ 60,000
Accounts Receivable (45 x $1,000 increase in daily sales)	=	$ 45,000
Total Increase in Component Investment	=	$105,000

The total cash capability required to fund the Growth Company's proposed acquisition is $305,000, or the cost of the investment plus the natural increase in other assets. Should the firm's total cash capability fall below $305,000, the investment will lead to a cash flow problem.

Note that the potential problem exists even if a proposed fixed asset investment does not relate to projected expansion. For example, upgrading your plant with modern equipment may require retraining your employees. You may suffer operating losses—a drain on your cash capability—during the training period. In another circumstance, merely replacing old equipment with new often requires a halt in production during installation. Again, you suffer temporary losses that increase the cost of the investment.

The cash capability required for an investment in fixed assets is seldom limited to the purchase price. Therefore, keep in mind:

Concept 34: Anticipate the total cash capability necessary for an investment in fixed assets.

Recognizing this fact can reduce the chances of an unhappy surprise, a cash flow problem.

Depreciation: The Basic Concept

In several instances, we have referred to the acquisition of fixed assets as an investment. With qualifications, this remains a realistic view. Fixed asset acquisitions should promise the same return as any other investment. But an investment in fixed assets has an important distinguishing characteristic.

With the usual exception of real estate, most productive fixed assets deteriorate. Indeed, most fixed assets have a limited life, and ultimately they become worthless. This fact moves a fixed asset acquisition from the realm of an investment into the category of a normal operating cost. Accountants and tax authorities define that cost as depreciation. A business recognizes the deterioration in any depreciable asset as an expense prorated over its useful life.

Without losing ourselves in complex accounting considerations, we will review the effect depreciation has on the income statement of a business. As an example, we will take the experience of the KBA Corporation, a small manufacturer of specialty steel products.

KBA began operations four years ago with an initial $100,000 cash investment in machinery and equipment. Original estimates indicated that those assets would have a five year life. At the end of that term, the original investment would have no value at all.

Relying on those projections, KBA's accountant recognized the average annual deterioration in the equipment with a $20,000 depreciation expense. Using the operating statement for the firm's fourth year in business as an example, that expense reduced the firm's $20,000 in operating profits:

Earnings before depreciation	$20,000
Depreciation expense	(20,000)
Net earnings	—

During its fourth year in business, KBA found that it had break-even operating results. That shows depreciation has the same effect on earnings as any other expense.

Depreciation as a Noncash Expense

Depreciation prorates the cost of a fixed asset over its useful life. However, it stands apart from most other operating expenses in a business. Depreciation is a noncash expense. From a different perspective, you can view depreciation as an addition to the annual cash flow in a business. To illustrate that view, let's note the effect depreciation has on the cash account at the end of the year of KBA's break-even operations.

Table 14-1 compares the fiscal year end balance sheets for KBA's third and fourth years in business. We will assume that the company's accounts receivable, inventory, and total liabilities remain constant from one year to the next.

Note that despite the break-even operating results in the fourth year, KBA's cash balance increases by $20,000. This cash represents the effect of depreciation on the company's income statement. Although recognized as an expense, no cash flowed out of the business to pay it. However, the cash that develops from the depreciation expense does not represent the return of KBA's original investment in fixed assets. Instead, it merely recognizes the annual expenses incurred from the natural deterioration in those assets. The cash left the business at the time of acquisition. Consequently, no cash flows out when the business recognizes these expenses on the income statement. This fact merits recognition in:

Concept 35: A depreciation expense does not represent a current cash outlay.

Note also that financing the acquisition of fixed assets has no effect on the cash that flows from the depreciation process. Of course, the apparent cash flow from depreciation contributes to the periodic note payments that result from external financing. In fact, the lender measures that potential as an element in his decision to extend fixed asset financing. At the same time, you relate those two elements—the cash flow from depreciation and your debt amortization requirements—in a cash flow budget, not in an operating statement.

Table 14-1
Effect of Depreciation on Annual Cash Flow
KBA Corporation

	Third Year	Fourth Year
Cash	$ 40,000	$ 60,000
Accounts Receivable	200,000	200,000
Inventory	200,000	200,000
Net Fixed Assets (Net of $60,000 accumulated depreciation in the third year and $80,000 in the fourth year)	40,000	20,000
Total Assets	$480,000	$480,000
Total Liabilities	$300,000	$300,000
Stockholders' Equity	180,000	180,000
Liabilities and Equity	$480,000	$480,000

Another implication suggested by the depreciation process is you must foresee the eventual need to replace your depreciable assets. You may not reserve the cash flow from depreciation specifically for that purpose, but you must maintain access to the cash capability necessary to replace worn-out equipment.

Returning to the concept of earnings as cash flow, remember that earnings become a direct increase in cash capability. We will interrelate that with depreciation in:

Concept 36: **Earnings plus depreciation measure the total annual cash flow generated by a firm's operations.**

This identifies the internal cash a business has to expand its reserves, invest in other assets, or reduce debt.

Depreciation as a Tax Shield

Depreciation is a source of cash for a business because the accounting process doesn't recognize a fixed asset acquisition as an expense at the time of the purchase. Instead, it is a periodic noncash expense. The cumulative cash that develops from the depreciation process merely matches the original cash outlay for any particular fixed asset.

At the same time, a profitable business realizes a tangible cash benefit from depreciation expenses. These noncash expenses reduce the firm's reported income and lower its actual income tax obligation.

To illustrate, let's compare two businesses designated as Corporations A and B. Both corporations generate $400,000 in income before depreciation and taxes. Both incur a 40% income tax assessment on their earnings. The only significant distinction between the two is that Corporation A has $100,000 in depreciation expenses, while Corporation B has none. That difference leads to the following view of the two firm's comparative operating results:

	Corporation A	Corporation B
Earnings Before Depreciation and Taxes	$400,000	$400,000
Depreciation	100,000	—
Earnings Before Taxes	$300,000	$400,000
Taxes (40%)	120,000	160,000
Earnings After Taxes	$150,000	$240,000
Plus Depreciation	100,000	—
Annual Cash Flow	$270,000	$240,000

The total cash flow generated by a business includes earnings after taxes plus depreciation. Here Corporation A enjoys $30,000 more in annual cash flow, or $270,000 minus $240,000. The difference develops from the $100,000 in income shielded by Corporation A's depreciation expense. This noncash expense saves $30,000 in taxes, which eventually shows up in the firm's cash flow.

An Overinvestment in Fixed Assets

By now, we can anticipate the effect an overinvestment in fixed assets has on cash capability. Any excess investment absorbs cash that might be used profitably elsewhere. Indeed, an overinvestment in fixed assets is analogous to an overinvestment in accounts receivable and inventory. However, an overinvestment in fixed assets is more difficult to cure.

Indeed, a tighter credit and collection policy can reduce a firm's investment in accounts receivable. A temporary reduction in purchases will encourage a drop in inventory. The rapid disposal of excess fixed assets typically stands as a more difficult task.

Sometimes the excess assets may be part of a production process that has capacity well in excess of the demands set by the firm's sales volume. The business can't eliminate any of the assets without eliminating all of the assets. Thus it must concentrate on expanding sales volume sufficiently to justify the higher productive capacity. In the interim, it must absorb the cost of carrying the excess investment. In other circumstances, a business manager lacks the time or expertise necessary to market unnecessary fixed assets. She absorbs the overinvestment until she stumbles into the sale of the assets, often suffering a significant loss in the process.

An overinvestment in fixed assets also is more expensive than an overinvestment in accounts receivable or inventory. Of course, the financial or opportunity cost from carrying excess assets in any instance is the same. Using a 10% annual rate, a $100,000 excess investment in fixed assets leads to a $10,000 reduction in earnings.

This detrimental effect is increased by the insurance, storage, and maintenance costs associated with the excess fixed assets. Analogous to inventory, it costs more to carry an investment in fixed assets than in accounts receivable. However, in a major distinction from accounts receivable and inventory, an overinvestment in fixed assets commits still further injury to the earnings in a business because of the higher depreciation expense from that overinvestment.

Thus, a $100,000 excess investment in fixed assets may lead to a $10,000 reduction in annual earnings. The reduction comes from the annual depreciation charge associated with that overinvestment, applying straight line depreciation over a ten year useful life. In any circumstance, higher depreciation charges lead to lower earnings.

An Underinvestment in Fixed Assets

An underinvestment in fixed assets should impose no direct cash flow problem. Fewer assets in one account leave cash capability available for use elsewhere. However, such an underinvestment often leads to direct and indirect costs that penalize a firm's earnings.

The higher direct costs can arise from an operation that, because of the underinvestment, remains less efficient than an operation with a larger investment in fixed assets. Higher labor costs and lower productivity associated with an inefficient manufacturing process inevitably shrink a firm's profit margin.

While the business may remain profitable, the earnings lost from the lower profit margin can be viewed as an opportunity cost. The firm earns less than it should. Another opportunity cost may come from sales lost as a result of inefficient or insufficient productive capacity. These opportunity costs may be difficult to measure, but they are real.

The Proper Investment in Fixed Assets

The proper investment in fixed assets relative to total assets will vary widely among businesses. A wholesaler may require no fixed assets except the shelves necessary to store her products and the trucks necessary to deliver them. Alternatively, a manufacturer may carry a larger investment in fixed assets than either accounts receivable or inventory.

Although the correct investment in any specific case involves many complex variables, we can demonstrate one fundamental financial tool that can orient your analysis. That tool, the sales to net fixed assets ratio, enables you to relate your sales volume to your net investment in fixed assets and to measure your fixed asset turnover rate. For example, a business with $1,000,000 in annual sales and a $100,000 net investment in fixed assets will relate the two totals as follows:

$$\text{Sales to Net Fixed Assets} = \frac{\text{Sales}}{\text{Net Fixed Assets}}$$

$$\text{Sales to Net Fixed Assets} = \frac{\$1,000,000}{\$100,000} = 10$$

The firm's sales volume exceeds its investment in fixed assets ten times. Or, the business turns its fixed assets ten times in the course of the year. The assets don't turn in the same way as accounts receivable and inventory, but the fixed asset turnover rate becomes the primary criterion for measuring the efficient use of fixed assets.

Perhaps the best use of that criterion again comes from a comparison with the fixed asset turnover rates demonstrated by your competitors (using, for example, Dun and Bradstreet ratios or Robert Morris Associates Annual Statement Studies). Should your fixed asset turnover rate fall below your competitors', you may have an overinvestment relative to your sales volume. Conversely, a turnover rate significantly above your competitors' may suggest an underinvestment.

In either case, the turnover rate is influenced significantly by the special characteristics of a business. Moreover, since the calculation relies on depreciated equipment values, turnover rates may vary significantly among businesses. The assets held in one business may be several years older than the assets held in another. That can lead to wide disparities in net fixed asset values.

Subject to logical qualifications, the fixed asset turnover calculation at least provides the starting point for identifying the appropriate investment level in a business.

Chapter 15

Structural Management: Two Break-Even Points

Most business managers recognize the concept of break-even analysis. That analysis identifies the sales volume where total revenue exactly matches expenses. At that point, the business neither makes nor loses any money. However, a business also has a break-even cash flow volume, a point where cash income exactly matches cash expenses.

Proper cash flow management requires a clear distinction between the two break-even points. This chapter demonstrates that distinction.

Basic Break-Even Analysis

Break-even analysis begins by dividing a firm's operating expenses into two categories. Every expense can be defined as either a fixed or a variable cost.

Fixed costs hold constant across a specific range of sales. For example, a business might increase sales from $1 million to $1.5 million without incurring any increase in rent, utility, or office salary expenses.

Variable costs fluctuate proportionately with any change in sales. Thus a 20% increase in sales produces a 20% increase in variable costs. Product expenses, sales commissions, and delivery charges are the more obvious examples of variable costs. A business doesn't incur a variable cost unless it generates a sale. Then, it incurs variable costs proportionately to any sales volume.

Contribution margin becomes the critical third element that enters into break-even analysis. Contribution margin represents the difference between the selling price and the variable cost per unit volume. Contribution margin represents the proportion of each sales dollar available to pay fixed costs and, ultimately, to provide any earnings the business might enjoy.

The relationship between contribution margin and a firm's fixed costs provides the arithmetic premise for break-even analysis. Let's examine that relationship from a couple of perspectives.

First, a business suffers a loss from operations so long as the total contribution margin from sales remains insufficient to cover fixed costs. Remember, fixed costs hold constant regardless of the sales volume generated.

Second, a business breaks even at that volume where the total contribution margin from sales exactly equals its fixed costs. Identifying that point stands as the obvious objective of break-even analysis.

Third, as sales move above the break-even point, the total contribution margin from sales exceeds fixed costs. The excess margin over fixed costs represents earnings. A business operating above the break-even point generates a profit. Figure 15-1 provides a conceptual view of the relationship between contribution margin and the break-even point.

Part a in Figure 15-1 sets the foundation for the illustration. The quantity in the rectangle on the left represents the total selling price for the product. That price is then separated into its two elements: contribution margin (CM) and variable costs (VC). The square on the right represents fixed costs, segmented by the number of unit contribution margins necessary to cover those costs. In this case, there are six.

Observe the relationship as the business begins to generate sales.

First, in part b, five unit sales leave total fixed costs uncovered. The firm's loss at that unit volume is equivalent to the contribution margin from a single sale.

Then, increasing sales by one unit, the firm reaches the break-even point, illustrated in part c. Six-unit sales provide the contribution margin that exactly covers fixed costs. At this point, total revenue equals total expenses and the business breaks even.

Part d shows the benefits of operating above the break-even point. The firm produces earnings equal to the contribution margin from each unit sold in excess of the break-even volume. After fixed costs are covered, the margin from each additional sale proceeds directly to the bottom line.

Let's translate this conceptual view into the calculation that actually identifies the break-even point in a business. That illustration uses the simplified circumstances of the Strong Electric Motor Company (SEMCO). SEMCO carries only one product, a small motor that sells for $7. Since the firm incurs a $4 variable cost from each unit sold, we find the contribution margin as:

Figure 15-1
Conceptual View of Break-Even Analysis

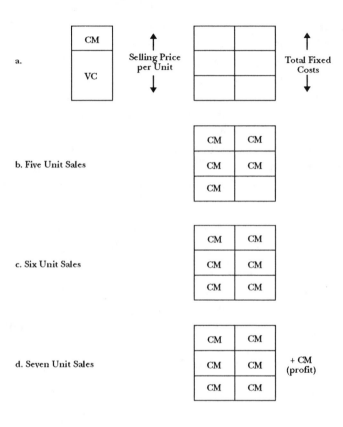

Contribution Margin	=	Selling Price	–	Variable Cost
Contribution Margin	=	$7	–	$4
Contribution Margin	=	$3		

Assuming that SEMCO's fixed costs total $90,000 per year, the contribution margin per unit can be used to calculate the firm's break-even sales volume. From Figure 15-1, we know that the break-even volume occurs at that point where the total contribution margin from all units sold exactly equals fixed costs. Arithmetically, that becomes:

$$\text{Break-Even Volume} = \frac{\text{Total Fixed Costs}}{\text{Contribution Margin per Unit}}$$

Entering SEMCO's data:

$$\text{Break-Even Volume} \quad = \quad \frac{\$90,000}{\$3} \quad = \quad 30,000 \text{ units}$$

SEMCO breaks even when sales reach 30,000 units. The company's sales price per unit translates that into an annual volume of $210,000 (30,000 x $7).

Now relate this example to two points asserted above. First, each sale in excess of 30,000 units per year contributes $3 to SEMCO's earnings. The margin in excess of fixed costs proceeds directly to the bottom line. Alternatively, should SEMCO sell fewer than 30,000 electric motors, it will suffer a loss. The total contribution margin will fall short of the amount necessary to cover fixed costs. The amount of the loss will be $3 for each unit that SEMCO drops below the 30,000 unit sales level. For example, sales of only 28,000 units will leave SEMCO with a $6,000 loss.

We can summarize the key role contribution margin plays in break-even analysis in:

Concept 37: A business breaks even when the contribution margin from sales exactly covers fixed costs.

Of course, most businesses carry a variety of items at different sales prices, different variable costs, and thus different contribution margins. That makes break-even analysis more complex, but it does not affect the essential concept.

Average Contribution Margin

An alternative approach to break-even analysis recognizes the difference in contribution margins among products with different sales prices and costs. It uses data extracted directly from a firm's income statement and relies on the average contribution margin that comes from each sales dollar. The Able Company's experience illustrates this approach to break-even analysis.

As shown in the summary of its income statement, the Able Company presently operates profitably:

Sales	$ 275,000
Variable Costs	(87,500)
Fixed Costs	(140,000)
Earnings	$ 47,500

However, John Able, the company's founder, is concerned about the uncertain economy and a potential reduction in sales. He wants to identify the sales decrease the firm can absorb without falling below a break-even level of operations. Since Able's product costs and sales prices vary widely, there will be a wide variation in the contribution margin that comes from the sale of different products.

Conceptually, of course, the alternative seeks the same objective. It identifies the sales volume where the firm's cumulative contribution margin from all sales exactly equals total fixed costs. But since the contribution margin varies among products, Able must use a three-step process to achieve that objective.

First, Able must calculate the total contribution margin included in the income statement:

$$\text{Total Contribution Margin} = \text{Total Sales} - \text{Total Variable Costs}$$

$$\text{Total Contribution Margin} = \$275,000 - 87,500 = \$187,500$$

The $187,500 total represents the contribution margin generated from all sales. So, the next step calculates the average contribution margin per sales dollar. That average measures a straightforward proportional relationship:

$$\text{Average Contribution Margin per unit} = \frac{\text{Total Contribution Margin}}{\text{Total Sales}}$$

$$\text{Average Contribution Margin per unit} = \frac{\$187,500}{\$275,000}$$

$$\text{Average Contribution Margin per unit} = 68\% \text{ (or 68 cents per dollar in sales)}$$

On the average, each dollar in sales provides 68 cents that contributes to the coverage of fixed costs—and ultimately to any earnings the firm realizes.

We can use that average contribution margin per unit to calculate Able's break-even point:

$$\text{Break-Even Sales Volume} = \frac{\text{Fixed Costs}}{\text{Contribution Margin as \% of Sales}}$$

$$\text{Break-Even Sales Volume} = \frac{\$140,000}{0.68}$$

$$\text{Break-Even Sales Volume} = \$205,882$$

The Able Company can suffer a drop in sales of approximately $75,000 and still not suffer an operating loss. At the same time, note that the calculation process applies to any business. If you can identify your average contribution margin per sales dollar, you can calculate your break-even point.

One major qualifying assumption applies to this alternative approach. It presumes that as sales fluctuate the proportionate product mix that makes up any volume remains constant. A change in that mix naturally will change the average contribution margin received from each sales dollar.

Obviously, this assumption is not totally realistic. As sales fluctuate, product mix varies. So this approach to break-even analysis is less precise than the fundamental calculation. Nevertheless, the calculation provides a satisfactory estimate for most management purposes.

Cash Flow Break-Even Analysis

Standard break-even analysis identifies the particular sales volume in a business where revenues equal expenses. However, not all expenses incurred within a particular operating period are cash expenses. Depreciation, as well as some less significant expenses, represents noncash expenses. Consequently, a business can have a cash flow break-even point—where the cumulative contribution margin from sales covers fixed cash expenses—that falls well below its financial break-even point.

Part a in Figure 15-2 shows the contribution margin provided by each unit sale, together with the firm's total fixed costs. Again, it is apparent that it requires six unit sales to cover fixed costs fully. However, here the total fixed costs include depreciation (D) equivalent to the contribution margin from two unit sales.

Note what happens as sales increase. A three unit volume, shown in part b, leaves the business well below both the financial and cash flow break-even points. That volume creates a negative cash flow from operations. Cash expenses exceed cash income. In part c, a four unit volume provides a break-even cash flow. The total contribution margin from sales covers actual cash expenses.

Finally, part d demonstrates the effect of one unit sale above the cash flow break-even point. That sale provides a positive cash flow from operations, even though it leaves the business below the financial break-even point. One more sale returns the business to the proper break-even point.

The major results can be summarized in:

Concept 38: **A business has a break-even cash flow when the contribution margin from sales exactly covers fixed cash costs.**

Figure 15-2
Conceptual View of Cash Flow Break-Even Analysis

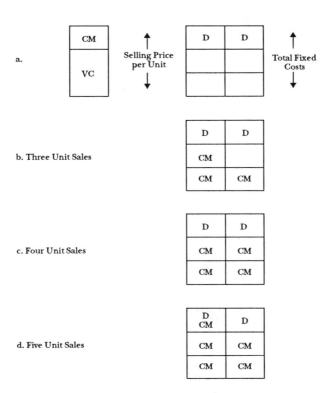

The calculation process that identifies the cash flow break-even point in a business is identical to that illustrated above. However, instead of using total fixed costs, the calculation recognizes only fixed cash expenses. Usually that amount is merely the total fixed expenses less depreciation.

For example, looking at SEMCO again, assume that the firm's $90,000 annual fixed costs include $30,000 in depreciation. To find its cash flow break-even point:

$$\text{Cash Flow Break-Even Point} = \frac{\text{Fixed Cash Expenses}}{\text{Contribution Margin per Unit}}$$

$$= \frac{\$60,000}{\$3.00} = 20,000 \text{ units}$$

SEMCO has a break-even cash flow when sales reach $140,000 (20,000 x $7).

If your business sells a variety of products with different contribution margins, you must use the latter calculation to find the cumulative contribution necessary to cover fixed cash expenses.

Break-even cash flow analysis is a useful management tool. But it has limitations because it relies on the accrual accounting process. Thus it does not reflect the actual timing of the cash flow into and out of a business. Indeed, only an actual cash flow budget anticipates the physical collection and disbursement of cash.

Over a relevant period, cash flow break-even analysis can still be valuable because it identifies the sales volume that matches cash revenues to cash expense. But keep it in perspective. You cannot equate accrual and cash flow accounting.

Fixed Assets and the Break-Even Point

Chapter 14 introduced the fixed asset turnover rate calculation, which helps identify the proper fixed asset investment level for a business. Break-even analysis contributes another important perspective. It recognizes depreciation as an element in total fixed costs. Thus the relationship between a firm's investment in fixed assets and break-even analysis follows logically.

As a business expands its investment in fixed assets, the higher depreciation charge that develops increases total fixed costs. That increases the sales volume the business must generate to achieve break-even operating results. Alternatively, a lower investment in fixed assets leads to a lower break-even point.

Of course, the relationship is more complex. A larger investment in fixed assets may lead to production efficiencies that reduce variable product costs, increasing the contribution margin available from each sales dollar. But that doesn't negate the basic relationship between the size of the investment in fixed assets and break-even analysis. Nor does it eliminate the implications for the fixed asset investment decision process.

Before making a fixed asset investment, measure how it will affect your break-even point. If you can't be assured of the additional sales necessary to offset the higher fixed costs from the investment, you may wisely defer the acquisition.

Alternatively, if you can operate efficiently with a smaller fixed asset investment, you lower the sales volume necessary to break even and reduce your operating risks. You also must measure the effect of your fixed asset investment on the contribution margin that you realize from each sale. This consideration falls naturally into the calculations that translate into break-even analysis.

The Benefits of Break-Even Analysis

Prudent business management often calls for the use of break-even analysis. But the manager must recognize it as a tool and know how to use it. It is more than a gauge of the effect that a firm's investment in fixed assets has on the break-even point. From the pessimist's viewpoint, break-even analysis identifies the worst circumstances that can exist without suffering a loss from operations. If the business doesn't generate a profit, at least it breaks even.

The realistic manager recognizes break-even analysis as a step toward improving the firm's performance. The analysis categorizes the critical relationships that determine whether or not a business operates profitably. Should a business fall below the break-even point, the manager can use the analysis to consider the alternative solutions to his problem. Although the obvious corrective action in any instance will appear to be a higher sales volume, that often may not be the best approach, and certainly it isn't the only approach.

The best alternative depends upon the operating constraints set by the external market and its internal operating requirements. Whatever the circumstance, break-even analysis isolates the major considerations and serves as a convenient tool for forecasting the results from any major change.

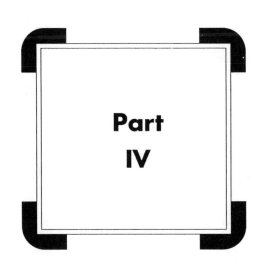

Part
IV

Leverage
Management

Chapter 16

Leverage: A Conceptual View

Leverage measures the percentage of a firm's assets supported by debt. For example, a business with $1,000,000 in total assets and $600,000 in debt has a 60% leverage factor. Understanding the concept of leverage as a basic principle of financial management will enable you to use leverage beneficially.

Measuring the Benefits of Leverage

You can use an increase in earnings to measure the benefits that a business realizes from the proper use of leverage. However, setting one earnings total against another can be misleading.

A more reliable criterion for measuring the potential benefits comes from calculating the return a business produces for its stockholders—the return on stockholders' equity, or ROE.

The ROE calculation measures the earnings a business generates as a proportion of stockholders' equity. For example, if a business with $200,000 in stockholders' equity earns $30,000 in a year, the calculation becomes:

$$\text{Return on Equity} \quad = \quad \frac{\text{Earnings}}{\text{Stockholders' Equity}}$$

$$\text{ROE} \quad = \quad \frac{\$30,000}{\$200,000}$$

$$\text{ROE} \quad = \quad 15\%$$

Leverage Management

On one level, the ROE calculation measures the increase in the value of the stockholders' investment from earnings. On another level, it becomes a tool for analyzing the comparative performance of different businesses. That is, a larger ROE suggests a better performance.

The earnings total used in the ROE calculation represents a firm's *after-tax* earnings. After all, only net earnings total actually benefits a business—and its stockholders. Also, the denominator in the calculation employs the stockholders' equity total as it stands at the beginning of the business year.

While that may appear obvious, some financial philosophers believe the calculation requires an *average* equity total, since earnings accrue incrementally throughout the year. But this approach complicates a straightforward concept. Using the equity total as it stands at the beginning of a business year provides a criterion more suitable for comparative analysis.

Leverage and Return on Equity

Leverage can increase the return on the stockholders' equity in a business. For an existing business, that result also leads to higher earnings. However, the two results are not necessarily synonymous.

Let's look at the experience of Beth Tallman, an entrepreneurial investor who recently considered a major investment in a new plumbing supply operation. Tallman centered her analysis on the following characteristics of the proposed investment:

1. The business required $1,000,000 in total assets to operate profitably.
2. Given those assets, the business promised earnings of $150,000 in the first year, excluding any potential interest expenses.
3. The cash was available to finance the $1,000,000 in required assets with an equal dollar equity investment.
4. Alternatively, he could use as little as $200,000 in cash equity and borrow the funds necessary to finance the difference in required assets.
5. Any borrowed funds will carry a 10% annual cost.

Recognizing her options, Tallman analyzed the proposed investment using four different financial structures. Table 16-1 measures the net earnings (after interest costs) and ROE that would result from each alternative.

As she increases the use of debt instead of equity, Tallman sees the projected earnings from the new venture drop. For example, using $1,000,000 in equity, with no debt, promises $150,000 in earnings. At the other extreme, coupling $800,000 in debt with $200,000 in equity, earnings from the venture drop to $70,000. The interest costs associated with the debt absorb the $80,000 difference.

Table 16-1
Leverage and ROE

| | Alternative Financial Structures | | | |
	1	2	3	4
Total Assets	$1,000,000	$1,000,000	$1,000,000	$1,000,000
Total Liabilities (10% annual cost)	—	200,000	500,000	800,000
Stockholders' Equity	1,000,000	800,000	500,000	200,000
Earnings Before Interest Costs	150,000	150,000	150,000	150,000
Interest Cost	—	20,000	50,000	80,000
Earnings	$ 150,000	$ 130,000	$ 100,000	$ 70,000
Return on Stockholders' Equity	15%	16.25%	20%	35%

When earnings are used as a criterion, leverage actually appears to be detrimental to a business. However, the ROE criterion contradicts that assessment.

Tallman increases the return on the dollars she invests in the business by using less equity and more leverage. Indeed, an 80% leverage factor raises her ROE on the minimum $200,000 investment to 35%, compared to the 15% return she gains by avoiding any debt at all.

We recognize that potential benefit in:

Concept 39: Leverage can increase the return a business produces on stockholders' equity.

If Tallman seeks the maximum possible return on her investment, she will select the option that requires the fewest equity dollars. That allows her to employ the difference in cash profitably elsewhere. Carried to the limit, an investor will never commit a single dollar more than necessary.

Let's look at the same concept from a more familiar perspective.

Leverage and Earnings

Leverage does not have to lower earnings to induce a higher return on equity. Indeed, the example of Beth Tallman's analysis was designed specifically to emphasize the critical relationship between leverage and return on the stockholders' investment. Here we will examine the benefits an existing business gains from using borrowed funds. Our illustration relies on an analysis performed by the Hopeful Company, a growing business seeking to expand. We will assume that the company will open the next business year with the financial structure illustrated in the first column of Table 16-2. That structure includes $1,000,000 in total assets, balanced by $500,000 each in liabilities and stockholders' equity.

Table 16-2
Debt vs. Equity Financing for Expansion
The Hopeful Company

		Equity Financing	Debt Financing
Total Assets	$1,000,000	$1,500,000	$1,500,000
Total Liabilities	500,000	500,000	1,000,000
Stockholders' Equity	$ 500,000	$1,000,000	$ 500,000
Earnings before Interest (15% of average investment in assets)	$ 150,000	$ 225,000	$ 225,000
Less: Interest Expense	(50,000)	(50,000)	(100,000)
Net Earnings	$ 100,000	$ 175,000	$ 125,000
Return on Equity	20%	17.5%	25%

Based on several assumptions, the company projected the results from financing the next year's anticipated growth with either debt or equity:

1. Earnings from operations (before deducting interest expenses) historically provide a 15% return on the firm's average investment in assets.
2. The projected expansion calls for a $500,000 increase in the firm's average investment in assets.
3. The firm can finance the increase in assets with either debt or equity; the firm absorbs a 10% average expense from the use of debt.

Proceeding from the beginning financial structure, Table 16-2 summarizes the effect that both debt and equity will have on Hopeful's earnings, as well as the return on the stockholders' investment. The company increases earnings in either instance. Certainly, proper financial management should use any external funds profitably, whether debt or equity. No other result justifies or attracts cash from either source. However, as might be anticipated, using debt to finance Hopeful's expansion provides a larger return on investment for the firm's stockholders. The illustration reinforces Cash Flow Concept No. 39.

Of course, leverage is not automatically beneficial. To use borrowed funds properly, you must work within some natural constraints.

One Limit on Leverage

To benefit from leverage, a firm's return on assets must exceed the cost of the borrowed funds. Before illustrating this natural limit, we should establish a common view of the term return on assets, or ROA.

ROA measures a firm's earnings as a percentage of its total asset investment. For example, if a business has $100,000 in earnings and $1,000,000 in total assets, the ROA calculation becomes:

$$\text{Return on Assets} = \frac{\text{Net Earnings}}{\text{Total Assets}}$$

$$\text{ROA} = \frac{\$\ 100,000}{\$1,000,000} = 10\%$$

In this instance, the total assets figure may represent the firm's investment at the beginning of the year, the end of the year, or the average that prevails throughout the year. The latter alternative, perhaps using monthly balance sheet totals to compute average assets, offers the more logical approach. At the same time, any of the three alternatives should prove satisfactory so long as you maintain consistency from one year to the next.

The Hopeful Company's analysis illustrates the relationship between ROA and leverage costs. The firm still projects a $500,000 increase in assets. Using leverage to finance those assets will impose a 10% annual interest expense. However, we will alter one point in the analysis and assume that the firm is unsure of the return it can anticipate from the incremental assets associated with the expansion. Consequently, the analysis considers the ultimate change in earnings across the three most likely outcomes—a 5%, 10%, and 15% ROA. Table 16-3 reflects the analysis.

Should the Hopeful Company realize less than a 10% return on the proposed incremental assets, the expansion will actually reduce earnings. However, should the return on assets exceed the cost of the debt (as in Column 3), the use of leverage leads to higher earnings. In that case, borrowing benefits the bottom line.

So, note one limit on leverage in:

Concept 40: **To benefit from leverage, a firm's return on assets must exceed the cost of debt.**

Table 16-3
How ROA Limits Leverage
The Hopeful Company

ROA ($500,000 in incremental assets financed with borrowed funds)	5%	10%	15%
Leverage Cost	10%	10%	10%
Incremental Earnings Before Interest	$ 25,000	$ 50,000	$ 75,000
Interest Expense (10%)	(50,000)	(50,000)	(50,000)
Net Change in Earnings	($25,000)	—	$ 25,000

Now, let's see how better asset management can improve the return a business produces on its stockholders' equity.

Asset Turnover and Return on Equity

Part II demonstrated the benefits that a business derives from a reduction in the average size of its investment in accounts receivable and inventory. A reduction in either instance reduces the total cash capability necessary to support those investments, contributes to a better cash flow, and leads to higher earnings. Now we can use the ROE calculation to measure those benefits from another perspective and find that a lower average asset investment for any constant sales volume increases the return a business produces for its stockholders.

Table 16-4 helps prove that point as it compares the ROE generated by two closely comparable businesses: Company A and Company B.

Both firms enjoyed $100,000 in earnings from a $2,000,000 annual sales volume, and each employs a 50% leverage factor. One half of each firm's assets is financed with debt. However, Company A carries a $1,000,000 investment in total assets, while Company B generates the same sales volume with only $800,000 in assets. By dividing annual sales by each firm's total investment in assets, Company B turns its total asset investment two and a half times a year, while Company A manages to turn its assets only twice.

Ultimately, the faster turnover rate reduces the stockholders' investment necessary to achieve any sales volume. As indicated in Table 16-4, Company B's stockholders enjoy a 25% return on equity, while Company A's investors earned 5% less. That should encourage you once again to exercise the tenets of competent component management. Turning the assets more rapidly—that is, using them more efficiently—increases the return on the stockholders' equity.

Table 16-4
Asset Turnover and ROE

	Company A	Company B
Total Assets	$1,000,000	$ 800,000
Total Liabilities	500,000	400,000
Stockholders' Equity	500,000	400,000
Liabilities and Equity	1,000,000	800,000
Sales	2,000,000	2,000,000
Profit Margin	5%	5%
Earnings	$ 100,000	$ 100,000
Asset Turnover	2	2.5
ROE	20%	25%

Leverage and Risk

The relationship between the cost of leverage and the return on a firm's assets implicates the other major limit on the use of leverage. While leverage can increase earnings and ROE, the opposite outcome always remains a possibility.

Using leverage imposes an unavoidable element of risk on a firm. On one level, leverage may lead to lower rather than higher earnings. On another, leverage may temporarily turn a profitable business into a losing operation. Carried to the worst extreme, the improper use of leverage can destroy a business. Remember this threat as:

Concept 41: Risk is a natural companion of leverage.

Financial analysts employ complex models to measure the degree of risk associated with various proportions of leverage in a firm's financial structure. However, complex models are not necessary to illustrate the fundamental relationship. We demonstrate that fact below with a simpler view of the relationship between risk and leverage. However, first let's look at the circumstances that make risk an unavoidable companion of leverage.

The Uncertainty in Futurity

A business seldom increases its leverage—debt as a percentage of total assets—merely to finance its current level of operations. Of course, it might use debt to replace obsolete or worn-out equipment. But in most instances, leverage usually precedes—indeed, anticipates—a projected increase in sales volume.

The process follows a logical course.

First, a business projects a larger sales volume. Perhaps it intends to expand into new areas, introduce a new product, or merely press for a larger share of its existing market. Then, as a necessary precedent to achieving any such projection, it must increase its investment in inventory. That, in turn, may also be preceded by an expansion in fixed assets. Using borrowed funds to finance the necessary increase in assets raises the leverage factor in the business.

Should the business achieve the projected sales increase, the leverage becomes beneficial. But should the higher volume fail to follow the projected course, the increased cost from the leverage may lead to lower earnings. The potential for more than one outcome defines the element of risk associated with leverage.

Uncertainty is a constant companion of futurity. A firm's projected volume is subject to all of the vagaries of an uncertain economic environment. A business may find resistance to projected expansion from a general economic decline or increased competition. Technological innovation or a change in consumer tastes may alter customer purchasing habits. A supplier strike may stymie any projection in the best circumstances. Whatever the source of the problem, the presence of such potential makes the use of leverage a risky proposition.

Of course, even the business that uses no leverage confronts risk as a natural element of the economic environment. When leverage enters a financial structure, the element of risk acquires greater importance. As leverage increases the return for the business that achieves its goals, it also increases the penalty inflicted on the business that falls below its projections.

Leverage, Risk, and Return

Our discussion of the impact leverage has on a business serves two functions. First, it demonstrates the interrelationships between risk, return, and the use of leverage. Although leverage can benefit a business that achieves its goals, when volume falls below projected levels, the business using leverage suffers a larger setback.

Second, as a logical extension of the basic concept, it shows how the risks associated with any operation increase as leverage increases. Low levels of leverage involve little risk; high levels of leverage involve high levels of risk. You must find the level for your business that provides the best return for the risk you are willing to accept.

Beth Tallman's analysis of her proposed investment in a new plumbing supply operation illustrates the fundamental relationships. Tallman's initial analysis compared the earnings and return on stockholders' equity from four alternative financial structures. However, the analysis proceeded on the assumption the new business would earn $150,000 before deducting any interest expense.

Recognizing the uncertainty inevitably associated with that expected outcome, Tallman expanded her analysis. She estimated the risk associated with the alternative financial structures based on the following assumptions:

1. At any level of sales, the new business would incur $200,000 in fixed costs.
2. Variable costs will average 50% of any sales actually generated.
3. In the worst circumstance, the new company will generate no sales at all; the most optimistic projection anticipates a $2,000,000 sales volume.

Tallman's analysis proceeded in two steps. First, she calculated the expected earnings the business would realize from four alternative sales volumes, ranging from the worst to the best possible outcomes. (The calculations measure Earnings Before Interest and Taxes, or EBIT.) Table 16-5 shows the calculations associated with each outcome.

Table 16-5
Four Potential EBIT Operating Results

	1	2	3	4
Sales	—	$ 500,000	$1,000,000	$2,000,000
Fixed Costs	($200,000)	(200,000)	(200,000)	(200,000)
Variable Costs (60% of sales)	—	(300,000)	(600,000)	(1,200,000)
EBIT	($200,000)	—	$ 200,000	$ 600,000

A glance at Table 16-5 shows that $500,000 stands as the operating breakeven point. Sales in excess of $500,000 will generate operating profits; sales below that level will leave the firm with an operating loss. Of course, that break-even point presumes that the firm uses no leverage at all.

As the second step in her analysis, Tallman completed the earnings and ROE calculations, using the four alternative leverage factors illustrated in Table 16-1: 0%, 20%, 50%, and 80%. Table 16-6 also includes those calculations in order.

Table 16-6
Leverage, Risk, and Return

Financial Structure 1: Zero Leverage

EBIT	($200,000)	—	$200,000	$600,000
Interest Expense	—	—	—	—
Net Earnings	($200,000)	—	$200,000	$600,000
ROE	20%	—	20%	60%

Financial Structure 2: 20% Leverage

EBIT	($200,000)	—	$200,000	$600,000
Interest Expense	(20,000)	($20,000)	(20,000)	(20,000)
Net Earnings	($220,000)	($20,000)	$180,000	$580,000
ROE	(27.5%)	(2.5%)	22.5%	72.5%

Financial Structure 3: 50% Leverage

EBIT	($200,000)	—	$200,000	$600,000
Interest Expense	(50,000)	(50,000)	(50,000)	(50,000)
Net Earnings	($250,000)	($50,000)	$150,000	$550,000
ROE	(50%)	(10%)	30%	110%

Financial Structure 4: 80% Leverage

EBIT	($200,000)	—	$200,000	$600,000
Interest Expense	(80,000)	(80,000)	(80,000)	(80,000)
Net Earnings	(140%)	(40%)	60%	260%

Tallman's analysis emphasizes the critical interrelationships among leverage, risk, and return. First, a higher sales volume increases earnings and return on equity. This holds true regardless of the financial structure. At the same time, as the firm achieves a higher sales volume, ROE increases dramatically because the financial structure includes greater leverage factors. If the firm achieves a $2,000,000 sales volume with a financial structure that contains an 80% leverage factor, the return on the stockholders' equity reaches a remarkable 260%.

However, that is the best possible outcome among a set of projections looking into an uncertain future. We will look at the other side of the picture and measure the risk associated with the leverage factors used in the prospective investment.

As leverage enhances the return from a successful venture, it also increases the loss should the firm achieve a minimal volume. Referring again to Table 16-6, examine the alternative outcomes should the business achieve only a $500,000 sales volume. If the firm has no leverage, that volume produces a break-even operation. Using leverage, however, converts the break-even results into a loss, and more leverage leads to losses.

Table 16-7 summarizes the return on equity that Tallman should anticipate from each sales volume, beginning with each financial structure distinguished by its leverage factor.

At the bottom of Table 16-7, note the range of expected outcomes associated with each leverage factor.

Thus when Tallman projects the results from using absolutely no leverage, the range between the best and worst possible outcomes is 80%. In the worst circumstance (no sales at all), she stands to lose 20% of her original investment. Should the new business achieve a $2,000,000 sales volume, however, using no leverage yields a 60% ROE.

Table 16-7
Risk, Return, and Leverage:
The Range of Potential Outcome

Range of Potential Sales Volume	Leverage Factor			
	0%	20%	50%	80%
	ROE at Each Leverage Factor and Sales Volume			
0	(20%)	(27.5%)	(50%)	(140%)
$ 500,000	—	(2.5%)	(10%)	(40%)
$1,000,000	20%	22.5%	30%	60%
$2,000,000	60%	72.5%	110%	260%
	Range of Expected ROEs: Low to High			
	80%	100%	160%	400%

Compare these outcomes to the range that results from the 80% leverage factor. In the worst circumstance, Tallman theoretically could lose 140% of his original investment. When the firm uses leverage, interest expense continues regardless of sales volume. At the same time, should the business generate $2,000,000 in sales, Tallman's ROE will reach 260%. In one year, she will realize a return that is more than two and a half times her original investment.

We acknowledge these trade-offs in:

**Concept 42:   Leverage imposes risk on a
business in exchange for the
promise of a higher return.**

With an 80% leverage factor, using ROE as a criterion, we find a 400% range in the anticipated results from the alternative possible sales volumes. That range is five times more than that using no leverage. The range differentials demonstrate the critical interrelationships among leverage, risk, and return. Thus a successful outcome returns larger benefits to the business that uses leverage. And an unsuccessful outcome leads to a larger loss.

Chapter 17

Leverage: A Mechanical View

This chapter outlines the three major categories of leverage available to a business and differentiates the mechanics involved with the extension and repayment of the borrowed funds. Adopting a mechanical view of the major borrowing alternatives is designed to help you better fit each lending method to the circumstance that raises the need for leverage. Each alternative form of leverage serves some purposes better than others.

The Single Payment Loan

A single payment loan requires repayment in full, including the interest charge, on a predetermined date. Typically, the repayment follows the granting of the loan by ninety days or six months. Less frequently, it may extend for only a few days or as long as a year. The lender specifies the required payment date in the loan document.

Before he extends the loan, a well-informed lender also knows the probable source of funds necessary to meet the payment schedule. The source isn't necessarily specified in the note, but it should be understood in advance. The maturity of a single payment loan should coincide with the purpose of the loan, coupled with a realistic projection of the date the funds will be available for repayment.

The more common single payment loans answer the seasonal needs of a business. For example, a business may borrow to build inventory in anticipation of its major selling season. The collection of the accounts receivable from the sales provides the cash to repay the loan on schedule.

The farmer remains the classic example of the seasonal borrower. He borrows to finance his spring planting and then raises (rather than buys) his inventory during the summer. He harvests his crops in the late summer or early fall. Then, he repays the lender from the proceeds of the sales. The terms and source of repayment are clearly recognized by both the borrower and lender on the day the loan is granted.

Many manufacturers and wholesalers also use seasonal loans. For example, lawnmower and fertilizer manufacturers and bathing suit and ski distributors need seasonal loans. Indeed, the single payment loan smooths the cash flow across many business cycles.

We recognize the primary purpose of a single payment loan in:

Concept 43: A single payment loan answers a specific business purpose that provides a well defined source of repayment.

Single payment loans also answer specific, short term purposes apart from the seasonal requirements that arise in a business. In one instance, a business might borrow to fill a temporary gap in its cash flow. Perhaps the inventory requirements for an unusually large sale drain a firm's cash reserve. Collection of the receivables that result from the sale provides the cash to retire the loan. Or a business might use a single payment loan to take advantage of a unique profit opportunity. The loan may facilitate the purchase of some bargain merchandise or enable the business to obtain quantity or trade discounts.

Calculating the Single Payment Interest Charge

The lender extending a single payment loan charges a stated annual interest rate, prorated for the fraction of the year that makes up the term of the loan. For example, assume a business borrows $100,000 from a lender who charges a 12% annual interest rate. If the loan extends for a full year, the interest charge totals $12,000. However, should the term of the loan be only six months, the interest calculation becomes:

1. $100,000 x 12% = $12,000
2. $12,000 x 0.5 (six months) = $6,000

Two traditional lender practices can make measuring the true cost of a single payment loan more complicated than it first appears.

First, lenders do not calculate interest charges based on the calendar year or specific fractions of that year. Instead, they measure the term in days, such as 90, 180, or 365 days.

Second, some lenders do not use an annual interest charge applied to the pro-rata portion of the year of the loan. Instead, they charge a daily rate derived from the annual stated rate. While that may imply a proper pro-rata application, the result may differ because of the calculation process that determines the daily interest charge.

Some lenders use a calculation that proceeds on the presumption a year has only 360 days. For example, using the 12% annual rate, the average daily charge is found as:

$$\frac{12\%}{360} = 0.00033\% \text{ per day}$$

The lender applies that charge to each dollar you use each day. Unfortunately for the business borrower, that daily rate exceeds the rate that would come from the same calculation using a 365 day year.

To illustrate the effect that difference has on the actual annual cost of borrowing, compare the actual dollar cost a business incurs from the daily rate versus a true 12% annual cost:

1. $100,000 x 0.00033% per day x 365 = $12,165
2, $100,000 x 12%   = $12,000

Incremental Cost $ 165

Using the 360 day year increases the cost of borrowing by $165.

Of course, this difference isn't significant to any business in a position to use substantial funds profitably. But the practice increases the lender's earnings at your expense.

Also note one advantage you gain when you employ a single payment loan. You seldom incur a prepayment penalty for retiring a loan prior to the original maturity date. For example, assume you obtained the $100,000 loan for a six month, or 180 day, period. However, forty-five days after obtaining the loan, you find you can repay the lender. The lender will charge you only for the forty-five days you use the funds, rather than for the 180 days. That is a logical, equitable approach for both the borrower and lender.

The Revolving Loan

A revolving loan is a natural complement to the cash flow cycle in a business.

A revolving loan begins with the lender's approval of a specified line of credit, which authorizes the advance of any loan amount up to that line. However, the revolving loan agreement involves more than a single advance followed by a scheduled repayment.

Instead, the loan fluctuates in direct response to the peaks and valleys in a borrower's cash flow cycle. Whenever the borrower foresees a demand that will exhaust his cash reserve, the lender advances funds sufficient to maintain a positive cash position. Conversely, as the natural cycle generates funds in excess of those needed for normal reserves, the business repays all or part of the funds advanced by the lender.

The process repeats itself as often as these peaks and valleys occur in the firm's cash flow. Figure 17-1 provides a simplified picture of that relationship.

Figure 17-1
The Revolving Loan and the Cash Flow Cycle

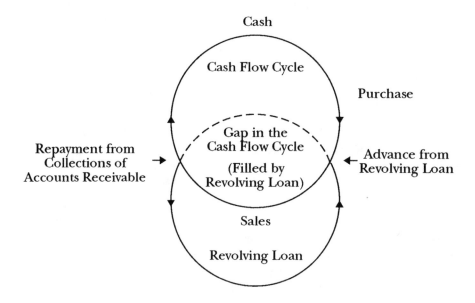

Figure 17-1 includes the normal cash flow cycle. However, as suggested by the overlapping circles, the normal collection of accounts receivable isn't sufficient to pay for the inventory purchases in a timely manner. Foreseeing that gap, the business obtains an advance from its revolving loan to maintain a prompt payment record. The eventual collection of the receivables repays the advance. However, while the size of the cash flow gap expands and contracts in response to fluctuating needs of the business, it seldom disappears completely.

The revolving loan stands as a source of flexible leverage that can answer a number of business needs that are not served by a single payment or installment loan.

One measure of flexibility comes from the elimination of any predetermined repayment schedule. Of course, a revolving loan is not a perpetual, open ended arrangement. The loan agreement usually matures one year after initiation. So long as the lender is satisfied with the relationship, he will probably allow annual extensions or renewals.

The revolving loan also provides flexibility as a source of growth money for the business that is projecting expansion. If the anticipated growth does not result, the firm suffers no unnecessary interest expense. Indeed, the revolving loan imposes no interest expenses except on the funds actually employed. Yet it provides assurance that the cash needs from expansion will not go unfilled. Remember the potential benefit as:

Concept 44:　A revolving loan provides a source of flexible leverage that answers a number of cash needs.

The flexibility to borrow or not to borrow suggests another advantage that comes with the revolving loan. The borrower pays a simple daily interest rate for the funds used. This provides reasonable incentive to borrow as little as possible and to repay as soon as possible. Moreover, that practice benefits both the borrower and the lender. The borrower can hold the cost of his credit consideration to a minimum, while the lender is assured that the loan will revolve as agreed. This fluctuation adds some measure of assurance to the lender regarding the borrower's creditworthiness.

A revolving loan does not provide permanent credit consideration. The loan has a specified maturity date when all unpaid advances fall due. While that usually results in an extension of the original agreement for another year, the borrower must meet certain continuing financial requirements. Also recognize that the lack of positive action to ensure renewal makes the total amount of the unpaid advances a single payment note on the expiration date of the revolving loan agreement.

The Installment Loan

An installment loan requires repayment of a fraction of the original loan at regular intervals. The fraction repaid usually comes on a monthly basis proportionate to the terms of the loan measured in months. For example, each payment on a $12,000 installment loan in one year will include $1,000 in principal repayment, plus a portion of the interest due to the lender. One year usually is the shortest term installment loan available to a business. While shorter terms exist, they are usually better served by single payment loans. At the other end of the continuum, it is not uncommon to see an installment loan extend for three, five, or ten years, depending upon the purpose and circumstance of the loan.

The repayment schedule that distinguishes the installment loan should reflect the purpose of the loan.

Most businesses use installment loans to purchase fixed assets. Typically those assets have a useful life that exceeds the term of the loan. So, a business might employ an installment loan repayable over three years to finance the acquisition of equipment with a five-year productive life. Of course, the productivity of the equipment purchased, measured by the cash flow from a rise in revenues or a reduction in costs, should be sufficient to meet the required loan payments and provide some bottom-line benefits for the business. The main purpose is summarized in:

Concept 45: **Installment loans finance the purchase of productive assets that should contribute a positive cash flow.**

When you analyze a prospective fixed asset acquisition, don't forget the cash that flows from the depreciation process. That remains a significant element in the analysis.

Hybrid Loans

Hybrid loans often combine one or more elements of the three categories of loans. For example, one hybrid loan might call for installment payments of $2,000 per month for twenty-three months, with a single "balloon" payment due in the twenty-fourth month. Alternatively, a revolving line of credit might reduce a firm's maximum credit line by $10,000 per month, allowing the business to fluctuate its loan within that maximum.

Most often, a lender designs a hybrid loan repayment schedule to correspond with some unique pattern in the borrower's cash flow. The installment loan with the balloon payment might reflect the borrower's limited cash flow in the early life of a fixed asset investment. Presumably, the eventual productivity of the asset will generate the cash necessary for repayment. Similarly, reducing the line of credit may coincide with the expectation that cash from projected earnings will reduce the need for borrowed funds.

Don't restrict your financial vision to the three basic types of loans. A creative lender adapts his credit consideration to your special needs.

Collateral Considerations

Few businesses borrow without pledging collateral to the lender to secure the loan. That pledge, which may include accounts receivable, inventory, or fixed assets, may be little more than a formality that adds confidence to the lender's credit decision. Or the collateral pledge may directly affect the firm's borrowing power.

Standing alone, a collateral pledge to secure a loan seldom justifies credit consideration. Instead, it provides the final margin of safety that protects a lender. The role that collateral plays in the credit decision becomes apparent as we review the rank it holds as the anticipated source of repayment for a loan.

The primary source of repayment of any credit consideration should come from the normal operations of the firm. The source of repayment for a single payment loan comes from the cyclical or seasonal liquidation of assets held in the cash flow cycle. Repayment for an installment or revolving loan should proceed from projected cash flow.

In the latter instance, the lender looks for a historical earnings trend that promises the future profitability necessary to retire any credit consideration. Those potential earnings also provide a secondary source of repayment for a single payment loan if the firm's cyclical asset liquidation does not proceed as planned.

Because earnings projections extend into an uncertain future, the lender looks for a potential source of repayment in addition to projected earnings. The strength held in the borrower's financial structure usually serves as that source. The lender also measures the ability of a business to absorb a financial setback without losing the ability to honor its credit consideration.

Finally, the lender seeks collateral as the final hedge against an error in judgment. If a business generates excessive losses that erode its financial strength too far, the lender can liquidate the collateral as the final source of repayment. Thus collateral doesn't justify credit consideration. It merely adds support for the lender's positive view of a borrower's creditworthiness. Collateral simply makes a good loan better.

Collateral and Borrowing Power

Although collateral does not directly justify the extension of credit, it often influences the amount of the credit. Thus an approved loan might become some proportionate amount of the full value of the pledged asset.

Numerous considerations interact to determine the advance rate, the maximum loan a lender will grant against any collateral. However, the credit-worthy borrower can expect the following general relationships to hold true:

Collateral	Advance Rate	Probable Loan Limits (per each $10,000 in collateral value)
Accounts Receivable	60-80%	$6,000-8,000
Inventory	20-50%	$2,000-5,000
Machinery and Equipment	70-90%	$7,000-9,000

The specific applicable advance rate varies widely with the circumstance. For example, a financially strong borrower qualifies for a higher advance rate than a business confronting a major cash flow problem. And the more certain the value held in the collateral, the more the lender is likely to advance.

The advance rate also will vary among lenders. Commercial finance companies feel comfortable advancing funds at rates that approach the high end of the ranges listed above. Alternatively, banks will be more likely to adopt the lower limits. Moreover, lenders within the same category often adopt different views.

Lenders still rely primarily on the profitability and financial strength of the borrower. Collateral doesn't justify a loan; it merely increases the probability of repayment.

Chapter 18

Leverage: A Practical View

Few business managers have the time or inclination to measure the risks associated with the use of leverage. Nor do they typically calculate the relationship between the cost and return on assets financed with any debt.

Instead, most adopt a practical, functional approach to borrowing. They use leverage to solve a problem or to serve a specific, profitable purpose. This chapter will identify the practical purposes that encourage businesses to borrow and illustrate the potential benefits.

The Need to Borrow

No business should incur any debt haphazardly. Any debt a business uses should serve a specific, well-defined purpose.

Borrowed funds may solve a problem, facilitate growth, or merely provide the cash capability to support a larger, more profitable investment in inventory. Whatever the circumstance, a clear purpose should precede the assumption of any obligation.

When you borrow, you accept the risk that the funds will not return an amount sufficient to pay the cost of borrowing. That failure will hurt your earnings.

You also accept the risk that your business might lack the capacity to honor its debt obligation in a timely manner. This is the risk of default. Should the lender allow an extension or renewal, you will suffer no more than a measure of financial embarrassment. Of course, chances are that the potential default will limit future credit consideration, limiting your firm's future prospects.

Finally, in the most unfortunate circumstance, you also accept the risk that the ultimate inability to honor your credit obligations satisfactorily will lead to financial failure. This is the risk of bankruptcy.

A business may borrow to satisfy any number of objectives. However, most circumstances fall into several categories. Businesses commonly borrow to:

1. Solve a cash flow problem,
2. Facilitate growth,
3. Generate supplier profits, and
4. Enhance financial flexibility.

Let's review some examples that illustrate each purpose.

Using Leverage to Solve a Cash Flow Problem

In the broadest sense, any use of leverage solves a cash flow problem. After all, the business with sufficient internal cash capability achieves its business objectives without external financing. However, borrowing to solve a cash flow problem seldom arises from a threat to a company's financial integrity. It might earn less because it grows more slowly or misses supplier discounts, but the lack of external financing doesn't cause financial embarrassment.

Let's consider the potential benefits a business derives from using leverage to (1) fill a gap in the cash flow cycle, and (2) gain the cash capability necessary to achieve a profitable level of operations. Although more than one potential solution exists for many of these problems, we will assume the business manager recognizes the fundamental precepts of component and structural management. Proceeding from that premise, she finds the use of leverage the logical solution to her problem.

Filling a Gap in the Cash Flow Cycle

A business has a gap in its cash flow cycle whenever it lacks the capacity to meet all of its obligations in a timely manner. The problem appears when accounts payable remain unpaid beyond the seller's original terms, or when scheduled note payments fall past due, or, in the worst circumstance, when the business fails to pay its employees promptly.

A simple example demonstrates a natural business circumstance that leaves a gap in the cash flow cycle. Leverage erects the natural bridge across that gap. The example also reestablishes a fundamental concept that remains critical to positive cash flow management.

The example comes from the experience of the Tyson Company, an architectural design firm. As a financially conservative operation, Tyson traditionally has functioned on a cash basis. The firm used no debt.

However, a recent management decision created a cash flow problem that necessitated a change in that policy. The problem came with the acceptance of a design contract that led to a $100,000 increase in the firm's monthly revenue. The terms of the contract, coupled with the special nature of Tyson's business, created an inevitable gap in the cash flow cycle.

One element of that problem stemmed from Tyson's employee payment practices. The firm paid its employees twice a month, on the fifteenth and the thirtieth.

The other element came from the terms of the new contract. Those terms restricted Tyson to a monthly billing schedule for work performed by the employees.

Moreover, the contract allowed Tyson's customer an additional thirty days for payment after the billing date. Table 18-1, a simple cash budget, identifies the gap in Tyson's cash flow that develops naturally from these circumstances.

Table 18-1
A Gap in the Cash Flow Cycle
Tyson Company

	Cash Out	Cash In	Cash Gap
9/15	$45,000	—	$ 45,000
9/30	45,000	—	90,000
10/15	45,000	—	135,000
10/30	45,000	$100,000	80,000
11/15	45,000	—	125,000
11/30	45,000	100,000	70,000

The firm must meet payroll and cash overhead requirements for three pay periods prior to receipt of payment for the first month's billing. The budget projects a maximum $135,000 gap in the middle of the second month. The gap drops to $80,000 after Tyson collects payment for the revenue billed at the end of the first month, then it builds again to $125,000.

Lacking adequate cash reserves, Tyson must use leverage to fill the gap or risk defaulting on the contract. That valuable contribution from borrowed funds earns recognition in:

Concept 46: Leverage can fill a gap in your cash flow.

A gap in cash flow may be more subtle than in the case of Tyson Company. A business may watch a prompt payment record deteriorate as a shrinking bank account forces a deferral of payments to suppliers. Or a business may find itself short of the cash required to retire a single payment note originally extended for ninety days. In fact, a business may have a large gap in its cash flow that is not directly apparent. The following section illustrates that circumstance.

Filling a Hidden Gap in the Cash Flow Cycle

A business with sufficient cash capability measured by the requirements set by its investment in operating funds, accounts receivable, and inventory can still suffer from a gap in its cash flow.

This hidden problem occurs whenever a business improperly matches the form of its debt to its needs. Table 18-2 summarizes the circumstance of Darnell, Inc., a modestly successful automobile parts distributor. The firm's cash flow cycle reflects three characteristics:

1. Darnell presently generates $90,000 a month in sales, which produces $3,500 a month in earnings.
2. A forty-five day average collection period (not subject to reduction) translates into a $135,000 investment in accounts receivable.
3. The $189,000 in inventory, sufficient for three months' sales, represents the minimum practical investment for the present sales volume.

Despite the firm's success, the balance sheet summary in Column 1 reflects haphazard leverage management that could lead to a serious cash flow problem. That problem could come from two sources.

First, supplier trade terms prevalent in the industry typically require payment thirty days after purchase. However, Darnell's accounts payable represent two months' purchases. Thus $63,000 out of that total is one to thirty days past due.

Second, Darnell's balance sheet includes a $74,000 single payment note. Whether that note is due in one day or ninety days is less important than the fact that Darnell lacks sufficient cash to honor it. The firm's investment in receivables and inventory is not subject to reduction; nor is a significant increase in cash reserves from earnings likely.

Table 18-2
Leverage Management: Matching Form to Circumstance
Darnell, Inc.

	Before Restructuring	After Restructuring
Cash	$ 11,000	$ 24,000
Accounts Receivable	135,000	135,000
Inventory	189,000	189,000
Total Assets	$335,000	$348,000
Accounts Payable	$126,000	$ 63,000
Single Payment Loan	74,000	—
Installment Loan	—	150,000
Total Liabilities	$200,000	$213,000
Stockholders' Equity	135,000	135,000
Liabilities and Equity	$335,000	$348,000

Darnell presently has a $137,000 gap in its cash flow. This represents the total necessary to honor the existing credit consideration as agreed. The indulgence displayed by the firm's creditors provides the cash capability necessary for a $90,000 monthly volume, but maintaining that volume remains subject to the whim of suppliers and a lender who may not renew or extend a single payment note.

Consider the potential benefit Darnell can derive from rational leverage management. Assume that the company negotiates a $150,000 installment loan repayable over seven years, perhaps guaranteed by the Small Business Administration (see Chapter 20). The company uses the proceeds from the loan to retire the single payment loan and pay all past due accounts payable. Also, Darnell gains a $13,000 contribution to its cash reserves.

In this instance, one form of leverage merely replaces another. But the alternative form eliminates the gap in the firm's cash flow. No accounts payable remain past due. Darnell has no risk of defaulting on a single payment note. The firm's earnings are more than sufficient to amortize the monthly payment required to repay the installment loan. So, Darnell no longer operates at the mercy of its creditors. The potential benefits from leverage in this instance can be summarized in:

Concept 47: A potential gap in a firm's cash flow is not always obvious.

Darnell's experience directly demonstrates the relationship between debt service requirements and the cash flow in a business. This relationship often becomes an important element in a lender's decision to extend credit consideration. It also should influence your decision to accept that consideration.

Achieving a Profitable Level of Operations

Leverage can help a business achieve a profitable level of operations. But that holds true only when insufficient cash capability is the only obstacle to profitability.

The case of Bayline Bolt Corporation in Chapter 11 illustrated this potential use of leverage. There the $100,000 used to start the business provided cash capability sufficient only for a break-even sales volume. The firm's natural cash flow cycle at that volume absorbed the full $100,000 in cash.

Then Bayline's founder negotiated $30,000 in trade credit consideration, which provided the cash capability necessary for a profitable sales volume. Remember, however, that this potential realistically exists only when limited cash capability is the only obstacle to a profitable sales volume. So remember:

Concept 48: Leverage may provide the cash capability necessary to achieve a profitable sales volume.

Cash Flow Concept No. 48 is most beneficial for a business operating within reasonable proximity of its break-even sales volume, as in Bayline Bolt's circumstance. In that event, a relatively small increase in sales can have a dramatic effect on earnings.

At the same time, the farther a business is from that break-even point, the more questionable the potential benefits from external financing. If the distance becomes too great, the business will be unlikely to find a lender to extend such financing.

Using Leverage to Increase Supplier Profits

Many businesses use leverage to facilitate profitable purchase and payment practices that help increase earnings. In general terms, these benefits are supplier profits.

The business with sufficient cash capability doesn't have to use leverage to benefit from supplier profits. Cash capability, not borrowing, provides the benefits. But a business often justifies the use of leverage and the associated cost to gain the cash capability to take advantage of substantial supplier profits.

Using Leverage to Take Cash Discounts

You will often find you can profit from using leverage to gain the cash capability necessary to take cash discounts suppliers allow for early payments. Let's examine a case that identifies the actual dollar benefits.

The Bonner Company purchases $200,000 in merchandise each month to maintain its investment in inventory at a level appropriate for its projected sales volume. Half of the firm's suppliers offer a 2% discount for payment within ten days, requiring payment in full in thirty days. Bonner is losing those discounts, although it has the cash capability to pay in thirty days. Presently, the discounts lost reduce Bonner's annual earnings as follows:

$$\$1,200,000 \quad x \quad 2\% \quad = \quad \$24,000$$

Recognizing the substantial profit penalty imposed by insufficient cash capability, management decides to borrow the funds necessary to take the 2% discounts.

Since half of the total monthly purchase includes the potential discounts, Bonner needs two-thirds of that amount to pay for all such purchases in ten days, leaving ten days' discount purchase constantly outstanding. Bonner needs $66,666 to achieve that objective.

Assuming the firm incurs a 12% annual borrowing cost, we can calculate the potential bottom-line benefits:

Total Annual Discounts Taken	$24,000
Annual Borrowing Cost ($66,666) x 12%	8,000
Net Bottom-Line Benefits	$16,000

Thus leverage leads to substantial bottom-line benefits when it provides the capability necessary to take cash discounts.

Note that Bonner would increase earnings even if the necessary leverage cost 24%, or even 30% per year. So don't let the presumed high cost of borrowing make you miss out on an increase in earnings. Always measure the actual dollar cost against the potential benefits.

Using Leverage to Take Quantity Discounts

Quantity discounts stand as a less obvious form of supplier profits that can justify the use of leverage. However, the potential benefits usually fall well below those from trade discounts. This follows logically when you remember that as you increase the size of your inventory purchases, you also increase the size of your average investment in inventory. This, in turn, increases the carrying costs associated with that component of the cash flow cycle. Adding leverage costs to carrying costs can significantly diminish the potential held in quantity discounts. Nevertheless, the potential does exist. In the proper circumstances, the financial benefits can be substantial.

The Assembly Company manufactures standard desk lamps. The company doesn't produce any of the component parts of the lamps. Instead, it purchases each component from various suppliers. Projections for the upcoming year suggest the realistic potential for the sale of 20,000 desk lamps. Beginning with that projection, the firm measures the potential increase in earnings available from suppliers' quantity discounts.

The analysis began with a look at the quantity discounts offered by the lamp base supplier. Table 18-3 includes the supplier's price structure. Thus the unit price drops from $4.00 to $3.10 when a business increases its order size from 1,999 to 10,000 units.

Beginning with that schedule, the Assembly Company proceeded with the analysis on the following assumptions:

1. The company could make twelve monthly purchases of 1,666 units each or two semiannual purchases of 10,000 units each.
2. The total acquisition and inventory carrying costs incurred in the two alternatives are exactly equal.
3. To purchase the lamp bases, the company will have to borrow an average of $20,000 for the year, incurring $2,400 in interest costs.

A glance at Table 18-3 finds that the Assembly Company reaps substantial benefits from the quantity discounts associated with the larger lot purchase, even after considering the leverage cost. We emphasize this potential benefit from borrowed funds in:

Concept 49:   Leverage can lead to supplier profits from cash and quantity discounts.

Table 18-3
Using Leverage to Obtain Quantity Discount
The Assembly Company

Lot Size	Unit Price
0-1,999	$4.00
2,000-4,999	$3.70
5,000-9,999	$3.40
10,000 +	$3.10

	Annual Cost Based on Twelve Monthly Purchase Orders (1,666 each)	Annual Cost Based on Two Semiannual Purchase Orders (10,000 each)
Total Units	20,000	20,000
Unit Cost	$4.00	$3.10
Annual Purchase Cost	$80,000	$62,000
Plus: Leverage Cost	—	2,400
Total Cost	$80,000	$59,600

Next, let's touch on the benefits that can develop when leverage provides a business with some financial flexibility.

Using Leverage to Gain Financial Flexibility

The flexibility that leverage provides enables a business to effect profitable decisions that otherwise might be precluded by a limited cash capability. Some of those decisions may involve special, one time opportunities for profit.

For example, a business might use its financial flexibility to take advantage of a special supplier discount in exchange for immediate cash payment. Or the firm may pursue a larger prospective customer, certain that it has the cash capability necessary to service the customer's needs.

Here we will emphasize the ongoing bottom-line benefits available to the business that properly exercises its financial flexibility.

A business might use that flexibility to eliminate discounts from its selling terms, using the cash capability from the leverage to carry the large investment in receivables that results from that policy.

If your profit margin warrants, your financial flexibility might allow you to carry that policy another step and extend longer selling terms to induce a higher sales volume. Obviously, you must carefully weigh the cost against the benefits. But if the potential profits and your financial flexibility prove sufficient, the longer selling terms may make good business sense.

In any event, note the point of these examples in:

Concept 50: **Leverage can provide financial flexibility that leads to bottom-line benefits.**

In other circumstances, you might use that financial flexibility to carry a larger investment in inventory, to move into other product lines, or to expand your geographical market. Even the conservative business manager benefits from the financial flexibility provided by leverage. She knows that she has the cash capability necessary to absorb a financial setback.

Using Leverage to Serve Special Objectives

A business might profitably use borrowed funds to increase sales, take discounts, or fill a gap in its cash flow cycle. In each instance, however, those benefits ensue because leverage serves as a natural complement to the firm's existing cash capability.

However, a business can also use leverage in cases that are not directly related to its normal operations and that don't contribute directly to an increase in cash capability or earnings. For example, a business might borrow to buy out some of its stockholders or to facilitate the acquisition of another operation. In another circumstance, debt may provide the cash to pay dividends.

Although such objectives may directly or indirectly benefit the business, they represent unique circumstances that exceed our concern. At the same time, recognize that any leverage a business employs inevitably affects the cash flow process. After all, the business that borrows must repay.

Chapter 19

Leverage from the Trade

A supplier contributes leverage to your business whenever he extends open account credit consideration. This credit consideration allows you to defer cash payment for a purchase in accordance with the supplier's standard selling terms.

Conceptually, trade credit provides the same benefits to a business as any other form of leverage. It increases your cash capability and enables you to satisfy objectives that might remain out of reach in the absence of external financing. However, it is more closely intertwined with the cash flow cycle than any other form of leverage.

The Mechanics of Supplier Lending

Properly managed, trade credit becomes a hybrid form of the three principal lending methods discussed in Chapter 17. Trade credit provides a permanent revolving loan in the form of an infinite series of single payment loans.

Rather than the borrower executing a formal note each time he makes a purchase, the credit consideration becomes part of the firm's accounts payable, the accounting record of amounts due to all suppliers. Each account represents a promise to pay for a purchase within the allotted time set by the supplier's payment terms.

However, trade credit can provide a constant contribution to the cash capability in a business. Accounts payable, a current liability, becomes permanent leverage. A brief look at the experience of the Boone Company with a single supplier demonstrates that potential.

The Boone Company, a regional manager of trailer axles, recently placed a $10,000 order for wheel bearings with a new supplier. The supplier approved open account credit consideration for the purchase in line with the industry's standard thirty day terms. Thus payment for the September 1 purchase falls due on October 1.

Concomitant with the payment scheduled on October 1, Boone repeats the $10,000 purchase on the same thirty day terms. The simultaneous transactions lead to a $10,000 continuous contribution to Boone's cash capability. The following transaction record illustrates that contribution:

Creditor's Contribution to Cash Capability

Date	Purchase	Payment	Capability
9/1	$10,000	—	$10,000
10/1	$10,000	$10,000	$10,000

Assuming that Boone continues the same purchase/payment cycle, the roll-over effect translates into a $10,000 revolving line of credit that becomes a permanent addition to the firm's cash capability. Similar consideration from a number of suppliers provides Boone with the support necessary to carry a profitable investment in inventory.

Before we take a closer look at the Boone Company, let's review an approach to analyzing the benefits held in the alternative supplier selling terms.

Comparing the Alternatives

Two interrelated factors ultimately determine the size of the contribution to cash capability that comes from a supplier's credit consideration. The primary influence comes from the supplier's estimate of his customer's creditworthiness. The higher the estimate, the larger the line of credit extended. That line sets the maximum credit consideration available to the customer at any point. Viewed from our special perspective, the line of credit sets the maximum contribution a supplier will commit to the cash capability in a business.

Of course, a business often qualifies for credit lines that exceed its purchase requirements. In such instances, the supplier's selling terms specify the cash capability the business draws from that consideration. Obviously, the longer a supplier allows for payment, the larger the contribution he makes to your cash capability.

We will illustrate the analytic approach that helps identify the appropriate supplier when cash capability is the primary consideration. However, this is not always the ruling factor that selects one supplier instead of another. Many businesses favor supplier discounts for early payment over the additional cash capability that comes from larger lines of credit or longer terms for payment. Our illustration also includes that alternative view as an element in the comparative analysis of supplier selling terms.

Table 19-1 summarizes an analysis performed by Any Company, a diversified conglomerate. The analysis begins with the following facts:

1. As a logical necessity for good employee relations, Any Company purchases $10,000 in toilet tissue each month for internal use.
2. Six potential suppliers (tagged by alphabetical designation in Table 19-1) can provide a competitive product.
3. The list purchase price from any of the six suppliers is the same.
4. Each supplier approves an unlimited line of credit for Any Company.

Despite its size and financial strength, Any Company follows a regular pattern of analysis when no price differential exists among prospective suppliers of the same product. That analysis examines the competitors' selling terms from two perspectives. Each perspective usually favors different suppliers. One perspective considers the bottom-line benefits that Any Company can gain from discounts allowed for early payment.

Table 19-1
Cash Capability and Profit Potential
Available from Alternative Credit Terms
(Assumes $10,000 in monthly purchases)

Supplier	Selling Terms	Maximum Potential Contribution to Cash Capability	Maximum Potential Contribution to Annual Earnings
A	Net 10 ROG (receipt of goods)	$ 3,333	—
B	1% 10, net 30	10,000	$1,200
C	2% 10, net 30	10,000	2,400
D	Net 30	10,000	—
E	Net 45	15,000	—
F	Net 60	20,000	—

Note in Table 19-1 that Supplier C's discount for payment in ten days rather than thirty gives that firm the advantage. Buying toilet tissue from Supplier C each month for a year yields a $2,400 benefit for Any Company.

The other perspective of Any Company's analysis contributes information to a contingency plan for operating in a tight money period. The plan calls for conservation of the company's cash as a singular corporate objective during such periods. Thus, if effected, Any Company will switch its preference from suppliers who offer discounts to those who provide the largest contribution to the firm's cash capability.

Note that Supplier F's sixty day credit terms will gain the firm Any Company's business in a tight money period. These terms provide the maximum potential contribution of $20,000 to Any Company's cash capability. That will contribute to the contingency plan's primary objective—retention of as much cash in the business as possible, without eliminating toilet tissue as an employee benefit.

Even though Any Company's circumstances remain hypothetical, the considerations involved in the alternative decision criteria remain valid. The firm with adequate cash capability will favor the profit potential available from discounts even though a business has to borrow to realize those benefits. Certainly, the cost of institutional credit seldom exceeds the cost of lost discounts.

Alternatively, the business suffering from a tight cash flow abandons trade discounts in favor of longer terms for payment. Longer terms contribute capability that can ease the strain imposed by a cash flow problem.

In both cases, you should remember the tenet held in:

Concept 51: Use the supplier credit terms that answer the needs of your business.

Typically, the analysis of alternative supplier credit remains less complicated than implied in Table 19-1. Suppliers in any industry usually have similar designated selling terms. Of course, compare any alternatives that do exist.

From another perspective, the analytic tasks increase in complexity when you look at implied terms rather than designated terms. Of course, prompt payment habits open the door to the maximum benefits available from supplier credit consideration. However, in the midst of a cash flow crunch, you might find welcome relief from a supplier who designates thirty days for payment but continues shipments to customers who fall thirty days or more past due.

Because implied terms are nebulous, they are less subject to objective analysis. Nevertheless, the careful manager can expand the cash capability in his business with the aid of lenient collectors. Don't abuse the privilege, but don't overlook the potential.

Average Payable Period

Average payable period measures the average length of time that you use each dollar of trade credit consideration.

To illustrate the calculation process and how it contributes to positive cash flow management, let's assume that the Control Company has $170,000 in total accounts payable at the end of the first quarter of operations for the year. During this quarter, Control received trade credit consideration for $240,000 in total purchases. In a ninety day quarter, that translates into $2,666 in average daily purchases. To calculate the average payment period for the accounts payable that remain unpaid at the end of the quarter, we can use the calculation:

$$\text{Average Payment Period} = \frac{\text{Accounts Payable}}{\text{Average Daily Purchases on Account}}$$

Using the Control Company's circumstance:

$$\text{Average Payment Period} = \frac{\$170,000}{\$2,666}$$

$$\text{Average Payment Period} = 64 \text{ Days}$$

Each dollar of trade credit consideration contributed to the Control Company remains in the business for sixty-four days before being returned to the supplier in the form of a cash payment.

We summarize the importance of that measure in:

Concept 52: **Average payable period defines the relationship between trade credit and the cash flow process.**

Recognizing that relationship becomes a critical consideration in cash flow management.

The Complete Cash Flow Cycle

A conceptual view of the cash flow cycle includes cash, accounts receivable, and inventory. However, this view is incomplete for most established businesses.

In most businesses, the cash flow cycle should include accounts payable as a natural component.

As the Boone Company's experience indicated, the business that maintains a prompt payment record gains a permanent contribution to its cash capability. Thus accounts payable (supplier credit consideration) substitute for the cash purchase of inventory. Sales convert that inventory into accounts receivable. Proceeds from the collection of the receivables provide the cash to retire the original credit consideration. Then the cycle begins again.

Of course, a supplier's selling terms seldom coincide with the cash conversion period in a business—the length of time it takes to convert a customer's order into a collected account. So accounts payable cannot substitute entirely for cash. Instead, they supplement the original cash invested in a business.

This leads us to a view of the complete cash flow cycle in Figure 19-1. The cash investment coupled with accounts payable provides the total capability necessary for the purchase of inventory. The cycle then proceeds normally. However, part of the cash collection retires the original supplier debt, with the remainder—the gross profit margin—returning to the firm's cash account. That cash pays expenses, while any excess buys more inventory. So long as the cycle operates satisfactorily, accounts payable remain a natural part of the complete cash flow cycle.

Figure 19-1
The Complete Cash Flow Cycle

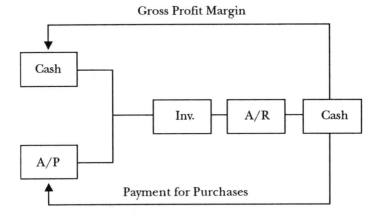

Let's further refine our view of the role trade credit plays in a properly managed cash flow cycle and interrelate the payable period with the requirements set by a firm's cash conversion period.

A closer look at the Boone Company and its present operating characteristics helps demonstrate the interrelationships:

1. Sales presently average $2,000 per day, or $60,000 per month.
2. A sixty-day average collection period leaves the firm with a $120,000 investment in accounts receivable.
3. Product costs average 75% of each sales dollar.
4. The company maintains inventory on hand sufficient for two months' sales; the sixty-day average investment period translates into $90,000 in inventory.
5. Experience indicates a forty-day average payable period satisfies supplier implied terms for payment.
6. Boone maintains a minimum $10,000 cash operating balance.

Figure 19-2 provides a view of Boone's complete cash flow cycle. The company has $220,000 in total assets revolving in the cash flow cycle. Accounts payable, with a forty-day average payment period, provides the cash capability for $60,000 of that amount. Purchases average $1,500 per day.

Figure 19-2
Trade Creditors Contribution to Cash Capability
The Boone Company

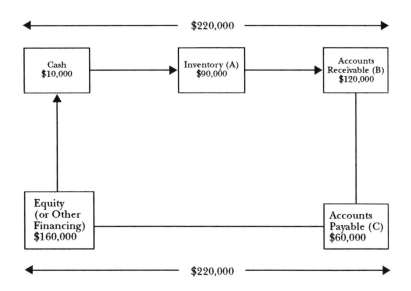

This leaves $160,000 in cash capability that comes from the company's original cash investment and retained earnings. Now, let's see how a change in the company's operations affects those interrelationships.

First, holding the above operating characteristics constant, let's see how an increase in sales affects the firm's financial structure in Figure 19-2. Assume that the company manages an instant 50% increase in sales. We can anticipate the effect the sales increase has on the company's assets. The investment in cash, accounts receivable, and inventory increases by 50% or a total of $110,000.

To maintain the necessary balance, other changes in the firm's financial structure must provide the cash capability to carry the higher asset investment. The support that comes from trade creditors emphasizes the natural place accounts payable hold in the complete cash flow cycle.

As sales increase, the cash capability contributed by trade creditors also rises in line with the higher volume. Of course, that increase occurs only so long as a business satisfies its supplier requirements for prompt payment.

The business must maintain an average payable period consistent with supplier expectations. In the Boone Company's circumstance, that means paying for all purchases in no more than forty days. At the same time, it must continue to satisfy the credit standards set by its suppliers. The firm must qualify for the higher lines of credit. However, presuming the business satisfies those constraints, trade credit usually expands in direct proportion to sales volume. Figure 19-3 demonstrates how that contribution affects Boone's cash flow cycle. We note this fact in:

Figure 19-3
Spontaneous Increase in Trade Credit

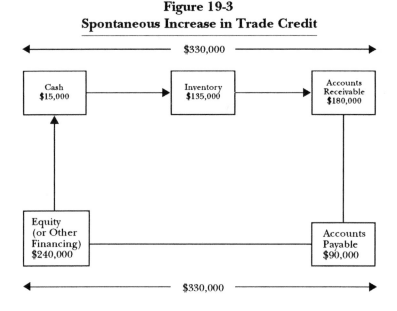

174

Concept 53: Trade credit provides a spontaneous increase in cash capability for a growing business.

The spontaneous increase in trade credit consideration provides $30,000 of $110,000 in cash capability necessary to support the higher investment in assets. Boone's financial strength and ability to maintain a forty-day average payable period encourages its suppliers to grow with the business. To support the sales increase, the Boone Company has to obtain $80,000 in cash capability from other sources. Nevertheless, the spontaneous increase in trade credit is a significant source of financing for expansion.

Trade Credit Criteria

The benefits you derive from trade credit partially depend on the line of credit each supplier approves for your business. Of course, that line comes from the supplier's estimate of your creditworthiness. Before extending any credit, he assesses your capacity to pay.

The complexity of the assessment depends upon the circumstances of the sale. A large sale to an existing customer or any sale to a new customer might call for extensive financial analysis similar to that performed by institutional lenders. However, most trade credit decisions center on one pivotal consideration—payment history. Presuming that past history predicts future performance, the supplier estimates the probable payment pattern for future purchases.

A long, prompt payment history makes trade credit consideration easily accessible for a business, while a record for slow payment may restrict a firm to little or no consideration. However, often a business achieves favorable results from a payment history that remains consistent, although it exceeds the supplier's designated terms. Table 19-2 helps demonstrate that fact with a review of the payment histories of three businesses that buy from the Large Company.

All three customers have purchased the same amount from the company in the last six months. All three also have recently entered new orders for $10,000 purchases. The company's credit manager approves immediate shipment to the Established Company. The firm's recent history indicates prompt payment in accordance with the Large Company's designated thirty-day terms.

The credit manager also approves immediate shipment to Controlled Growth, Inc. Although Controlled Growth does not pay within the designated terms, it does follow a consistent payment pattern. The firm lets no payment fall more than thirty-days past due.

Table 19-2
The Supplier's Credit Decision

Month	Purchases	Outstanding at Month's End	Current	1-30 Past Due	31-60 Past Due	60-90 Past Due
		The Established Company				
January	$10,000	$10,000	$10,000			
February	12,000	12,000	12,000			
March	15,000	15,000	15,000			
April	10,000	10,000	10,000			
May	20,000	20,000	20,000			
June	10,000	10,000	10,000			
		Controlled Growth, Inc.				
January	$10,000	$20,000	$10,000	$10,000		
February	12,000	22,000	12,000	10,000		
March	15,000	27,000	15,000	12,000		
April	10,000	25,000	10,000	15,000		
May	20,000	30,000	20,000	10,000		
June	10,000	20,000	10,000	10,000		
		The Problem Company				
January	$10,000	$10,000	$10,000			
February	12,000	12,000	12,000			
March	15,000	20,000	15,000	$5,000		
April	10,000	25,000	10,000	15,000		
May	20,000	40,000	20,000	10,000	$10,000	
June	10,000	45,000	10,000	20,000	10,000	$5,000

This illustrates a critical point. Many trade credit decisions rely as much on consistent payment as on prompt payment, even though the consistent pattern may exceed the boundaries set by the creditor's designated terms. Such consistency usually improves a firm's potential credit consideration.

A look at Large Company's third customer, the Problem Company, suggests the rationale behind that presumption. The firm's prompt payment record has deteriorated over its recent six month history. Indeed, it is ninety days past due for some purchases. That changing pattern probably disqualifies the Problem Company from any new credit consideration. The slower payment record suggests a cash flow problem approaching serious proportions.

Payment history isn't the only element in a supplier's credit decision, but consistent payment habits in accordance with the designated terms, or at least within a reasonable period, help reassure a supplier. Practicing consistent payment habits can increase the cash capability a business gains from trade credit.

Supplier Relations

A discussion of the elements that contribute to a sound relationship between a business and its suppliers may seem out of place in a book that concentrates on cash flow management. But the working relationship you have with your suppliers has a direct influence on your cash capability. That relationship affects both the amount and the terms of the credit consideration your business receives.

Making a major purchase from any supplier involves considerations that proceed beyond any potential credit consideration. Price structures, product lines, delivery schedules, and service capabilities also remain relevant. However, most businesses eventually establish ongoing relationships with their major suppliers. Once a business establishes such relationships, it should seek to develop and maintain the maximum potential cash capability from each supplier's credit consideration.

Two management practices contribute to good supplier relations. First, practice consistent payment patterns. Erratic payment upsets even the most patient suppliers. So long as they know when to expect payment for purchases, even if persistently late, they can feel comfortable with the relationship.

Second, keep the lines of communication open. The more a supplier knows about your business, the more he can respond to your needs. After all, your purchases presumably represent profitable sales for his business. The better he responds to your needs, the more bottom-line benefits he realizes.

From a positive perspective, inform major suppliers of your purchasing plans. Tell them if your projected requirements for credit consideration exceed presently approved lines. In this way, you can lay the groundwork for approval by giving your suppliers the information that will facilitate the credit decision process.

From another perspective, open lines of communication can help you slip unscathed through a cash flow problem. Don't let a supplier learn about that problem from a break in your payment pattern. Instead, inform him in advance that you cannot pay according to your usual pattern. Explain your circumstance and your problem. Then offer the best estimate of your revised payment schedule. Most trade creditors can live with a past due account.

Of course, the best supplier relations will not lead to unlimited credit consideration or to a cure for every cash flow problem, but they often can lead to more credit consideration and less pressure for prompt payment.

Chapter 20

Leverage from the Bank

When a business manager seeks leverage in excess of the amount available from trade creditors, she first looks to her banker. In fact, bank loans are the second largest form of external financing used by businesses. This chapter discusses bank credit consideration as an element in cash flow management.

Cash Capability and the Single Payment Loan

The single payment loan serves a specific purpose and has a predetermined source of repayment. Of course, the purpose may not be fulfilled as predicted, nor does the repayment always follow promptly. Nevertheless, the premise that justifies a single payment loan identifies each.

The experience of Fawn Chemicals, Inc., demonstrates the contribution that a single payment loan makes to a business and emphasizes the proper relationship between the purpose of the loan and the ultimate source of repayment.

Fawn Chemicals manufactures fertilizer for sale to large agricultural producers. The operating characteristics of the business require a seasonal, single payment loan. Fawn purchases the chemicals necessary for the fertilizer manufacturing process in January of each year. Chemical suppliers allow Fawn thirty day terms, so all accounts payable must be retired by the end of February.

Fawn's customers purchase the fertilizer during the planting season in March and April. However, the producers command terms that allow six months for payment. This means they defer payment until after they sell their harvests in September or October.

Table 20-1 summarizes the natural chain of events that justifies the use of a single payment loan. The successive financial structures reflect the following additional characteristics of Fawn Chemicals:

1. Fawn ends each year with no investment in accounts receivable or inventory, and it has no debt. At 12/31/90, that left the firm with $400,000 in cash, $100,000 in fixed assets, and a $500,000 net worth.
2. Projections indicate that Fawn will earn $140,000 from a $1,000,000 sales volume in the upcoming year.
3. That sales volume will require the purchase of $560,000 in agricultural chemicals.
4. The firm's operating expenses, including interest costs, average $20,000 per month.
5. The firm incurs $100,000 in manufacturing expenses, all paid in February.

Table 20-1
The Mechanics of a Single-Payment Note
Fawn Chemical Company

	(Fiscal Year End)				
	12/31/90	**1/31/91**	**2/28/91**	**4/30/91**	**10/31/91**
Cash	$400,000	$280,000	$160,000	$ 120,000	$540,000
Accounts Receivable	—	—	—	1,000,000	—
Inventory	—	560,000	560,000	—	—
Fixed Assets	100,000	100,000	100,000	100,000	100,000
Total Assets	$500,000	$940,000	$820,000	$1,220,000	$640,000
Accounts Payable	—	$460,000	—	—	—
Bank Loan	—	—	$460,000	$460,000	—
Total Liabilities	—	$460,000	$460,000	$460,000	—
Stockholders' Equity	$500,000	$480,000	$360,000	$760,000	$640,000
Liabilities and Equity	$500,000	$940,000	$820,000	$1,220,000	$640,000

Let's trace the chain of events that justifies the need for the single payment loan and also provides a natural, predictable source of repayment.

First, in January, Fawn purchases the $560,000 in chemicals necessary for the projected sales volume. The company pays $100,000 in cash for part of the inventory, while suppliers allow the balance to be paid in February. As indicated in Column 2, that leaves the firm with $460,000 in accounts payable due by February 28. Even the firm's healthy $280,000 cash balance is insufficient to satisfy the obligation.

(Observe the $20,000 cash drain imposed by operating expenses for the month of January. The lack of any revenue during that period translates that into a matching $20,000 reduction in the stockholders' equity account.)

In February (Column 3), Fawn obtains a $460,000 bank loan to retire the entire amount due to suppliers. The bank extends the single payment loan with repayment required on or before October 31, 1991. Of course, Fawn incurs $20,000 in operating expenses again in February; also the firm must absorb the $100,000 in fertilizer manufacturing expenses. The 2/28/91 financial statement registers the effects that those expenses have on both the cash and equity accounts.

As predicted, Fawn sells its entire inventory by 4/30/91. The firm registers those sales in the form of $1 million in accounts receivable. All of the accounts come due no later than October 31.

Column 4 reflects the impact the sales have on Fawn's financial structure. Note, in particular, two elements in that structure. First, the accrued profits on the sales raise Fawn's equity account to $760,000. At the same time, the monthly operating expenses drain another $40,000 from the firm's cash reserves. This monthly cash drain continues until September, when the producers begin paying for their purchases as agreed. Indeed, by 10/31/91 Fawn collects all of its accounts receivable, retires its bank loan, and has a respectable $540,000 cash balance. The $20,000 in monthly operating expenses will reduce that balance to $500,000 by year's end, when the cycle begins again.

Fawn's experience clearly demonstrates the proper use of a single payment loan. The loan answered a specific need, providing the cash capability necessary to pay for inventory purchases. As sales converted the inventory into accounts receivable, the loan then helped support the investment in receivables. The ultimate collection of those accounts served as the necessary source of repayment.

Obviously a business does not have to be seasonal to benefit from a single payment loan. The loan can enable a business to take advantage of a special inventory purchase or generate an unusually large sale. However, both you and the lender must relate the loan directly to the purpose and ultimately to the repayment source.

Cash Capability and the Installment Loan

Chapter 14 suggested that a business should use external financing as the source of the cash capability required to purchase fixed assets. Then Chapter 17 narrowed that perspective, indicating that the source of external financing usually should be an installment loan. An installment loan allows a business to repay on a schedule that coincides with the cash flow generated by the investment. Now we relate the cash that flows from a new investment in fixed assets to the amortization requirements associated with an installment loan.

From the lender's perspective, to justify installment loan credit consideration, the annual cash flow in the borrower's business must equal or exceed the principal amortization requirements set by any installment loan. The lender relates that practical requirement to the firm's total installment debt service, existing as well as proposed.

This requirement can be clarified with a look at the Collins Company, a small tubing manufacturer that presently operates at a break-even level. The company is contemplating the purchase of a $400,000 automated assembly line that promises a return to profitable operations. The reduction in production costs should translate into $80,000 a year in earnings.

In conjunction with the proposed acquisition, Collins has requested a $400,000 bank loan to finance the purchase and installation of the new line. Despite its break-even operation, the company satisfies the bank's basic credit criteria. However, final approval of the credit consideration hinges on the relationship between Collins's annual cash flow and the amortization requirements for the proposed loan. That phase of the analysis proceeds on several assumptions:

1. Estimates indicate that the new machinery and equipment will have a ten year useful life.
2. The application of straight line depreciation to the new assets will contribute $40,000 per year to Collins's cash flow.
3. The existing fixed assets are fully depreciated and have no effect on annual cash flow measurements.
4. Collins presently has no other fixed debt requirements.
5. The bank's credit policy precludes extending any installment loan that will not be repaid in five years or less.

Collins's banker analyzed these facts in two simple steps. First, she found the annual cash flow necessary to amortize the $400,000 loan over a five year term. That amount came from the basic calculation:

$$\text{Annual Cash Flow Requirements} = \frac{\text{Loan Amount}}{\text{Term (in years)}} = \frac{\$400{,}000}{5} = \$80{,}000$$

Consequently, Collins will need to produce an annual cash flow of at least $80,000 to meet the debt service requirements on the proposed loan. We ignore interest expense in this instance, since it would fall into the category of normal operating expenses included in the projected earnings calculations.

Second, the banker measures the annual cash flow anticipated from the company's operations. However, recognizing the uncertainty inevitably associated with the proposed transformation of the business from a break-even to a profitable operation, the banker considered three alternative outcomes: pessimistic, optimistic, and an average view.

	Cash Flow from Earnings	Cash Flow from Depreciation	Total Annual Cash Flow	Amortization Requirement	Loan Decision
Pessimist	—	$40,000	$ 40,000	$80,000	Decline
Optimist	$80,000	40,000	120,000	80,000	Approve
Average	40,000	40,000	80,000	80,000	?

The pessimist's view presumes that the new investment will have no effect on Collins's operating results. The firm will remain a break-even operation. The annual cash flow will be equal to the annual depreciation.

The optimist's view accepts the company's projections. It presumes that the firm will produce $80,000 a year in earnings and a $120,000 annual cash flow—the earnings plus $40,000 in depreciation.

Logically, the average expectations split the difference between the optimist and the pessimist. This view anticipates future earnings of $40,000 per year, which, when coupled with depreciation, produces an $80,000 annual cash flow.

The optimistic view encourages approval of the credit consideration. The prospective cash flow from that perspective stands as 150% of the amount required for debt amortization. The bank adopting that view will extend the loan.

The pessimist will decline the loan. Since half of the cash flow necessary to retire the debt comes from projected earnings, he foresees a $40,000 annual shortfall.

Finally, the lender who holds the average view is left without any clear decision criteria. Indeed, this view projects an annual cash flow exactly equal to Collins's debt service requirements. However, a slight drop in earnings below the $40,000 projected reduces the firm's annual cash flow below the required

$80,000, so the average view must rely on other factors to justify the final credit decision.

Perhaps surprisingly, the ultimate credit decision in the Collins Company's circumstances actually may depend upon the banker's individual perspective: whether she is a pessimist, an optimist, or something in between. Whatever her attitude, however, when she analyzes a prospective installment loan, she will look closely at the relationship between the firm's annual cash flow and fixed debt amortization requirements.

The logic of this attitude recognizes that the principal repayment of a loan is not a business expense. It does not appear in the income statement. Instead, the repayment merely returns borrowed cash capability. The cash for repayment must come from the liquidation of assets, from funds borrowed from another lender, or from the annual cash flow from operations.

Lenders who approve an installment loan automatically tie themselves to the borrower for the term of a note that usually extends several years. In addition, they recognize that a business might be unwilling or unable to liquidate other assets to meet its fixed debt requirements. And the lender cannot depend on some other creditor to provide the cash necessary for installment debt service.

The business with a tight cash flow isn't the most welcome prospect for a loan. So the bank (or other lender) looks for an annual cash flow from operations that is sufficient to meet the debt service requirements. The business that fails to satisfy that requirement usually has trouble obtaining installment loan credit consideration.

Cash Capability and the Revolving Loan

A revolving loan provides flexible leverage for a business. The business gains the discretionary use of the lender's funds up to the limit set by its line of credit. Table 20-2 presumes that the bank approves a $500,000 line of credit for a business, extending from the beginning to the end of the calendar year. The business uses the line during that term as a complement to its normal cash flow cycle. Thus the borrower obtains $300,000 on January 15 and another $200,000 on March 7. Reflecting a cyclical operation, the firm generates the cash to repay $400,000 on April 7. The firm obtains another $300,000 on July 26 and then retires the full amount of the loan in three payments during the last quarter of the year.

The flexibility available from a revolving loan is apparent. Unfortunately, only the stronger, more creditworthy borrowers qualify. Since such firms most often have resources that preclude the need for such consideration altogether, the revolving loan becomes a convenience rather than a necessity.

Table 20-2
A Revolving Line of Credit ($500,000 Maximum)

Date	Borrowed	Repaid	Loan Balance	Available Cash Capability
January 15	$300,000	—	$300,000	$200,000
March 7	200,000	—	500,000	—
April 7	—	$400,000	100,000	400,000
July 26	300,000	—	400,000	100,000
October 1	—	100,000	300,000	200,000
November 9	—	200,000	100,000	400,000
December 7	—	100,000	—	500,000

The True Cost of Bank Borrowing

Without properly measuring the costs, a borrower can't determine how profitable leverage is for her business. Nor can she properly compare the costs among the alternative forms of leverage.

The interest charge sets the basic, or apparent, cost of a bank loan. To measure the true cost, you must recognize the expenses that arise from compensating balances, commitment fees, restrictive covenants, legal fees, negotiating renewals, and annual cleanups.

Of course, every borrower does not absorb all of these costs. But when incurred, they can add substantially to the apparent cost of bank borrowing represented by the stated interest rate.

The Compensating Balance Requirement

A deposit relationship is usually necessary before a bank approves a loan. A business that borrows from a bank must have, or agree to establish, an operating account with the lender. This requirement serves two objectives.

First, a prospective borrower's cash management practices enter into the credit criteria that guide the lending decision. The business that maintains a comfortable cash balance has the first line of defense against the threat of financial reverse. This adds an element of confidence to a lender's decision to extend credit.

From a different perspective, the business that holds little cash relative to its sales volume constantly confronts the risk of a financial setback. A supplier pressing for payment of past due accounts, or a major customer who defers payment for large purchases, can translate that risk into reality. Consequently, the business has less chance of receiving bank credit.

In either case, the bank's requirement for the borrower's operating account allows the bank to monitor the firm's cash management practices. It also enables the bank to update that estimate regularly. So it becomes an important element in a continuing lending relationship.

The second objective, however, probably stands higher in the banker's mind. That is, it enables the bank to obtain a compensating balance which increases a bank's earnings. The cash a business holds for normal transactions often satisfies a bank's compensating balance requirements. But if the average deposits are too low, the bank will require the borrower to carry additional, idle cash sufficient to make the compensating balance equal to 20 to 30% of the credit consideration. The compensating balance provides the bank with additional funds for profitable lending elsewhere.

As the compensating balance requirement increases the bank's earnings, it also increases a firm's cost of borrowing. That hurts its earnings. This follows naturally, since the necessity for a compensating balance forces a business to borrow more than it actually needs. For example, a business that needs $400,000 in additional cash capability might have to borrow $500,000 to satisfy the bank's requirements for a 20% compensating balance. The firm pays for $100,000 in credit consideration, which lies idle in its checking account.

You measure the cost of a compensating balance by relating the actual dollar cost of bank credit to the funds you actually employ. Assume a bank approves a $100,000 single payment loan for a business, repayable at the end of one year. The bank charges a 10% annual interest rate for that consideration, but it requires a 20% compensating balance for the term of the loan.

The compensating balance requirement raises the firm's apparent cost of borrowing:

1. Annual Cost of Borrowing at 10% = $10,000

2. Interest Rate Based on = $\dfrac{\$10,000}{\$80,000}$ = 12-1/2%
   Funds Actually Used

The inability to use 20% of the total bank credit consideration raises the apparent cost of borrowing by 2-1/2%.

Table 20-3 charts the effect of various compensating balance requirements on a firm's apparent cost of borrowing across a range of interest rates.

The Commitment Fee

A business may obtain a line of credit from a bank merely to provide a cushion of cash capability to contend with any unforeseen problems. A preapproved line of credit often makes good business sense. But a business manager should recognize that she can incur a cost of borrowing even if she never uses the committed funds.

Table 20-3
Effect of Compensating Balances on the
Cost of Bank Credit Consideration

Stated Rate	Compensating Balance Requirements				
	10%	20%	30%	40%	50%
	True Rate				
6%	6.6	7.5	8.5	10	12
6-1/2%	7.2	8.1	9.3	10.8	13
7%	7.8	8.8	10	11.7	14
7-1/2%	8.3	9.3	10.7	12.5	15
8%	8.8	10	11.4	13.3	16
8-1/2%	9.4	10.6	12.1	14.2	17
9%	10	11.25	12.8	15	18
9-1/2%	10.6	11.9	13.6	15.8	19
10%	11.1	12.5	14.3	16.7	20
10-1/2%	11.7	13.1	15	17.5	21
11%	12.2	13.8	15.7	18.3	22
11-1/2%	12.8	14.4	16.4	19.2	23
12%	13.3	15	17.1	20	24

Many banks charge a commitment fee for establishing a line of credit. The fee typically totals 1/4% to 1/2% of the unused portion of the approved line. Consequently, a business that uses only $100,000 of a $200,000 line of credit will pay an interest charge for the borrowed funds, plus a $250 to $500 fee for the funds committed but not employed. A commitment fee may be a small cost to pay for a cushion of cash capability. But recognize it increases the apparent cost of bank borrowing.

Restrictive Covenants

A bank often includes restrictive covenants as conditional elements associated with a term or revolving loan agreement. Violation of a covenant by a borrower allows the bank to make immediate demand for repayment of any credit consideration outstanding.

Common restrictive covenants preclude a borrower from incurring additional debt, paying dividends, increasing the investment in fixed assets, or even increasing officers' salaries. The bank also might require the business to satisfy certain financial constraints.

For example, a bank may expect a business to maintain current assets (cash, accounts receivable, inventory) that total at least twice the firm's current liabilities. Similarly, the firm's total debt in any circumstance might be restricted to an amount that doesn't exceed the total stockholders' equity in the business.

From the banker's perspective, restrictive covenants encourage a borrower to avoid any action that could prevent her from eventually repaying the credit consideration. However, the borrower often finds restrictive covenants become another addition to the apparent cost of bank credit. The business incurs that cost when the covenant delays or precludes management actions that can benefit the business.

Certainly, a bank can waive any covenant that hampers a borrower. However, while waiting for that waiver, the business might lose a profitable business opportunity to a competitor with the capacity for prompt action. And no matter how much promise an opportunity may hold, the bank may ultimately refuse to bend the restrictive covenants. The business may find its potential limited or stymied altogether.

The cost from restrictive covenants may be difficult to measure. But that cost can become a substantial, if indirect, opportunity cost. Remember that fact before you accept such binding credit.

Legal Fees

The larger and more complex the lending arrangement, the more likely you will incur legal fees in addition to the apparent cost of bank financing. In some instances, those fees arise when a cautious business manager employs her attorney to review a loan agreement before execution. In other instances, the bank passes the cost of preparing loan documents on to the borrower. In either case, the legal fees often translate into a substantial increase in the true cost of bank credit consideration.

Negotiating Renewals

On occasion, a business may be unable to retire a single payment loan as originally agreed. Perhaps the purpose that justified the loan remains unfulfilled. Or a changing business environment necessitates a decision that absorbs the cash earmarked for the repayment.

The failure to meet the repayment obligation seldom becomes a cause for serious concern, so long as the borrower maintains the appropriate credit-worthiness. However, negotiating an extension or renewal of the loan becomes another element in the cost of bank financing. You measure that cost in terms of the management time devoted to the negotiating process. It is another opportunity cost.

If negotiating a renewal requires no more than a phone call or a brief visit to the bank, the cost remains small. It can be considered a part of your normal operating expenses. But as the management time devoted to obtaining renewals (or new loans) increases, the cost of negotiating rises rapidly. After all, a business manager can't employ her management talents while she is locked into loan negotiations. Too much time negotiating for credit consideration can damage the bottom-line of a business. The more valuable your time, the larger the cost of negotiating renewals.

Annual Cleanups

Many banks expect their borrowers to repay all loans—that is, to operate free of any bank credit consideration—for thirty to ninety days each year. This requirement for an annual cleanup period can become another element in the true cost of bank credit consideration.

This requirement doesn't pose a problem for the seasonal business. The natural business cycle generates the cash necessary to satisfy the cleanup requirement. However, the business with a level or expanding sales volume may find the requirement a burden. Indeed, to satisfy the call for a cleanup, the business either must obtain comparable credit consideration elsewhere, usually from trade creditors, or temporarily scale down its operations.

If the burden falls on trade creditors, the business may lose trade discounts that it previously took with the aid of the bank financing. In the extreme circumstance, the business may suffer injury to its credit rating. That can restrict future operations even further. Alternatively, should the business scale down its operations for the cleanup period, it will suffer another opportunity cost—the potential profits on lost sales. In either case, the cleanup period can prove costly.

In any event, recognize that potential cost as one more item that increases the real cost of bank credit consideration. We recognize the cumulative costs in:

Concept 54: A business manager should measure all of the costs associated with bank credit consideration.

Now, let's take a look at the credit criteria that orient most bank lending decisions.

Bank Credit Criteria

A banker's credit decision evolves from a number of interrelated factors. First, the banker estimates the management ability of the business and its prospects within its industry and within the larger economic environment. Ultimately, however, the credit decision focuses on the financial characteristics of the business. The banker estimates not only the firm's ability to repay the potential credit consideration but also its ability to absorb an unforeseen financial setback.

Earning Power

The banker begins her credit analysis with a look at the prospective borrower's earnings performance. Then she evaluates the probability of whether the performance will hold constant or improve in the future. The term *satisfactory earnings* may seem to be a nebulous credit criterion. But the lender expects earnings to remain realistic relative to sales volume, perhaps compared to other firms in the borrower's industry. Moreover, the earnings must be substantial enough to offer the reasonable promise the credit consideration can be repaid over a realistic period.

Occasionally a bank may extend credit to a business with a recent history of losses rather than earnings. Special circumstances must justify that consideration, but the banker seldom proceeds farther in her analysis if the business lacks the prospective earning power sufficient to justify loan approval.

Cash Flow

A profitable operation does not necessarily generate a positive cash flow. While a business must demonstrate satisfactory earnings, it must also have a cash flow satisfactory to meet all obligations on time. This means the borrower should have cash capability to pay all trade creditors promptly, service any debt requirements, and maintain cash reserves sufficient to absorb disruptions in its cash flow cycle.

From a broader perspective, the bank also estimates the prospective borrower's *liquidity*, measuring the firm's total investment in cash, accounts receivable, and inventory against the obligations due to creditors in the near term future. This comparison of current assets against current liabilities, the *current ratio*, helps the banker estimate the probability that the firm will be able to meet its obligations satisfactorily, even in the event of some business reverse.

For example, a business with $500,000 in current assets and $250,000 in current liabilities (a two-to-one current ratio) has little risk of defaulting on its immediate obligations. Alternatively, a business with $500,000 in current assets and $500,000 in current liabilities has little margin for error. This doesn't necessarily imply any immediate financial distress, but it does raise the potential for problems. And the larger the potential for problems, the less likely it is credit will be extended.

The Debt/Equity Ratio

As the third major element in her credit analysis, the banker examines the borrower's debt to equity ratio. That ratio compares the borrower's total debt to the total stockholders' equity. For example, a business with $200,000 in total liabilities and $100,000 in equity has a debt/equity ratio of two-to-one. As debt increases relative to equity, the ratio rises.

A banker will usually be reluctant to lend to a business with a debt/equity ratio that exceeds two-to-one. Naturally, her reluctance increases as the debt/equity ratio rises. Conversely, a lower ratio lends reassurance to any positive credit decision.

The debt/equity criterion adds two elements to the banker's credit analysis: one psychological, one financial. From the psychological perspective, as a firm's debt/equity ratio rises above two-to-one, stockholders have less than one dollar invested in the business, compared to every two dollars (or more) supplied by creditors. So stockholders have much less to lose than creditors. And the more liabilities increase relative to equity, the more likely a business is to take higher risks. The psychological implications of gambling with someone else's cash—that is, the creditors'—tends to reduce the fear of failure.

From the financial perspective, a debt/equity ratio of two-to-one (or lower) generally allows the business to absorb a short term setback. A drop in sales or a rise in costs that leads to a temporary loss from operations does not push the borrower to the brink of financial disaster.

One negative element in the analysis will not necessarily disqualify a business from credit consideration. Unusual strength in one area can overcome a weakness in others. For example, the prospects for a strong earnings performance can offset the detrimental influence that comes from tight cash flow and a high debt/equity ratio. Collateral considerations also often add strength to the decision to extend credit consideration.

A banker often may extend credit to a business even though it fails to meet the standard credit criteria. This often occurs when the potential promise in a young business exceeds the bounds set by its financial circumstances. When the credit consideration can help the business achieve its potential, the banker might justify the loan with the aid of a guarantee from the Small Business Administration (SBA).

SBA Loans

Insufficient cash capability often stands as the primary obstacle to profitability. That obstacle grows larger if a weak financial structure precludes standard bank credit consideration. However, many business managers can overcome that obstacle with loans that are funded or guaranteed by the Small Business Administration. SBA loans fall into two categories: (1) the direct SBA loan and (2) the indirect SBA guaranteed loan.

The direct SBA loan means that the SBA accepts the application, approves the request, and extends the credit consideration. No intermediary is involved. Unfortunately, we can dispense with this category as a potential source of cash capability with two brief comments.

First, a business typically qualifies for a direct funded SBA loan only when other reputable avenues to credit consideration are closed. Such loans may provide start-up cash for the new, untested business or disaster financing for the business on the brink of failure. However, relatively few firms qualify.

Second, few direct funded SBA loans are available relative to the number of applicants. Indeed, budget cutbacks have pushed direct funded SBA loans to the verge of extinction. This precludes practical consideration of this alternative source of funds.

In contrast, the indirect SBA guaranteed loan remains readily available from many banks. Such loans are extended directly by the bank. The borrower's promise for repayment is supported by a guarantee provided directly by the Small Business Administration. That guarantee usually ensures repayment of at least 75% to 90% of the credit consideration.

Don't presume that the SBA's guarantee eliminates a bank's concern about a borrower's creditworthiness. The bank still expects the borrower to demonstrate a fundamentally sound financial status. But that status may still not satisfy the requirements set by the bank's normal credit criteria. Perhaps the firm's debt/equity ratio is somewhat higher than usual for normal bank credit consideration. Or the firm may be losing money, held back by insufficient cash capability. Or the prospective borrower's promise may exceed its past performance.

In such circumstances, the SBA's guarantee enables the bank to meet the needs of a worthy customer who fails to qualify for normal credit consideration. An SBA guarantee does not make a bad loan good; instead, it makes a good loan better.

One unfortunate myth associated with this category of SBA loans should be dispelled. Many business managers still shy away from SBA loans because they fear that there are mountains of paperwork or government interference. In reality, neither obstacle exists.

After the initial application process, which is no more tedious than most other loan applications, the only paperwork is the monthly repayment (most SBA guaranteed loans come in the form of five to seven year installment loans). The imaginary mountain of paperwork becomes lost in the normal administrative process. Because you obtain the loan from your bank and work with your banker, your contact with the SBA is minimal.

Bank funded SBA guaranteed loans should not be overlooked as potential sources of credit consideration. Often such loans are the logical answer to a firm's external financing requirements.

Bank Relations

A sound banking relationship is essential for the long term success of a business. Indeed, that relationship can ensure that the business has a source of external financing to fill a gap in its cash flow cycle. Also, an experienced bank can provide valuable counsel.

Of course, you don't establish a sound banking relationship in your first meeting with a banker. Nor does that relationship automatically follow the extension of bank credit consideration. Instead, a business builds a bank relationship over a long period and in a manner that is mutually beneficial for both the business and the bank. As with any other lender, the cornerstones of a sound banking relationship are (1) open lines of communication, (2) timely financial information, and (3) adequate lender compensation.

The communication process operates most effectively, if not most efficiently, when it relies on personal contact. The better your personal relationship, the better your bank relationship. To enhance the personal relationship, you should provide the bank with timely financial information about your business. You should give the bank your most recent balance sheets and income statements as soon as they are prepared. The more the banker knows about your financial circumstances, the more she can contribute to your business.

You also should communicate any actual or potential financial setback to your banker immediately. She cannot feel comfortable with a relationship that reveals financial difficulties thirty, sixty, or ninety days after the fact. So long as you maintain open lines of communication, whether the news is good or bad, your bank will have incentive to help solve your problems.

Finally, a bank deserves reasonable compensation for its services. While you should know the true cost of borrowing, you should not try to reduce that cost unnecessarily and make your account unprofitable for the bank. When the bank finds your account profitable, your lines of communication open, and your financial information timely, you have set the structure for a sound, mutually profitable relationship.

Chapter 21

Leverage from the Commercial Finance Company

Many business managers view the commercial finance company as the lender of last resort, a source of leverage to be used only when other lenders refuse credit consideration. Unfortunately, this attitude most often arises from ignorance. It becomes an obstacle to the success or to the full potential of many businesses.

This chapter reviews the two major sources of credit consideration provided by commercial financing companies: factoring and accounts receivable financing.

The Collateral-Based Loan

Before extending any loan, a prudent lender assesses the borrower's creditworthiness. A commercial finance company is no exception. But rather than approving a specific loan, it agrees to advance funds, subject to a realistic upper limit, in direct proportion to the amount of collateral pledged to secure the credit consideration.

For example, a commercial finance company might approve an 80% *advance rate,* secured by a borrower's investment in accounts receivable. The borrower gains access to cash capability in any amount up to the limit set by the proportional relationship. In this circumstance, a $100,000 investment in accounts receivable warrants $80,000 in credit consideration. Should the borrower's receivables increase to $150,000, the potential loan rises to $120,000 (80% x $150,000). Alternatively, a reduction in that investment to $50,000 reduces the firm's borrowing power to $40,000 (80% x $50,000).

The total credit consideration extended by the finance company will not exceed the collateral value set by the specific advance rate. Collateral-based loans secured by accounts receivable comprise the major portion of the credit consideration extended by the commercial finance industry.

With some modification, lenders employ the same concepts to provide leverage secured by inventory and, less frequently, by equipment. The lender extends credit secured by assets that revolve through the business.

Revolving the Collateral-Based Loan

Unless financing the purchase of fixed assets, many borrowers pledge collateral only to secure single-payment loans. A business may pledge $100,000 in accounts receivable to secure an $80,000 bank loan. Collections from the pledged accounts ultimately repay the loan. Should its cash requirements continue, the business obtains another loan secured by a new set of accounts receivable. Continuous requirements call for a series of repetitive single-payment loans.

However, factoring and accounts receivable financing both proceed beyond the limits set by a series of successive single payment notes. Instead, each translates collateral-based lending into a fluid, revolving relationship that becomes cash flow financing. Figure 21-1 illustrates this relationship. View A shows another perspective of the normal cash flow cycle. After sales convert inventory into accounts receivable, the business must wait for the term of its average collection period to obtain the cash to pay expenses or reinvest in inventory.

The collateral-based revolving loan, as shown in B, eliminates the waiting period and enables a business to obtain the bulk of its cash from sales immediately. On a continuous basis, as it generates sales, a business can obtain cash secured by receivables up to the limit set by its advance rate. A business with an 80% advance rate generates $8,000 in borrowing power from $10,000 in new sales. That much cash is available immediately for profitable reinvestment.

At the same time, the ongoing collection of the borrower's receivables completes the revolving loan cycle. Logically, the collections provide the cash necessary to repay previous advances from the lender. The collateral-based revolving loan becomes cash flow financing because the sales-borrowing-repayment cycle operates continuously. In essence, the system accelerates the cash flow process.

Cash Flow Financing in Action

The collateral-based revolving loan accelerates cash flow. The borrower obtains the immediate use of a major portion of each sales dollar without waiting to collect the accounts receivable from those sales. To illustrate, let's look at the experience of the Crandall Company, an expanding wholesale operation.

Crandall's growth rate recently led to increasing cash needs that exceeded the bounds set by standard bank financing. Consequently, the firm arranged for an accounts receivable revolving loan from a commercial finance company. The finance company agreed to advance Crandall cash in amounts up to 80% of its eligible accounts receivable. Table 21-1 tracks the first five days in the operation of the loan.

Figure 21-1
Normal Cash Flow Cycle

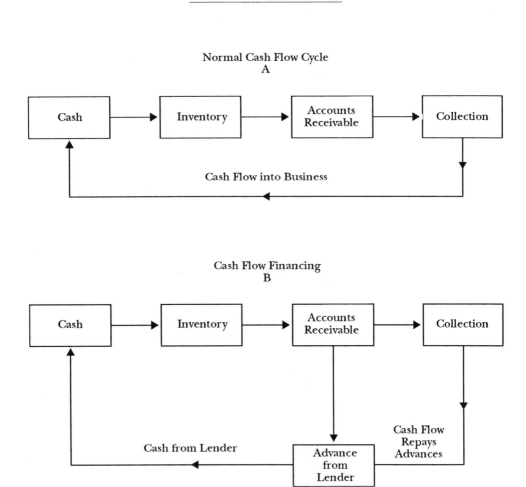

Normal Cash Flow Cycle
A

Cash Flow Financing
B

Table 21-1
Cash Flow Financing
The Crandall Company

Day	Sales	Collections	A/R Balance	Total Cash Capability	Daily Cash Advance	Loan Outstanding	Unused Cash Capability
1	—	—	$300,000	$240,000	$240,000	$240,000	—
2	$50,000	—	350,000	280,000	40,000	280,000	—
3	—	$40,000	310,000	248,000	—	240,000	$8,000
4	30,000	—	340,000	272,000	20,000	260,000	12,000
5	—	—	340,000	272,000	5,000	265,000	7,000

On day 1, when the revolving loan agreement begins, Crandall's accounts receivable total $300,000. The 80% advance rate provides the firm with $240,000 in borrowing power. Initially, Crandall exercises its option to obtain the full amount of the cash available. It uses that cash to retire its bank debt and perhaps to pay some past due trade credit.

On day 2, after initiating the loan agreement, Crandall generates $50,000 in sales but receives no collections from accounts receivable previously outstanding. So the firm's total investment in receivables increases to $350,000, which raises its total borrowing power to $280,000 ($350,000 x 80%).

Crandall again exercises its options and gains an additional $40,000 in cash from the lender. The sales create new receivables that increase the collateral-based borrowing power available from the lender.

On day 3, Crandall generates no sales. However, the company does receive $40,000 in payments on account from its customers. Since the receivables stand as collateral for the credit consideration, Crandall remits the collections to the lender. Application of the collections to the firm's outstanding loan balance completes the revolution of the loan. New sales create new borrowing power; collections on account reduce any existing loan balance.

Observe the first three days and measure all of the results that come from the $40,000 in collections. Of course, the firm's total investment in receivables drops to $310,000. Simultaneously, the collections reduce Crandall's total loan balance to $240,000. But observe that, despite the lack of any new sales, the collections produce $8,000 in new cash capability, or borrowing power, for the firm.

This new borrowing power develops naturally from the characteristics of the revolving loan. The lender advances cash only up to 80% of each sales dollar. However, collections usually represent 100% of each sales dollar. Thus the collection "overpays" the original advance. The borrower sees the effect of the overpayment in a rise in his borrowing power equal to 20% of the collected amount.

On day 4, Crandall receives no collections but generates $30,000 in new sales. The new sales increase the firm's cash capability by $24,000 ($30,000 x 80%). We presume that Crandall's cash needs will absorb $20,000 of that capability. This suggests another critical point. The borrower using cash flow financing does not have to use the full amount of the cash capability available from the lender. He can use all of it, none of it, or part of it as his cash needs dictate.

It is easy to see how cash flow financing provides an element of flexibility for the business with fluctuating cash needs. So long as the excess capability exists, the business can use leverage in direct response to its cash needs. Indeed, the collateral-based revolving loan fluctuates in direct response to the sales, collections, and cash requirements in a business.

On day 5, Crandall generates no new sales and receives no new collections. However, at the close of the previous day, the company enjoyed $12,000 in unused cash capability. Crandall obtains $5,000 from that amount on day 5.

The actual administration of the collateral-based revolving loan is more complex than the illustration suggests. But the Crandall Company's experience demonstrates the basic concept and suggests some of the potential benefits that can come from cash flow financing. Our illustration also should encourage you to adopt a different perspective of the cash flow process.

A New Definition of Cash Flow

The collateral-based revolving loan changes the concept of cash flow. No longer is it totally dependent on collections; instead, it becomes primarily dependent on sales. Moreover, it fluctuates on a daily basis depending upon the interrelationship of sales, collections, borrowing power, and the needs of the business.

A straightforward relationship identifies the specific cash flow in a business using every dollar available from the collateral-based revolving loan. Presuming the business has an 80% advance rate, its cash flow becomes 80% of sales plus 20% of collections. That cash flows naturally from the mechanical process that revolves the loan. The borrower obtains up to 80% of any new sales in cash. This is 80% of the cash flow equation. Subsequently, as indicated in Crandall's experience, collections provide another 20% in cash capability, since they reduce the loan dollar for dollar.

Different advance rates change the cash flow equation. For example, with various advance rates, the cash flow becomes:

Advance Rate	Cash Flow	
70%	70% of sales plus	30% of collections
75	75	25
80	80	20
85	85	15
90	90	10

To the extent you can predict your sales and collections, you can reasonably estimate the cash flow and benefits you might derive from the collateral-based revolving loan.

Note the business with excess cash capability gains a unique benefit from this financing method. It can gain complete control over its cash flow. For example, assume a business has $320,000 in borrowing power from an 80% advance rate applied to a $400,000 investment in accounts receivable. However, the company only uses an average of $200,000 of that borrowing power, leaving $120,000 in excess or unused cash capability. Here the company can exercise complete control of its cash flow. It requests cash only when necessary for actual expenditure. It controls its borrowing in direct response to its cash requirements.

Factoring and Accounts Receivable Financing

So far we have categorized factoring and accounts receivable financing as analogous forms of cash flow financing. Although either alternative activates the same fundamental concepts, three critical characteristics distinguish these two financing methods: (1) the matter of notification, (2) credit and collection services, and (3) the element of cost. As we examine the basic distinctions, the advantages and disadvantages of each alternative will become apparent.

The Matter of Notification

Both accounts receivable financing and factoring rely on the pledge of a firm's receivables to a lender (or factor) to secure a loan. In both, the total cash capability available from that pledge comes from the application of the contractual advance rate to the firm's eligible accounts receivable. (Some receivables that fall too far past due or whose ultimate collectibility is questionable may receive no consideration at all in the cash capability calculation.)

Also, in both cases, the loan revolves as the lender advances funds against the accounts receivable created by new sales, and as he applies the collections from outstanding accounts against the existing loan balance. However, the first distinction between the two alternatives arises from the factor's standard practice of *notification*.

The factor accepts the pledged accounts as collateral. At the same time, however, he directs the borrower's customers to remit payment directly to him rather than to the borrower.

For example, assume that the Best Company factors its accounts receivable. Using a $10,000 sale as an example, the factoring process proceeds as follows:

1. Prior to the actual shipment, the Best Company obtains the factor's approval of the sale to the Better Company.
2. Subsequent to the shipment, the Best Company issues an invoice to the Better Company as evidence of the sale with the designated terms for payment.
3. The Best Company obtains an advance from the factor, up to $8,000, using the Better Company's promise to pay as collateral.
4. However, the invoice issued to the Better Company requires remittance directly to the factor.

This summary oversimplifies the factoring process, since the factor often provides services that proceed well beyond the basic cash advance. But what is important here is the recognition that a factor notifies your customers to remit payment directly to him.

Many business managers believe that notification carries a stigma of financial distress. Consequently, they eliminate the factor as a potential source of credit consideration. However, factoring offers other benefits that can offset the negative effects of this imaginary stigma.

In contrast, accounts receivable financing operates on a *nonnotification* basis. The lender accepts the receivables as collateral for the loan but allows the borrower to continue the normal credit and collection process. The lender receives copies of sales invoices that support the specific pledge, and the borrower remits collections on accounts to the lender for application against the loan balance.

However, barring financial disaster on the part of the borrower, his customers—the debtors whose promises to pay serve as collateral for the loan—remain unaware of the financing relationship. Nonnotification preserves the confidence of the financing transaction. We can sum up this basic distinction in:

Concept 55: The matter of notification distinguishes accounts receivable financing from factoring.

Now, let's turn to another consideration that distinguishes factoring from accounts receivable financing.

Credit and Collection Services

Credit and collection services are usually included in a factoring arrangement. The borrower agrees not to extend credit to any customer without the factor's prior approval. Then, as a logical extension of the notification process, the factor also becomes responsible for the collection of the firm's receivables. Any uncollected accounts ultimately become bad debt losses for the factor, rather than for the borrower. This arrangement eliminates the need for a firm's credit and collection staff. Instead, those functions are provided by the factor's own experienced staff.

We mark this characteristic of factoring in:

Concept 56: The factor typically supplements cash flow financing with credit and collection services.

In another direct contrast, the lender who provides accounts receivable financing contributes little to the borrower's credit and collection effort. The borrower makes the credit decisions and manages the necessary collection effort. He absorbs any loss from bad debts. At the same time, the lender may refuse advances against some accounts receivable if he considers the collateral value to be questionable. But the decision to extend credit consideration to any customer remains in the hands of the borrower.

The Element of Cost

You incur a borrowing cost when you use accounts receivable financing or factoring as a source of leverage. If you use the factor's credit and collection services, you pay an additional fee.

Lenders who provide cash flow financing typically charge 4% to 7% over the prevailing prime lending rate. The uninitiated often consider such rates to be exorbitant. However, you should recognize two critical facts about that charge.

First, the lender properly charges a firm only for the actual dollars borrowed each day. Thus a 12% annual interest rate becomes a 1/30 of 1% daily charge. Using $100,000 for one day costs the borrower $33.33. Since a borrower's cash usage usually fluctuates on a daily basis, the actual dollar cost of cash flow financing often falls below comparable bank financing. This holds true even though the bank's stated annual interest charge is significantly lower.

For example, assume that a business foresees a peak need for $150,000 over a thirty day period. A bank may satisfy that need with a $150,000 loan for thirty days at a 10% annual interest rate. The monthly charge for the bank's funds totals $1,250. However, the business also recognizes that its actual need for borrowed funds fluctuates from day to day. That need never exceeds $150,000, but it often drops as low as $50,000. Projections indicate that the average daily cash needs for the month actually total only $100,000.

Should the business use cash flow financing at a 12% annual interest rate, the monthly charge for the $100,000 average loan balance totals $1,000, or $250 below comparable bank financing. Note that the difference becomes larger if we recognize the cost of a bank's standard compensating balance requirement.

Second, even when the actual dollar cost is higher, you might still find cash flow financing preferable to bank financing if it leads to larger net bottom-line benefits.

The cost of borrowing from a factor seldom exceeds the cost of accounts receivable financing. However, in addition to any financing charge, you pay the factor a commission of 1% to 5% out of each sales dollar to compensate for the credit and collection services included in the factoring arrangement. The specific commission rate paid to a factor arises from many interrelated considerations, such as invoice size, administrative effort, sales volume, and negotiation. Since it includes credit and collection services, factoring exceeds the cost of accounts receivable financing. We recognize that fact in:

Concept 57: Cost distinguishes factoring from accounts receivable financing.

The higher cost of factoring should not preclude it from consideration as a source of leverage. The factor's total commissions may be well below the cost of a competent credit and collection effort.

The Contribution from Flexible Leverage

Cash flow financing often leads to net bottom line benefits that exceed those available from bank financing. This holds true even though the actual dollar costs associated with cash flow financing appear higher. The potential advantage arises from the flexibility of the lending method and of the lenders who provide it. Compared to other forms of leverage, cash flow financing can contribute more cash capability, expanding cash capability, and permanent cash capability.

More Cash Capability

In many circumstances, collateral-based revolving loans provide more cash capability to a business than alternative financing methods. First, commercial finance companies employ liberal credit criteria. They are not restricted to the traditional lending limits on the size of bank loans. Second, the pledged collateral determines the cash capability available to the borrower. As the total collateral increases, the firm's borrowing power increases.

The experience of Marvel Products, Inc., an electronic parts distributor, demonstrates the benefits. Column 1 in Table 21-2 reflects Marvel's financial structure as it stood at 12/31/90.

That structure reflects the following characteristics about Marvel's circumstances:

1. A forty-day average collection period translates the firm's $2,000 daily sales volume into an $80,000 investment in accounts receivable.
2. To preclude excessive stock-out costs, Marvel maintains an investment in inventory sufficient for two months' sales.
3. The firm's suppliers allow credit consideration equal to the inventory level necessary for two months' sales.
4. Marvel's bank provided an additional $40,000 in cash capability at 12/31/90.

These characteristics left Marvel with a satisfactory financial structure. However, increasing demand for electronic parts encouraged Marvel to expand its sales volume. In fact, over the six months following 12/31/90, the firm pushed sales up to $4,000 per day.

Unfortunately, the higher sales volume devastated Marvel's financial structure. As receivables and inventory increased in line with the higher volume, the firm no longer paid suppliers on time. As shown in Column 2, the firm's effort to observe that policy exhausted its cash reserve.

Table 21-2
Benefits of Increased Cash Capability
Marvel Products, Inc.

	12/31/90	6/30/91	6/30/91
Cash	$ 20,000	—	$ 40,000
Accounts Receivable	80,000	$160,000	160,000
Inventory	80,000	160,000	160,000
Total Assets	$180,000	$320,000	$360,000
Accounts Payable	$ 80,000	$280,000	$160,000
Bank Loan	40,000	40,000	—
A/R Financing	—	—	128,000
Total Liabilities	$120,000	$248,000	$288,000
Stockholders' Equity	$ 60,000	$ 72,000	$ 72,000
Liabilities and Equity	$180,000	$320,000	$360,000

Not surprisingly, Marvel's higher debt/equity ratio at 6/30/91 precluded additional bank credit consideration. Indeed, the firm's banker demanded repayment of the $40,000 already committed.

Column 3 shows how cash flow financing solved Marvel's problem. Since the firm's total borrowing power comes from the collateral value (80% x $160,000), Marvel gains the cash adequate to maintain a consistent trade credit record. In addition, the company has excess borrowing power that it uses to expand its cash reserves.

Expanding and Permanent Cash Capability

The collateral-based revolving loan expands in direct line with a borrower's growth rate. As sales increase, so does the firm's borrowing power. Both factoring and accounts receivable financing can provide the cash necessary to fuel rapid growth. In addition, cash flow financing can provide permanent cash capability for a business.

This fact stands out as:

Concept 58: A collateral-based revolving loan can become a permanent source of expanding cash capability.

Each new sale provides new cash capability to offset the natural reduction in that capability from collections. Consequently, the borrower isn't concerned with the cash drain enforced by the maturity of a single payment note. Also, lenders who provide cash flow financing do not require annual cleanups, so the borrower can concentrate on sales and not worry about financing.

Credit Criteria

The commercial finance company's credit analysis proceeds in the same direction as any other lender's. It begins with an evaluation of the applicant's prospects within its industry and in the general economic environment. The analysis then proceeds to an analysis of the firm's past operating results, present financial condition, and projected cash flow. Finally, it considers the collateral that provides the critical insurance for eventual repayment.

However, the commercial finance company approaches the major portion of any credit analysis from a different perspective than that of traditional lenders. Often, a commercial finance company will approve credit consideration other lenders might deny.

Financial Credit Criteria

The financial credit criteria employed by a commercial finance company appear to be remarkably liberal. Neither a high debt/equity ratio nor a low current ratio necessarily eliminates a prospective borrower from credit consideration. The commercial finance company may disregard ratio analysis altogether and instead concentrate on two basic financial considerations.

First, the business should have reasonable expectations of profitable operations. While this seems obvious, the requirement does not disqualify the business with a recent history of operating losses. In fact, the favorable elements presented by a business in the midst of a turnaround often justify cash flow financing.

Second, a prospective borrower should demonstrate financial strength measured by tangible net worth. This is the difference between a firm's real assets and liabilities. It excludes assets that have no realistic liquidation value. That includes intangible assets such as goodwill, leasehold improvements, and loans to officers. Tangible net worth provides a reasonable estimate of the fundamental financial foundation in a business.

In general terms, the commercial finance company expects a business to have a tangible net worth sufficient to absorb an ordinary financial setback without threatening its survival. Some lenders set a minimum requirement, such as a $50,000 or $100,000 tangible net worth. Others relate the firm's total debt to tangible net worth, with no specific debt/equity ratio automatically requiring a negative credit decision. A liberal flexibility describes the financial criteria that orient the commercial finance company's credit decision.

Cash Flow Credit Criteria

A commercial finance company expects a borrower to have a cash flow satisfactory for normal operations. However, the finance company will include the proposed credit consideration in its examination of the borrower's cash flow projections. Presuming approval of the proposed cash flow financing, the business must then demonstrate the capacity to meet all obligations on time. It must show the ability to pay trade creditors within the designated terms and to meet debt repayment requirements, as well as retire all normal operating expenses on schedule. The business that can't satisfy these requirements, even with the proposed credit consideration, does not have a cash flow satisfactory for normal operations.

Collateral Credit Criteria

Collateral analysis ultimately becomes the pivotal element in the commercial finance company's credit decision. Two logical considerations justify that fact. First, collateral analysis identifies the potential borrowing power available to the business. Should the borrowing power prove to be inadequate to satisfy the cash flow credit criteria, the business doesn't qualify for cash flow financing. Second, the liberal financial and cash flow criteria require reliance on the value of the collateral pledged to secure the cash flow financing. This pivotal requirement can be summarized in:

Concept 59: A commercial finance company's credit decision centers on the fundamental value of the borrower's collateral.

The collateral value must be sufficient to offset the lack of financial strength and tight cash flow allowed by the other criteria.

Ultimately, the collateral value comes from the creditworthiness and payment habits of the firm's customers. The more likely the customers are to pay for purchases as agreed, the better the quality of the collateral that justifies cash flow financing.

Lender Relations

The collateral-based revolving loan contract specifies the rights and obligations of the borrower and the lender. In addition, it clearly defines the terms of the borrowing relationship, such as advance rate, credit line, and interest charge. Consequently, the borrower's personal relationship with the lender has little influence on the cash capability available to the business.

However, this does not diminish the need for a good working relationship with the lender. Because the administrative process associated with cash flow financing typically requires daily contact, the need for a sound relationship actually becomes even more significant. Open lines of communication provide the foundation for that relationship. When you satisfy the lender's need for information about your business, you allow him to satisfy your need for cash capability. Open lines of communication ensure a sound relationship for both parties.

Chapter 22

Leverage from Investors

Occasionally, a business may need external financing in excess of that available from institutional lenders. The need could arise from the cash demands set by rapid expansion, or because an unbalanced financial structure precludes institutional credit consideration.

Whatever the justification, the sale of an equity interest in the business may become the only source of additional cash capability. This chapter discusses that alternative and weighs the advantages and disadvantages of equity financing. It also reviews the basic instruments of external financing, including common stock, preferred stock, and convertible securities. The discussion also touches on potential sources of equity for independent businesses.

Equity as Leverage

Equity represents the owner's net financial interest in a business. In simplest terms, the difference between assets and liabilities measures the size of that interest. The net equity includes the common stock, the capital surplus, and retained earnings included in a firm's financial structure.

Most businesses begin with 100% of the ownership interest vested in the hands of the founder. Of course, the founder typically tries to maintain complete ownership. However, the cash needs in a business can exceed the contribution available from its creditors. If the owner lacks the financial capacity to meet these needs, she can generate cash by selling some portion of her ownership interest. In other words, she might seek external equity financing.

From the owner's perspective, using external equity financing to increase the firm's cash capability is no different from using credit or borrowed funds. In both cases, the external investor commits her funds to the business in exchange for the promise of some return on that investment in the future. The business then employs those funds in a way that will keep that promise, as well as increase the return on the original equity investment. The new equity serves as leverage for the old.

The Advantages of External Equity Financing

In comparison with leverage, external equity financing as a source of cash capability offers some distinct advantages for a business. For example, it does not require repayment, it has no scheduled interest payments, it enhances creditworthiness, and it imposes no personal liability on the original ownership.

In direct contrast to leverage, a business has no obligation to repay external equity financing on some predetermined date. Indeed, it provides a permanent contribution to the cash capability of the business. The investor naturally anticipates a profitable return from her contribution, but she expects that return to come from the appreciation in the value of her investment, perhaps enhanced by future dividend payments.

The business doesn't guarantee any return on the investment. Neither the lack of price appreciation nor the failure to receive dividends allows the investor to withdraw her cash contribution. Dividends and price appreciation of the investment remain a hope, not a promise.

In another contrast with leverage, external equity financing from the sale of common stock imposes no fixed charges on the business. The business does not irrevocably commit any portion of its future earnings to compensate the external investor. However, external equity financing from the sale of preferred stock or convertible bonds does impose fixed charges on the firm. The elimination of the fixed charge obligations comes only from the sale of common stock.

External equity financing also enhances the creditworthiness of a business. This benefit comes from the increase in financial strength generally represented by a higher net worth. As the business increases the size of its equity base with the aid of external financing, it becomes a more attractive risk for its creditors. Ultimately, it can expand its cash capability beyond the amount contributed by the external investors.

The first column in Table 22-1 shows the balance sheet of a business that has exhausted its potential for additional credit consideration. Using a fundamental credit criterion, the firm's $1 million in liabilities and $250,000 in equity translate into a four to one debt/equity ratio. Certainly, that exceeds the limits set by most creditors.

Table 22-1
How External Equity Financing
Enhances Creditworthiness

Total Assets	$1,250,000	$1,250,000
Total Liabilities	1,000,000	750,000
Stockholders' Equity	250,000	500,000
Liabilities and Equity	1,250,000	1,250,000
Debt/Equity Ratio	4 to 1	1.5 to 1

In the second column, observe the benefit that comes from raising $250,000 in cash from the external equity financing. Presuming all of the cash reduces the firm's liabilities, that total drops to $750,000. The firm's equity account rises to $500,000. The interrelated effects leave the business with a 1.5 to 1 debt/equity ratio. This new relationship should justify additional credit consideration.

The business can obtain $250,000 in additional cash capability from creditors without exceeding the two-to-one debt/equity relationship, the critical bench mark for many lenders. Each dollar invested in the firm translates in this instance into a potential $2 increase in cash capability. This enhances the direct cash contribution that comes from external equity financing.

Note that using the sale of equity to increase cash capability doesn't affect the personal financial liability imposed on the original owners. When a closely held corporation, one owned by one or a few stockholders, incurs institutional debt, the lender usually requires the personal guaranty of the individual(s) who controls a majority of the outstanding stock. That guaranty encourages the proper disposition of the cash advanced to the corporation. Each time the business increases its institutional debt, the owner also increases her total personal liability for the firm's financial obligations.

Equity financing has no effect on the original stockholders' personal financial liability. The new investor accepts the risk of loss in exchange for a potentially substantial return on her investment. Should the business collapse, she loses her investment. She cannot look to the founders for recovery.

The Disadvantages of External Equity Financing

Before you decide to use external equity financing to expand your cash capability, you should recognize some potential disadvantages: (1) it dilutes ownership control, (2) it often is difficult to obtain, (3) it costs more than debt, and (4) it becomes inflexible financing.

The first disadvantage is usually the most apparent to the entrepreneurial business manager. Selling a portion of her business to external investors obviously dilutes her right of ownership. At the same time, she may lose some management control.

So, when she decides to sell an interest in her business, the business manager confronts the prospect of splitting future profits with outsiders. This can become a psychological burden to the manager who has labored, worried, and risked her financial wherewithal to build a business. Indeed, the prospect of sharing the future earnings often becomes the obstacle that eliminates external equity financing from consideration as a source of cash capability.

Similarly, along with their equity interest, external investors usually expect a voice in corporate affairs. That voice may express itself only in the form of representation on the firm's board of directors, or it may be raised in day-to-day operations. Naturally, the volume of the voice increases according to the proportion of ownership assumed by the investors.

The original owner can retain controlling interest in the business, but she cannot ignore the legal rights of the minority shareholders. External interference that begins as a nuisance often becomes a severe management problem. The problem becomes even more severe because of the difficulty the small or medium size business has in obtaining external equity financing. The number of equity financing sources is limited. Moreover, the business reluctant to yield a significant ownership position will find the potential limited even more.

An external investor seldom will make a major cash commitment for a 5% interest in a business. However, her interest increases as the prospective proportion of ownership increases. Consequently, the business that seeks external equity financing usually will be successful only if the investor obtains a significant fraction of the total ownership. As the size of that fraction increases, so does the probability of interference from the new investors. The business manager must confront one disadvantage or the other.

High cost can become another major disadvantage of external equity financing. This may appear to contradict our assertion that the lack of fixed debt service is an advantage of external equity financing. However, a successful operation eventually incurs more cost from external equity financing than from comparable amounts of leverage. That cost comes from two sources.

First, selling an interest in a business invites interference from external investors. Not only does this become a management problem, it also can become an operating expense for a business. Part of the expense arises from the commitment of management time to nonproductive concerns. Communication may be necessary, but it often becomes a time consuming expense. And this expense increases in proportion to the external investors' efforts to influence the firm's actual management. The interference soon translates into a material expense.

Second, the investors' justifiable expectation of dividends on their investment can become a perpetual rising expense for a business. The successful business must pay a portion of its earnings to investors in the form of cash dividends. The amount paid typically increases as the business becomes more successful. Unlike debt service, dividends continue—and grow—over the life of the firm. In addition, a dollar paid out as a dividend is more expensive than a dollar paid out as interest expense on debt. Interest payments are tax deductible, while dividends flow from after tax earnings. Thus the cost of external equity financing is even more expensive than it appears at first glance.

Another disadvantage is that external equity financing is the least flexible source of cash capability. Once it is obtained, it cannot be used arbitrarily to repurchase the investor's interest. Any repurchase ultimately negotiated becomes an expensive proposition.

In contrast, a business usually has the option to prepay debt. Early payment of some fixed debt may involve a prepayment penalty, but the penalty will seem modest compared to the premium commanded by an external investor for the repurchase of her stock.

Of course, inflexibility may not disqualify external equity financing as a source of cash capability for a business. But before proceeding with any effort to obtain leverage from investors, consider the advantages and disadvantages.

Equity Instruments

Equity financing can take a variety of different forms. In fact, the variations are limited only by the imaginations of the business manager in need of equity financing and the investors who provide it. Nevertheless, the more familiar equity financing instruments fall into three major categories: (1) common stock, (2) preferred stock, and (3) convertible securities. Of course, you shouldn't employ any of these instruments without measuring the legal and financial ramifications. Proper consideration of any external equity financing requires professional advice.

Common Stock

Most external equity financing comes from the sale of common stock. A share of common stock represents the fundamental unit of ownership in a business. Thus the business that sells common stock to an external investor yields some ownership interest to her. As a simple example, assume an investor purchases 100 shares of common stock in a corporation with 1,000 total shares outstanding. The investor obtains a 10% ownership interest in the business. This interest automatically provides the investor with some significant rights.

The stockholder obtains the rights to the net income in the business in proportion to her pro-rata ownership. Of course, the earnings may not be paid out. Instead, the business may retain its earnings to finance future operations. But when they are distributed, the stockholder is legally entitled to her share.

A common stockholder also receives the right to cast a vote on certain company matters, such as the election of the board of directors. Each share of stock entitles the investor to one vote. Consequently, the more shares an investor holds, the more influence she exerts.

A common stockholder also may receive a privileged position in terms of her rights to buy any new stock issued by the corporation. This preemptive right gives her the first option to purchase any new shares and ensures that management cannot subvert the position of present stockholders by selling shares to other investors without offering them to the existing ownership. This protects the stockholder against unfair dilution of her ownership interest.

Preferred Stock

Preferred stock remains an alternative to common stock as an instrument for external equity financing. However, certain undesirable characteristics reduce its potential value as a source of funds for a small business.

First, preferred stock provides no ownership interest in the firm. The investor receives the right to a predetermined, fixed dividend, but she obtains no residual ownership.

Second, while the sale of preferred stock preserves the existing owner's position, the dividends payable come from after tax earnings. That makes it substantially more expensive than debt. So, preferred stock may be attractive to both the business and the investor only when it is issued as a convertible security.

Convertible Securities

In contrast to straight preferred stock, convertible securities can become useful instruments for external equity financing. A convertible security, either a bond or a share of preferred stock (designated as convertible when issued), can be converted into common stock at the option of the holder. Securities offer the investor two complementary advantages.

First, she receives a predetermined, fixed income on her investment, either in interest payments or in preferred dividends. When the business prospers, the investor can convert her holdings into common shares at a predetermined conversion ratio. She has the option to maintain her position as a debtor or she can become an owner.

Second, convertible securities offer a significant advantage to the business. The business obtains the investor's cash capability without yielding any management control. Convertible securities seldom carry voting rights until formally transformed into common stock.

As the business achieves its objectives, holders of convertible securities will exercise their options to obtain common stock. However, that conversion eliminates the requirement for interest or preferred dividend payments. Convertible securities may offer a realistic alternative that enables a business to balance the advantages and disadvantages of external equity financing.

Sources of External Equity Financing

The decision to use external equity financing often proves to be difficult for the entrepreneurial business manager. However, making the decision may be less difficult than searching for financing, since few sources of external equity financing are available to the small business. Usually, the business is limited to the potential equity investment from informal (noninstitutional) sources, suppliers or customers, venture capital companies, or small business investment companies.

Informal Sources

Rarely can a young, small business obtain external equity financing from institutional sources. Instead, the business manager most often must turn to informal sources—to friends, relatives, or business acquaintances.

From one perspective, obtaining equity financing from informal sources can be beneficial. Personal relationships can overcome some of the problems that arise from investor interference in the business. And the informal source may accept a smaller ownership position than that normally accepted by institutional investors.

From another perspective, using personal relationships to generate external equity financing can lead to problems. Should the business ultimately fail, the investor's loss may sour the personal relationship. At best, the relationship will suffer severe stress.

Leverage Management

The availability of external equity financing from informal sources remains a matter of circumstance. The business manager who has no contact or personal relationships with investors will find herself shut out from this source. Nevertheless, begin your search for external equity financing close to home. The farther you proceed from that base, the more difficult the search becomes.

Suppliers and Customers

Occasionally, the business that shows extraordinary promise can obtain equity financing from major customers or suppliers. The major customer of a small business might commit equity financing to ensure a dependable source of supply for a necessary element in its production line. The equity interest encourages preferred service. Alternatively, a major supplier might venture an investment in a growing concern to ensure the demand for its product. Helping the customer grow with an injection of cash ultimately helps the supplier expand her own operation. Of course, both sources of external equity financing expect a profitable return on their investment as the business prospers.

Venture Capital Companies

With the exception of small business investment companies, venture capital companies offer little potential as a source of external equity financing for most businesses because they have such restrictive selection requirements. Most venture capital companies invest only in businesses that display established credentials, exceptional prospects, and extraordinary management ability. The venture capital company also must foresee a realistic potential for a substantial return on its investment, usually from a public offering of stock. A business with modest prospects, however satisfactory to the ownership, will receive little aid from most of these companies.

Small Business Investment Companies

Among venture capital concerns, the Small Business Investment Company (SBIC) usually is more accessible to the business in need of external equity financing. Indeed, SBICs are unique among privately organized venture capital companies. The distinction arises from the source of the bulk of the funds SBICs have for investment. As entities licensed and regulated by the Small Business

Administration, SBICs have access to long term federal loans as a source of cash for venture capital investments.

Not surprisingly, SBICs operate under some restrictions set by the Small Business Administration. But these restrictions typically favor the business seeking financial aid.

First, an SBIC seldom makes a direct equity investment in a business. Instead, the equity financing usually comes in the form of convertible bonds. The business pays interest to the SBIC until conversion. But the initial commitment in the form of debt also preserves the potential for repayment. The original ownership ultimately may preserve its equity position.

Second, the SBIC cannot obtain more than a 49% interest in a business. While that substantial interest may require active participation in major management decisions, it still leaves final control of the business in the hands of the original owners.

Third, as regulated institutions, SBICs have limits on the amount of funds they can commit to any single operation. Many also have relatively low investment limits, such as $50,000 to $200,000. Consequently, they must seek the bona fide small business as a prospect for investment.

Certainly, SBICs hope to profit from their investments, but their operating limitations force them to adopt a more realistic view of the term required for that return.

Chapter 23

Leverage: Comparative Analysis

The comparative criteria that should encourage the use of one form of leverage over another can be confusing. When should a business employ trade credit in preference to institutional leverage? What can make a bank loan more desirable than leverage from the trade? When does a collateral based revolving loan become most appropriate for a business?

Unfortunately, no single answer exists for any of these questions. A specific form of leverage that benefits one business may prove detrimental to another. However, some common considerations should enter into the leverage decision process. This chapter reviews those considerations. The discussion will not necessarily make the leverage decision process a simple task, but it should help orient the decision process.

The major comparative criteria of the alternative forms of leverage can be separated into five major categories: availability, profitability, reliability, flexibility, and risk.

Availability

The form of any debt employed in a business should be appropriate for the purpose. A business seeking funds to finance a temporary increase in inventory will not consider leasing as a realistic source of leverage. Neither is a collateral-based revolving loan the appropriate method for financing the purchase of fixed assets. Recognizing the need to match the form of the leverage to the purpose it serves inevitably reduces the number of alternatives that enter into the comparative analysis.

The lenders' standard credit criteria also may reduce the sources of leverage available. The business with a high debt/equity ratio may not be eligible for bank credit consideration. Similarly, the business that lacks an investment in accounts receivable usually can discount the commercial finance company as a potential source of leverage.

A business also should consider the acceptability of the alternative forms of leverage. For example, management may consider external equity financing to be an undesirable alternative. Or a business may not use leasing as a matter of financial policy. Or the stigma associated with notification may eliminate factoring as an acceptable form of leverage. Eliminating both the unavailable and unacceptable sources of leverage can quickly narrow the list of candidates for external financing.

Profitability

A business often employs leverage to solve a cash flow problem. In such instances, the solution takes precedence over profitability as a borrowing objective. More often, however, a business obtains leverage because the additional cash capability opens the door to higher profits.

Logically, the business in that circumstance should use the source of leverage that ultimately provides the largest contribution to its earnings. Unfortunately, many business managers approach this management objective from the wrong perspective. They concentrate on the comparative costs of the alternative forms of leverage and decide that the least costly must be the most profitable. This approach can lead to a false conclusion. In some instances, leverage with a higher apparent cost ultimately may be most profitable.

Assume that a business needs external financing up to $100,000 over the next six months. However, the maximum need occurs only five days out of each month, or a total of thirty days out of the total six month period. Cash requirements fluctuate during the other twenty-five days each month, but they average $50,000 per day.

The business has eliminated all but two sources of leverage. It can obtain a $100,000 single payment bank loan at an 8% annualized rate for the full six month period, or it can obtain an accounts receivable loan that carries a 12% annual charge.

A straightforward comparison of the annual interest charges makes the bank loan the preferable alternative. But the business that uses accounts receivable financing borrows only to meet its daily cash requirements. Then it pays a daily rate (1/365 of the annual rate) for the funds employed.

Now let's compare the actual dollar cost of bank financing with accounts receivable financing:

<u>**Cost of Bank Financing:**</u>	
$100,000 at 8% for six months	$4,000
<u>**Cost of A/R Financing:**</u>	
$100,000 at 0.033% per day for 30 days	$ 990
$50,000 at 0.033% per day for 150 days	<u>$2,475</u>
	$3,465
Advantage from A/R Financing	$ 535

Repeat the experience for another six months and the net bottom line benefits from accounts receivable financing becomes more than $1,000 higher!

Also, this example doesn't consider the other costs that may arise from bank borrowing, so the advantage gained from accounts receivable financing may become even larger.

That potential receives emphasis in:

Concept 60: **Leverage profitability analysis concentrates on the net bottom-line benefits available from the alternative sources of external financing.**

Comparative leverage analysis may find a relatively expensive lease more desirable because it leaves funds free for a more profitable investment in inventory. Or one source of leverage may promise a higher line of credit than another, again leading to higher net bottom-line benefits. Always proceed beyond the simple comparison of direct costs, since the leverage that costs more may be worth more.

Reliability

Leverage contributes cash capability to a business. The borrower employs that capability to increase its investment in accounts receivable, inventory, or fixed assets. Any unanticipated withdrawal of the lender's contribution can leave the business with a severe cash flow problem. Consequently, comparative leverage analysis should include an estimate of the reliability of the prospective lenders. The estimate measures the potential for sudden withdrawal of the lender's credit consideration.

Reliability is seldom a concern when the leverage comes from an installment loan. So long as the borrower meets the repayment schedule set in the installment note, the lender must honor the original agreement.

However, lender reliability becomes a larger concern for the business that uses a revolving loan or anticipates the renewal or extension of a single payment note. In either case, continuation of the credit consideration is to some extent subject to the discretion of the lender. The lender can extend it or end it.

The borrower's estimate of the lender's reliability should proceed on two levels: one financial, the other personal.

The borrower should be certain that the lender has the financial capacity to continue the credit consideration. Is the lender subject to excessive strain in a tight money period? Does the lender have the financial strength to guarantee the cash advances anticipated from a revolving loan agreement? The business relying on those funds needs affirmative assurances in both instances. Special expertise is necessary to evaluate financial institutions, but raising the questions with prospective lenders will usually provide satisfactory responses.

A borrower also should estimate the reliability of the lending officer handling his firm's account. He has a major influence on the lender's credit decision. The borrower should seek a strong, reliable representative to ensure that credit decisions are not subject to the whims of an anonymous committee.

Personal relationships often have a strong influence on the quality and quantity of consideration a business receives from its creditors. Never take them for granted.

Flexibility

Lender flexibility refers to the capacity to adapt to the fluctuating needs of a business operating in a volatile economic environment. Among other considerations, the analyst should measure the lender's flexibility by its repayment requirements, its restrictive covenants, and its potential for expanded credit consideration.

In response to changing circumstances, a flexible lender readily alters the repayment requirements established by an original agreement. Should the purpose that called for a single payment loan remain unfulfilled, the lender provides an extension beyond the regular due date. Alternatively, should installment loan payments become a burden, the flexible lender develops a revised repayment schedule that fits the firm's actual cash flow. The revolving loan provides the maximum flexibility for a borrower. The business employs and repays cash capability in direct response to its own needs.

The tighter the restrictive covenants in a loan agreement, the less flexible the lender. Indeed, the borrower may become bound by rigid restrictions that exclude the potential for numerous profitable business opportunities.

A business should estimate each lender's response to the expanding cash requirements of a successful operation. A growing business needs increasing, not decreasing, amounts of cash. So, a rapidly growing concern should not lock itself into an inflexible source of leverage that restricts the potential for growth. An inflexible lender can hamper the success of any operation.

Risk

We define risk narrowly here as the potential for default that arises from the inability to meet repayment obligations as agreed. A business naturally should exclude any form of leverage that raises that risk too high. Because of future uncertainty, a business often finds it difficult to measure the risk of default. However, some estimate of that risk can develop from a look at the firm's sales stability (or predictability), financial condition, and profitability. Of course, the more stable (predictable) the sales volume in a business, the less the risk of default from any form of leverage.

In a broad sense, sales stability is directly related to the industry in which the business operates. The less subject that industry is to technological and economic disruptions, the more predictable the sales volume of a business becomes. From a narrower perspective, a business must recognize its position within the industry. The more secure that position, the more predictable the sales. That in turn reduces the risk of default.

For example, a business operating in the volatile electronics industry might avoid fixed debt requirements in favor of short term debt that can be paid quickly from liquidating accounts receivable and inventory. Alternatively, a wholesale grocer can accept fixed debt obligations, secure that his business will remain relatively stable whatever the state of the economy.

The characteristics of the firm's financial structure also affect the risk associated with leverage. The borrower should assess his financial condition no less rigorously than he would a prospective lender's. Often a lender will approve credit consideration that the business will be ill advised to accept. The business must assess both the profitability and the dangers that come with any credit consideration.

A business should not accept debt without considering the level of profitability that will be necessary to meet the interest and amortization requirements. While this may seem obvious, many borrowers assume debt in an effort to turn a losing operation into a profitable one. From a positive perspective, this decision may provide the cash capability necessary to achieve that objective. The borrower should recognize that such debt ultimately can become a burden for the marginal operation. The interest and repayment requirements can leave the business deeper in a financial hole than before the debt was incurred.

The risk of default depends upon the types of leverage being considered. An installment loan, for example, imposes fixed obligations on the business. Without lender flexibility, financial setbacks cannot relieve the firm of its obligations. Indeed, fixed debt requirements compound other financial problems.

Alternatively, single payment or revolving loans actually may impose less financial risk. This holds true so long as the business maintains the collateral adequate to liquidate the debt. The business may not prosper, but the potential transformation of the collateral into cash reduces the risk of default.

Undoubtedly, a comparative analysis of the various forms of leverage may be tedious and time consuming. But it can reduce the potential for cash flow problems and increase your earnings. Moreover, you gain assurance that you have chosen the proper kind of leverage for your needs.

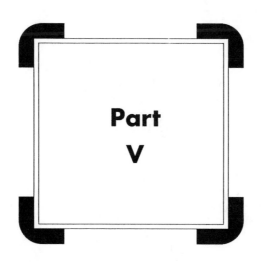

Part
V

Improving
Your
Cash Flow

Chapter 24

Accelerating Cash Inflow

A credit decision must precede an open account sale. A customer seldom pays for a purchase until he receives an invoice. A past due account pays more promptly when you politely remind the customer of his delinquency.

However obvious these facts appear, many business managers overlook the impact that they have on the rate cash flows into a business. That impact is illustrated in this chapter, as well as some principles that will help you to accelerate the cash inflow into your business.

The Cash Conversion Period

In Part II, we analyzed the rate of cash flow into a business using the average collection period and turnover rate calculations. A lower average collection period or a higher turnover rate indicated a more rapid conversion of accounts receivable into cash. However, the collection period and turnover rate calculations don't take into account all of the factors that affect how rapidly cash flows into a business. Both calculations measure cash flow from the date that a business generates a sale to the date that it receives payment. This limitation precludes the sequence of events before and after the sale that affect the cash flow into a business.

To measure the rate of cash flow properly, we need to adopt a broader perspective defined here as the *cash conversion period*. This period measures the total time lapse between each customer's decision to purchase a product and the date the payment for that purchase becomes cash.

Figure 24-1 lists the factors that enter into the total cash conversion period. Between the purchase decision and the cash collection are most of the administrative tasks usually required to complete a sale. You accelerate the cash flow into your business as you complete each administrative task more efficiently.

**Figure 24-1
Cash Conversion Period**

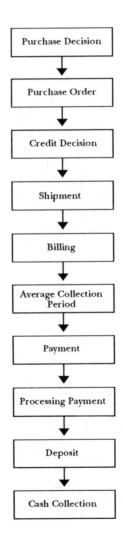

In terms of their influence on the cash flow process, we can identify the common problems that tend to stretch the cash conversion period. We also suggest some practical principles that compress that period.

The Purchase Decision and Purchase Order

A customer's decision to purchase your product initiates the cash conversion period. Encouraging the most rapid communication of the customer's purchase decision to your business—that is, making it as quick and easy as possible for her to place an order—is the first step in compressing your cash conversion period. A purchase order serves as the medium of communication. The nature and complexity of the business dictate the format of the purchase order. But regardless of the format, your customer should be able to transmit her order to you as rapidly as possible.

The need for rapid communication usually eliminates the postal system. Even in the best circumstances, using the mail extends your total cash conversion period from one to three days. Often the delays in mail delivery reach seven days or more. Of course, for items that don't affect your earnings, the postal service still provides the most efficient service because of its low cost. But remember any delay in receiving your customer's purchase order affects your bottom line. To overcome the deficiencies in mail service, you should provide an alternative for your customers.

For significant purchase orders, make electronic communication available. That can include telephone, a data phone wire service, or facsimile transmission. Unfortunately, many business managers concentrate on the personnel and equipment costs involved in these alternatives. They overlook the one to seven day reduction in their cash conversion periods that results from eliminating mail delays. Certainly that benefit often is more difficult to measure.

Electronic communication of purchase orders generally is suitable only when you have an ongoing relationship with a customer. But repeat customers usually make up the bulk of a firm's sales. So using electronic communication for them helps you improve service and accelerate your cash flow.

After you receive a purchase order, you should complete the sale smoothly and with a minimum of paperwork. However, the flow of paperwork often is less of an obstacle to the completion of a sale than the credit decision that must precede it.

The Credit Decision

A credit decision remains a necessary precedent to an open account sale. So, a business should expedite credit decisions for all significant orders. Each day a business delays that decision lengthens the cash conversion period.

Whenever possible, approve *lines of credit* for major customers in advance. Anticipate their needs *before* they exceed their credit limits.

You lose little if a customer does not use her full credit line. However, customers that do increase their purchases will find their orders delivered more promptly. Preapproved credit facilitates the completion of a sale and improves your service capability. A faster response inevitably offers a competitive advantage.

You can use the same procedure for prospective new customers. Check the creditworthiness of a significant new account in advance, before you receive a large order. Obtaining the information for a credit estimate—bank checks, supplier checks—can take several days. That lengthens your cash conversion period. If you delay too long, you risk losing the sale to a competitor with a more efficient credit decision process.

Of course, don't sacrifice reliable credit analysis for speedy approval. Even a modest increase in bad debt losses can offset the benefits from a shorter cash conversion period. At the same time, any element in the administrative environment that delays the completion of a sale hampers the smooth flow of cash into your business.

The Shipment

To avoid delays in shipment, you should have a well organized shipping department that meshes with your administrative environment. Inefficient shipping procedures seldom become a major problem for most businesses, but a less obvious administrative problem may interfere with prompt shipment. That occurs when a business has an inefficient inventory control system.

An inventory control system should answer two essential needs in a business: (1) it should maintain a current record of the amount of each item in stock and (2) it should locate that stock. Neither element should be left to chance or memory.

Accountants refer to this as a *perpetual* inventory. The system logs the sale and purchase of each item in inventory as it occurs. At any time, the log specifies the total inventory of each item held in stock. The log also should identify the exact location of the items.

Computerized inventory control systems now make a perpetual inventory control system a competitive necessity in most businesses. Indeed, the business without such a system operates at a competitive disadvantage.

The perpetual inventory system offers another benefit for the business that seeks an efficient administrative environment: When you apply EOQ analysis to the major items in your inventory, you can specify the reorder point for each item in stock. When the inventory falls to the reorder point, the "buy signal" tells you to restock, thus avoiding unnecessary stock-out costs.

The Billing

Issuing the invoice remains the final step in the administrative process that completes a sale. The invoice identifies the merchandise sold, the shipment date (usually supported by a copy of the bill of lading or other evidence of shipment), and the amount due from the purchaser. For two reasons, the prompt completion and transmission of the invoice is an important element in the cash conversion process.

First, few purchasers will pay for merchandise prior to receipt of the invoice. The invoice typically serves as the trigger for the payment process in the accounting system in most businesses. Second, the invoice date usually initiates the payment period defined by a firm's selling terms.

To illustrate the significance of timely invoice preparation, we will assume that your designated selling terms call for payment within thirty days from the date of the invoice. If your administrative structure delays preparation of an invoice for seven days after shipment, for example, you actually allow the customer thirty-seven days for payment. The invoice preparation period lengthens your cash conversion period by seven days.

Your administrative environment should allow for the completion and transmission of every invoice as soon as possible after shipment, preferably on the same day. Each day's delay reduces the rate at which cash flows into your business.

Unless precluded by industry standards, you should require payment for purchases in accordance with your designated invoice terms. That means that you should not render a monthly statement of account to trigger customer payments.

Rendering statements is a costly, time consuming, and self-defeating administrative process. And allowing customers to pay in response to monthly statements rather than to purchase invoices adds from one to thirty days to the cash conversion period. Customers will ignore invoices and wait for monthly statements. That can extend your cash conversion period significantly. It also can damage your earnings, even though you may have the cash capability to support the associated increase in accounts receivable.

Average Collection Period

The average collection period usually remains the largest fraction of the cash conversion period. So, you need a competent credit and collection effort. Thorough research into a prospective customer's credit history will lengthen the cash conversion period, but that is preferable to an increase in bad-debt write-offs. You should seek a balance between the need for an efficient decision process and the need to exercise sound credit judgment.

You should complement your credit decision with a collection effort that encourages payment within your designated terms. Select the average collection period that satisfies your earnings objectives within the constraints set by your cash flow. Then design and use a collection policy that supports your cash flow needs.

The Payment

The prompt collection of your accounts receivable naturally is important, but a customer's method of payment also affects your cash conversion period. Usually the customer mails a check to your office on the date payment is due. Of course, any postal delay lengthens your cash conversion period.

You may reduce that delay from one to three days by using a post office box as your business address. The rental fee typically remains an incidental expense compared to the benefits from a shorter cash conversion period.

An alternative payment method eliminates any reliance on the postal system. The *wire transfer* process transmits payments through the electronic network that unites the banking system. This process can transfer money from your customer's bank account to your bank account in a matter of hours.

Wire transfers eliminate the delays that can arise from the postal system, the administrative structure in your business, or the check clearing process. Unfortunately, your cash conscious customers will be reluctant to approve your request for payment by wire transfer. The system improves your cash flow, but it hurts theirs. Because the benefits are significant when large accounts are involved, you may want to make an effort to persuade them.

Processing the Payment

The wire transfer collection system allows collections to be deposited before they are processed through the firm's accounting system. The business that receives payments directly should also deposit collections before processing the accompanying paperwork. After all, your cash capability remains unchanged until they are deposited.

A business should have an efficient accounting system for recording customer payments. However, that recording process can proceed from remittance advice or photocopies, instead of from the check itself. Use any procedure that reduces your cash conversion period and accelerates your cash flow.

Chapter 25

Cash Collection Services

Improving cash flow is always a desirable management objective. But there are practical limits on the improvement you can gain from even the most concerted direct management effort. So, you may find it beneficial to complement your internal effort with the contribution available from third party, cash collection services.

The major third party services that can improve cash flow come from three sources: banks, factors, and collection agencies. Each source provides facilities or expertise that is not available or economical within many businesses.

Bank Collection Services

Bank services that can improve the cash flow into a business fall into two categories. One includes lockbox services, which are most beneficial to businesses with geographically dispersed customers. The other describes services that bypass part or all of the normal check payment and clearing process.

Lockboxes

Two interrelated circumstances lengthen the cash conversion period in a business with geographically dispersed customers. Together, those circumstances can severely affect cash flow.

One circumstance arises from the delays inherent in the postal system. Such delays become more significant as the distances between a business and its customers increase. A business may wait three days for a payment mailed by a customer located 500 miles away. That wait may increase to seven days if the customer is located 3,000 miles away.

Bank lockbox services can reduce the delays in both directions. Essentially, a lockbox represents a post office box that is controlled by a bank. A distant business with customers in the bank's area directs remittances to the lockbox. The bank collects and immediately deposits the customer payments, forwarding the remittance advice to the business by mail.

The lockbox service reduces mail delays because the bank is located close to the firm's customers. In addition, the service reduces processing delays, since the bank deposits collections into the payee's account immediately. The remittance advice (or photocopies of the checks) provides the business with the information necessary for the accounting process.

Lockbox services also accelerate the check clearing process. Since the payers are located in the bank's vicinity, their checks will clear rapidly. That reduces the waiting period for collected funds. Those funds then are wire transferred regularly to the recipient's primary bank.

Lockbox services can reduce a firm's average cash conversion period by five to ten days, depending upon the location and distribution of its distant customers. If the payments from those customers are an important proportion of a firm's cash flow, the lockbox services can provide a valuable cash collection service.

Check Truncation

Any method that truncates (shortens) the normal check payment and clearing process can improve cash flow. Banks offer three approaches to check truncation: preauthorized checks, preauthorized debits, and wire transfers.

Preauthorized checks are signatureless demand deposit instruments that allow a business to draw directly against customer checking accounts for scheduled payments. Naturally, a customer must approve the payment process and provide the business with the preauthorized checks or with the authority to obtain them. Additionally, the customer's bank must enter into the arrangement with a formal approval of the signatureless payment process.

Preauthorized checks accelerate cash flow by eliminating the wait for the postal system to deliver customer payments. A business merely deposits the checks on the scheduled payment dates.

While it improves cash flow, a preauthorized check payment system also can provide other benefits. First, the system makes cash flow more predictable. A business holding preauthorized checks isn't concerned about the various circumstances that can delay the receipt of customer remittances. A more predictable cash flow reduces the potential for cash flow problems. Second, the system can reduce billing costs and collection expenses and improve earnings. Indeed, billing becomes unnecessary for the business holding preauthorized checks. Certain payment eliminates the potential need for any collection effort.

Logically, the system is most suitable for fixed dollar repetitive payments. Thus it is usually employed by businesses that provide scheduled fixed fee services or those selling higher priced products that customers purchase with installment loans. However, it can be adapted to any circumstance where a business has an ongoing relationship with its customers.

Preauthorized "debits" eliminate the need for checks from the payment system. Here a debit represents a scheduled "checkless" draw against a customer's account. With proper authorization, a bank develops a computerized register of a firm's scheduled customer remittances. The register includes the information necessary to charge the customers' accounts electronically on the scheduled payment dates. Again, the system is most suitable for fixed dollar, repetitive payments.

Preauthorized debits represent a significant improvement over the preauthorized check payment system. Using electronic fund transfers eliminates mail float from the payment and check clearing process. At the same time, they eliminate physical check processing for a business and its bank. That eliminates any delays inherent in either accounting system.

While still in its incipient stages, preauthorized debits are the forerunner of the process that will eliminate checks from the payment system. Eventually, all payments will occur as electronic fund transfers from one account to another. Efficient electronic fund transfer systems (EFTS) will make this a "checkless" society.

Wire transfers also eliminate checks from the payment system, and funds are transmitted electronically on the same day remitted. In contrast with preauthorized debits, they must be initiated by the customer remitting payment. Once remitted, a business gains the same benefits as the preauthorized debit payment system.

Factor Collection Services

Chapter 21 discusses factoring as a source of cash flow financing. The factoring arrangement creates a revolving loan secured by a firm's receivables. While also providing credit and collection services, the factor advances funds secured by the firm's uncollected accounts receivable. The collections then retire the prior advances. Traditionally, that specific financing arrangement is defined as "advance" factoring.

In several respects, maturity factoring operates in a similar way to the advance factoring arrangement described in Chapter 21:

1. Upon receipt of an order, a business submits it to a factor for credit approval.
2. After credit approval, the business ships the order.
3. The firm bills its customers in the usual manner, except that each invoice carries a printed notice requesting that payment be made directly to the factor.

At this point comes the primary distinction between advance and maturity factoring arrangements. The business using maturity factoring does not obtain cash advances secured by the uncollected receivables. Instead, the factor remits payment on invoices to the business on the predetermined maturity date.

The maturity date typically is defined as the date when the invoice should be paid in practice by customers. It is based on historical analysis of a firm's average collection period. Consequently, the maturity date employed in the factoring arrangement may not agree with the invoice selling terms.

Maturity factoring makes cash flow predictable. Indeed, the factor is obligated to remit payments on the specified maturity date. That obligation exists whether or not the factor has collected the actual customer payments. At the same time, he does not remit payment equal to the full face value of a firm's sales invoices. Instead, he holds back reserves equivalent to 10 to 20% of a firm's receivables. That reserve absorbs credits created by merchandise returns and allowances for discounts.

A business also gains another benefit from maturity factoring. The factor assumes all of the expenses associated with the credit and collection function. Indeed, maturity factoring normally operates on a nonrecourse, notification basis. That is, the factor purchases the receivables outright and absorbs any losses from bad-debt write-offs. Thus the business using maturity factoring does not incur the personnel and operating expenses necessary to conduct the credit and collection effort. It shifts those expenses onto the factor, along with the risks of incurring any bad-debt write-offs.

A business must compensate a factor for his services. The specific cost of maturity factoring varies with the type of industry, annual sales volume, average sales amount, number of customers, and the maturity date employed in the factoring process. The cost typically varies from 3/4 of 1% to 3% of a firm's annual sales volume. Of course, a factor also charges interest for any funds advanced as loans—or advance factoring.

Although many businesses can benefit from maturity factoring, the cumulative benefits from it should justify the costs.

Collection Agency Services

Almost every business has some slow paying customers. A conscientious collection effort helps prevent most of those customers from falling too far past due. Occasionally, however, the effort to collect an excessively past due account becomes an expensive, time consuming burden. In that case, it may be beneficial to employ a collection agency.

Collection agencies specialize in the pursuit of overdue accounts for a fee. Thus they seek payments using correspondence and telephone contacts; larger past due accounts may warrant a personal visit by a professional collector.

Experience indicates that the same efforts by a collection agency produce better results. An impartial agency, drawing on its experience with a wide variety of difficult debtors, often can collect with fewer follow-ups than the business that extended the credit. Most businesses, if financially able, prefer not to have a reputation of being dunned by collection agencies. So they often respond rapidly.

A business incurs little risk from the decision to use a collection agency. When an account appears to be uncollectible, a firm's final collection letter or phone call should notify the delinquent debtor that his account will be assigned to a collection agency if payment isn't made within a specified time (usually ten days).

Collection agencies typically allow a "free demand period" after receiving an assignment. That period, usually ten days, waives any collection fee if the customer makes payment within that time. If payment results from the collection agency's efforts, a business pays a proportion of the amounts collected as a fee.

Fees for collecting small accounts often are as much as 50% of the amount collected. The proportionate fee then drops as the amount collected rises. For example, a collection agency may expect a 25% fee (or $250) for collecting a $1,000 account. The pro-rata fee then may drop to 20% for amounts collected in excess of the $1,000 amount.

Sometimes even a collection agency cannot collect a past due account. So many agencies retain attorneys who specialize in credit collection lawsuits. When warranted by a sound claim and the financial ability of the customer to pay, a lawsuit will ensue (with the claimant's approval).

When an account appears to be uncollectible, a business has little to lose by employing a collection agency. While the commission for any collection might be

20% to 50% of the amount paid, the business still may realize significant net cash benefits. We recognize the potential contribution from those services in:

Concept 61: Cash collection services can help accelerate the cash flow into a business.

Don't turn to a collection agency every time a customer falls a few days past due. But a collection agency may help when a customer resists a normal collection effort to pursue a past due payment.

Chapter 26

Delaying Cash Disbursements

While accelerating cash inflow, a business also should delay its cash disbursements. A business should delay disbursements as long as possible in order to extract the maximum benefit from every dollar that flows through the firm. This chapter reviews the management techniques that contribute to that objective while preserving a firm's creditworthiness.

Liability Management

Conscientious liability management defers cash outflow. This effort proceeds on an obvious premise: Pay no bill before it is due. Never abuse a creditor's consideration, but never prepay a liability. Retain every dollar as long as possible.

Some additional considerations also enter into liability management:

1. The potential for longer credit terms from competitive suppliers.
2. The trade-off between missing trade discounts and deferring payments to suppliers.
3. The potential for deferring payment of accrued liabilities.

Before we examine the considerations, let's review a basic tool that gauges the benefits a business obtains from effective liability management.

The Complete Average Payment Period

Deferring liability payments enables a business to use its creditors' dollars for a longer time. Calculating a firm's average payment period provides an important perspective of the benefits that can develop from that effort. The calculation measures the average length of time a business employs each dollar in credit consideration, exclusive of direct loans. Chapter 19 illustrated that calculation using only accounts payable. While that perspective remains useful, the illustration here encompasses all day to day credit consideration.

The average payment period calculation proceeds though six steps:

1. Identify the total credit purchases made during the year.
2. Identify the total annual operating expenses that originally appeared as accrued liabilities, such as accrued salaries, taxes, and rental obligations.
3. Combine the totals found in Steps 1 and 2.
4. Divide the sum in Step 3 by 360; this measures the average daily credit consideration (ADCC) received by the business.
5. Combine current outstanding accounts payable and accrued liabilities.
6. Divide the sum found in Step 5 by your average daily credit consideration.

Assume that a firm's open account purchases for the year totaled $3 million. Also, $500,000 in operating expenses originally appeared in the form of accrued liabilities. The firm's average daily credit consideration can be calculated as:

$$\text{ADCC} = \frac{\text{Annual Purchases} + \text{Annual Accrued Liabilities}}{360}$$

$$\text{ADCC} = \frac{\$3,000,000 + \$500,000}{360}$$

$$\text{ADCC} = \$9,722$$

The firm obtained a daily average of $9,722 in credit consideration from one source or another during the year.

Finally, note that the accounts payable and accrued liabilities total $350,000. This enables us to complete the average payment period calculation:

$$\text{Average Payment Period} = \frac{\text{Accounts Payable} + \text{Accrued Liabilities}}{\text{Average Daily Credit Consideration}}$$

$$\text{Average Payment Period} \quad = \quad \frac{\$350,000}{\$9,722}$$

$$\text{Average Payment Period} \quad = \quad 36 \text{ days}$$

The firm employed the average dollar in credit consideration for thirty-six days. Each day that liability management can extend the payment period defers $9,722 in cash outflow. We also can say that each day's extension in the average payable period provides that much incremental free financing for the business. Table 26-1 provides a view of the benefits that can develop from extending the average payment period.

Table 26-1
Extending the Average Payment Period

Average Daily Credit Consideration	Incremental Average Payment Period				
	1	3	5	10	20
	Total Deferred Cash Outflow				
$ 1,000	$ 1,000	$ 3,000	$ 5,000	$ 10,000	$ 20,000
3,000	3,000	9,000	15,000	30,000	60,000
5,000	5,000	15,000	25,000	50,000	100,000
8,000	8,000	24,000	40,000	80,000	160,000
10,000	10,000	30,000	50,000	100,000	200,000

For example, a business that employs $5,000 in average daily credit consideration defers $40,000 in cash outflow when it extends its average payment period by eight days. That represents $40,000 in free financing the business can use to reduce other liabilities, increase other assets, or replenish cash reserves. The benefit from the effort can be summarized in:

Concept 62: Delaying cash disbursements increases the cash capability in a business.

Recognizing the major tenet that helps extend a firm's payment period — pay no bill before it is due — let's look at the other major considerations that enter into liability management.

Negotiated Payment Terms

Most suppliers in a particular industry have comparable selling terms. Whenever significant differences in those terms exist, a business should extend its average payment period by buying from the supplier who allows the longest terms. Even if no differences exist, a business often can negotiate longer selling terms from its suppliers. Some suppliers may allow longer payment terms to secure a larger order. Others may exchange longer payment terms for customer loyalty. Suppliers are sometimes willing to sacrifice a better cash flow for the profitability that grows out of long term business relationships.

Never assume that a supplier's selling terms are etched in stone. With sufficient justification, any supplier will extend her standard terms. Negotiating longer terms can allow you to extend your average payment period.

Cash Discounts Versus Deferred Payments

A business should delay payment for a purchase until the due date set by the supplier's selling terms. This defers cash outflow and extends the average payment period. However, when a supplier offers a cash discount for early payment, compare the potential gain from that discount against the benefits of deferred payment.

For example, assume that a business buys $10,000 in merchandise each month from a supplier who offers 1% 10, net 30 day payment terms. The supplier allows a 1% discount, or $100, if the business pays for each purchase within ten days. But the business must pay the full purchase price if it defers payment until the end of the thirty day credit term.

Over the course of the year the business can accumulate $1,200 in cash discounts. Standing alone, this does not justify making the payment for each purchase in ten days rather than thirty. Instead, the business should identify the annualized interest rate it earns by taking the cash discount. If that yield exceeds the firm's borrowing cost, the discount is worth taking. If the cost of borrowing exceeds the interest yield, the business should abandon the discounts and pay the full purchase price at the end of the thirty day term.

The logic of viewing discounts as interest income asserts that a supplier actually borrows money from its customers when it allows a cash discount for early payment. The discount becomes the interest charge for the loan. When a business pays its supplier in ten days rather than thirty, the early payment becomes a twenty day loan. The supplier's 1% discount represents the interest charge for using the firm's funds for that period. The supplier doesn't have the use of those funds for that twenty day period when the business takes thirty days to pay. But neither does she have to pay any interest in the form of a cash discount.

If we view an early payment in exchange for a cash discount as a short term loan to a supplier, we should then focus on the annualized interest yield the business earns from that loan. That yield can be identified with the formula:

$$\text{Interest Yield from Cash Discount} = \frac{\text{Discount \%}}{100\% - \text{Discount \%}} \times \frac{360}{\text{Final Due Date} - \text{Discount Period}}$$

Note that the difference between the final due date and the discount period measures the term of the "loan" to a supplier when a business takes a cash discount. Using the example above, we can determine the yield the business obtains from a 1% discount:

$$\text{Interest Yield from Cash Discount} = \frac{1\%}{100\% - 1\%} \times \frac{360}{30 - 10}$$

$$\text{Interest Yield} = \frac{1\%}{99\%} \times \frac{360}{20}$$

$$\text{Interest Yield} = 1.01\% \times 18 = 18.2\%$$

The business that receives a 1% cash discount for paying a supplier in ten days instead of thirty earns an 18.2% annualized rate from the funds used to make that payment. Thus the business should take that discount so long as its borrowing cost remains below that level. Then the benefits from the 1% discount rate exceed the real or opportunity costs the business would incur from deferring payment until the end of the thirty day credit term.

Usually a business should take all cash discounts of 1% or more when the suppliers require full payment in thirty days. If a supplier offers extended terms, it may become beneficial to forego an early payment cash discount. Always compare the direct or opportunity cost of the funds to be employed with the annualized earnings rate from taking the discount.

The more traditional perspective of the cost of a cash discount presumes that the cost a business incurs when it misses a discount matches the yield it earns by taking one. When a business fails to take a discount, the firm pays the supplier for the privilege of taking the full credit term allowed for payment. The business should balance that cost against the cost of the funds invested in the operation by creditors and stockholders.

Deferring Payment of Accrued Liabilities

A business can use its accrued liability accounts to defer cash outflow. For example, a less frequent employee payment schedule can make a significant contribution to that objective. The business that pays its employees weekly should explore the possibility of a biweekly payment schedule. An existing biweekly schedule may open the door to a monthly pay schedule. Limits exist on the length of time a business can defer payment for any accrued liability, but a business should take advantage of any realistic opportunity.

Float

Most business managers recognize how float benefits the business that finds itself temporarily short of cash.

To take advantage of supplier discounts or other profitable opportunities, you can make payments with checks that exceed your actual cash balances. Of course, you should realistically expect to have the cash inflow necessary to pay those checks before they clear through the banking system.

Float can be defined as the difference between a firm's internal record of its prevailing cash balance and the amount registered by its bank. For example, assume that a firm's current checkbook balance is $50,000. On the same day, bank records show that the business has $100,000 on deposit. This means the business has $50,000 in uncleared checks outstanding, or $50,000 in float.

A comparative look at the cash transactions recorded by a business and its bank clarify the definition of float. Assume that a business begins a week with a $100,000 actual bank balance. The firm's own records also register a $100,000 balance. In an unusual departure from the norm, the two totals agree.

During the week the business collects and deposits $100,000 in customer payments. It also writes $50,000 in checks *each day* to pay its own suppliers. As the week ends, the firm's records show that the business has a $50,000 negative cash balance.

Only $150,000 in checks reach the firm's bank for payment during the week, so as the week ends, bank records show that the business still has $50,000 in cash on deposit. The difference between the firm's account and the bank record represents the creation of $100,000 in float. A summary of the week's transactions provides another view of that benefit:

	Corporate Books	Bank Books
Beginning Balance	$100,000	$100,000
Deposits	100,000	100,000
Checks	(250,000)	(150,000)
Ending Balance	($ 50,000)	$ 50,000
Float	$100,000	

Here the business actually employs only half the available float. This may represent the limit set by anticipated cash collections, since the business must garner sufficient deposits to pay the outstanding checks before they reach the bank for payment. That benefit can be summarized:

Concept 63: Float management helps increase a firm's cash capability.

Before illustrating the techniques for effective float management, let's first look at another view of the benefits of using float. Indeed, float contributes more to a business than a temporary cure for a cash shortage. Often it becomes a permanent fixture in a firm's financial structure.

The Phantom Asset

The Aggressive Corporation demonstrates the benefits that can develop when a business enjoys the continuous use of a specific amount of float. Aggressive's financial structure is illustrated in Table 26-2, Column 1. Although the firm's financial structure is relatively sound, note the apparent need for a $100,000 bank loan.

Also note that the corporation writes $300,000 in checks each month to pay for inventory purchases and operating expenses. Since purchases and expenses occur evenly throughout the month, the firm writes an average of $10,000 in checks each day. The discovery of the float inherent in that pattern eliminates the need for a $100,000 bank loan.

Aggressive's accountant found that the average day's payments required seven days to clear through the banking system. Of course, many checks cleared more rapidly, whereas others traveled up to two weeks before reaching the bank for payment. But the average clearing time for all payments was seven days. That created $70,000 in permanent float for the corporation. While Aggressive's books registered a $70,000 cash balance, there was $140,000 in the firm's bank account.

After recognizing this, the Aggressive Corporation decided to retire its $100,000 bank loan, which reduced its actual checking account balance to $40,000. The new financial structure is shown in Table 26-2, Column 2. The difference between the $30,000 cash deficit apparent in that structure and the $40,000 positive bank balance comes from the $70,000 in float.

The corporation's float actually becomes a phantom asset. It enables the corporation to conduct its normal operations with $70,000 less than actually appears necessary. In Aggressive's case, float helps to eliminate the need for external financing. When managed properly, float can make a valuable contribution toward the effort to defer the cash flow out of a business.

Table 26-2
Adding Float to the Financial Structure
The Aggressive Corporation

	Disregarding Float	Using Float
Cash	$ 70,000	($ 30,000)
Other Assets	430,000	430,000
Total Assets	$500,000	$400,000
Accounts Payable	$150,000	$150,000
Bank Loan	100,000	—
Total Liabilities	$250,000	$150,000
Stockholders' Equity	250,000	250,000
Liabilities and Equity	$500,000	$400,000

Float Management

Float measures the time lapse between the date you write a check and the date that check reaches your bank for payment. Determining the float available to a business is a simple but tedious task. To make that estimate, a cash flow manager charts the date she writes the check to pay her creditors and compares those dates to the time the checks actually reach her bank for payment. The latter date is stamped by the bank on the back of each check. Assuming that her monthly payment habits remain regular, the manager can measure her float with enough precision to make it a profitable management tool.

Table 26-3, a simplified approach to float management, tracks the actual movement of cash into and out of a business and interrelates that movement with that cash capability that comes from float.

On 8/1, the business begins with $100,000 in collected cash in its checking account. No unpaid checks are presently outstanding. On 8/2, the business writes and mails $30,000 in checks to pay suppliers. Although the checking account balance drops to $70,000, the actual cash held in the bank account remains unchanged. The checks are in the mail and are not affecting the firm's cash account. While the checks are outstanding, the business could use the cash in its bank account. Consequently, the float in this instance raises total cash capability to $130,000.

On 8/3, the business writes no more checks but receives $25,000 in cash collections on account. That raises the checking account balance to $95,000 and the actual bank balance to $125,000. (We assume here that the bank allows the customer immediate credit for all deposits, not an unrealistic expectation for the business that carries a reasonable collected balance throughout most of the month.)

Coupled with the float from the $30,000 in checks written on 8/2, the firm's total cash capability rises to $155,000. On 8/4, the business writes and mails another $60,000 in payments to suppliers, which raises the total float to $90,000 and the cash capability to $215,000.

Then, on 8/5, the $30,000 in checks written on 8/2 reach the bank for payment. We assume a conservative four day average float period in this instance. That lowers the firm's bank balance to $95,000 and its cash capability to $155,000. The $60,000 reduction measures the total of the unpaid checks no longer outstanding, plus the actual reduction in cash required to pay the checks.

On 8/6, the firm writes another $75,000 in checks. This lowers the checkbook balance to a negative $40,000. The company has a book overdraft, although the actual bank balance remains a comfortable $95,000. Now we can estimate the real significance of float management.

Perhaps the payments mailed on 8/6 enable the firm to take 2% discounts that would be missed if the firm delayed payment until it received the actual cash collections necessary to honor the checks. Or the firm may be observing payment within the supplier's terms in order to maintain its credit rating. In either case, the firm gains benefits that would be lost without the use of float.

Continuing the example set in Table 26-3, on 8/7 the company writes another $25,000 in checks. This raises the book overdraft to $65,000. On the same day, the firm's actual bank balance drops to $35,000 as the $60,000 in checks reach

Table 26-3
Float Management

	Beginning Checking-Account Balance	Checking-Checks Mailed	Ending Actual Cash Deposits	Total Cash Account Balance	Checks Cleared	Bank Balance	Total Float	Capability (6) + (7)
8/1	$100,000	—	—	$100,000	—	$100,000	—	$100,000
8/2	100,000	$30,000	—	70,000	—	100,000	$30,000	130,000
8/3	70,000	—	$25,000	95,000	—	125,000	30,000	155,000
8/4	95,000	60,000	—	35,000	—	125,000	90,000	215,000
8/5	35,000	—	—	35,000	$30,000	95,000	60,000	155,000
8/6	35,000	75,000	—	(40,000)	—	95,000	135,000	230,000
8/7	(40,000)	25,000	—	(65,000)	—	95,000	160,000	255,000
8/8	(65,000)	—	—	(65,000)	60,000	35,000	100,000	135,000
8/9	(65,000)	—	150,000	85,000	—	185,000	100,000	285,000
8/10	85,000	—	50,000	135,000	75,000	110,000	25,000	135,000

the bank for payment. However, the firm's total cash capability remains at $135,000 on the same day.

Finally, on 8/9, the business receives $150,000 in collections, easily sufficient to cover all checks outstanding. The bulk of the firm's float evaporates on 8/10 as the $75,000 in checks written on 8/6 reach the bank for payment.

Obviously, you can't manage your float with the precision presumed in Table 26-3. Some checks clear in two days, some in ten. Absolute predictability is impossible. Nor can you be sure that your bank will provide instant credit for collections. However, this is the usual procedure so long as you don't continuously demand the use of the balances represented by your uncollected checks.

Proper float management also can increase your earnings. Indeed, you don't need to suffer from a cash flow squeeze to benefit from float. If your business has adequate cash for normal operations, you can improve your earnings by investing the cash equivalent of float.

Also recognize that two separate components make up the total float available to a business. One component, postal float, measures the length of time it takes for a payment to be delivered to a creditor. The other, bank float, registers the length of time it takes your creditors' deposits to reach your bank for payment.

Of course, you have no influence over bank float. You can estimate the time it takes for your check to clear, but you can't extend it for your benefit. At the same time, the perceptive manager will anticipate the potential in lengthening postal float. She doesn't mail her payments to her supplier's post office box, but to her firm's street address. This increases the delivery time by a day or two, thus adding to your total float. So long as your payment is postmarked on the due date, most suppliers will consider your payment as prompt.

Never abuse a creditor's consideration, but use float to expand your cash capability and increase your earnings.

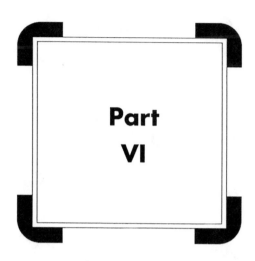

Part
VI

Positive
Cash Flow
Management

Maximum cash generation is usually the primary objective of the cash flow manager. This objective develops from the assumption that a business benefits from any action designed to improve its cash flow. However, cash flow management is not an isolated task in the operation of a business. It interrelates with every aspect of it. So any management effort must first serve the basic objectives of the business, even though those objectives may conflict with the idea of maximum cash generation.

This chapter considers the major implications that this requirement raises for the cash flow manager. Specifically, we discuss the appropriate cash flow management perspectives when the primary objectives of a business become survival, profitability, growth, and maximum earnings.

Of course, a business often works toward several objectives simultaneously. In fact, it can aim toward all four. The priorities may vary, but they ultimately remain compatible with one another. At the same time, identify one primary objective to orient your management decisions.

Perspectives for Survival

Survival becomes the primary objective for the business suffering financial distress of any degree. The temporary inability to pay all obligations promptly measures one level of distress. So long as creditors accept deferred payments, the problem may pose little threat to the survival of the business. Of course, the threat increases if the term of the deferred payments falls too far past due. Suppliers may cease shipments of replacement inventory. Without products to sell the business will quickly fail.

The threat becomes even more severe when suppliers seek recourse by forcing a business into bankruptcy. Although suppliers seldom recover significant amounts from bankrupt concerns, the threat often forces many businesses into voluntary bankruptcy actions. The bankrupt business rarely returns to active operations.

The most immediate threat to the survival of a business occurs when it cannot meet payroll requirements. Suppliers accept deferred payments more readily than employees. No doubt the employee who isn't paid on Friday won't return to work on Monday.

From the cash flow manager's perspective, the desire for survival encourages the original objective of cash flow management—maximum cash generation. Thus the manager seeks to convert the firm's investment in receivables and inventory into cash as rapidly as possible. He also seeks that objective even though it temporarily damages sales and profits. Obviously if the business doesn't survive the short term, long term prospects become irrelevant.

The desire for survival again raises the specter of risk as an element in the operation of a business. Even if a business is not faced with any immediate threat to its continued operations, risk should be a relevant consideration. This means that the desire for growth and profitability may become secondary if achieving either objective threatens the survival of the firm.

A measure of risk is involved in every business operation, but the size of the risk should be commensurate with the size of the potential reward. An imbalance in favor of risk could lead to a firm's ultimate demise.

Perspectives for Profitability

The higher the profits a business generates, the more successful it is. However, the drive for higher profits often raises higher levels of risk. As the firm stretches for a more rapid increase in earnings, it inevitably risks its survival. This encourages many businesses to accept a "reasonable" level of profits. The business earns less, but it is more likely to survive.

The business that seeks a reasonable, satisfactory level of profits isn't necessarily eliminating growth or maximum profits as business objectives. Instead, it may be building those objectives into the foundation for long term stability.

No standard definition identifies the satisfactory level of earnings. A proportionate increase of 5%, 10%, or 15% over the previous year's results may be satisfactory to some businesses. Others may look for a specific dollar increase in earnings each year. Still others may measure the return as a percentage of their anticipated sales volume. However defined, the satisfactory earnings level recognizes two facts of business life.

First, earnings must be sufficient to offset the detrimental effects of inflation. The business that fails to match the rate of inflation falls behind, even though it registers an apparent increase in profits.

Second, the business sets its satisfactory earnings level in line with some measure, however imprecise, of the risk associated with its operations. It will not chase earnings if that effort would impose risk beyond the acceptable level. Again, this recognizes that the size of the risk and the potential return in any operation tend to increase proportionately.

The cash flow manager who seeks satisfactory earnings without inordinate risk adjusts his activities accordingly. His cash management decisions seek to preserve the financial integrity of the business without seriously impairing its desired earnings level. He will not risk a gap in the firm's cash flow in exchange for an extra dollar of earnings beyond the desired level. Neither will he allow an overinvestment in receivables or inventory merely because they promise more rapid growth. Indeed, he constantly seeks a balance between profitability and the security that comes from a healthy cash position.

Perspectives for Growth

Rapid expansion often orients the drive of the ambitious entrepreneur. He measures success not in terms of profitability, but by this year's sales volume, and inevitably he either accepts or ignores the risk that is a natural companion to accelerated growth.

Rapid growth is accompanied by a need for external financing that actually expands more rapidly than a firm's sales volume. The limit on the financing available to a business becomes the primary restriction on its growth potential. At the same time, as a business increases the use of external financing relative to equity, it raises the risk of a major financial setback. Broad swings in operating results naturally accompany the use of higher degrees of leverage.

The cash flow manager serving his growth objective adjusts his approach accordingly. He first discounts the value held in excess cash reserves that provide insurance for survival. A business cannot grow without committing itself to a rising investment in inventory and accounts receivable, even at the expense of its cash reserves.

Next, he designs a credit and collection policy that encourages sales, even at the expense of carrying a larger investment in receivables. In fact, the growth oriented business may suffer a lower profit margin per sales dollar because of the carrying costs involved in its investment in receivables and inventory.

Finally, the cash flow manager in the rapidly growing business cannot overlook the use of leverage. Leverage is the single necessity for the expanding concern. The business can accept lower earnings and higher risks, but without expanding its use of borrowed funds, it will not continue to grow.

Perspectives for Maximum Earnings

A business might ignore all other objectives in its pursuit of maximum earnings. The business manager who selects this objective is less concerned with growth than with an immediate increase in earnings (although the two typically are interrelated). He also blinds himself to much of the risk involved in the drive toward maximum profitability.

In this case, the cash flow manager must allow profitability to take precedence over the desire for efficient cash flow. Thus a more liberal credit policy that increases earnings might be acceptable, even though it absorbs cash reserves. Similarly, the business might add to that strain by expanding its investment in inventory in the pursuit of profitability.

The desire for every last dollar of profits should not push the firm toward a cash flow disaster. Sound business sense recognizes the limits on any objective. But the cash flow manager must recognize and accept the higher risk of a cash flow problem that naturally develops when a business selects maximum profitability over liquidity as its primary objective.

In any event, recognize this as another perspective that reminds us of:

Concept 64: **The cash flow manager must orient his effort toward the fundamental objectives of the firm.**

Each firm's objective will have a significant influence on its cash flow management effort.

Chapter 28

Cash Resource Management

While day-to-day cash flow management should remain your primary focus, you should also recognize the need to maintain the proper balance among the sources and uses of cash capability. Failure to do that can lead to cash flow problems. Consequently, this chapter discusses the fundamental elements of *cash resource* management.

Cash resource management adopts a comprehensive view of a business's cash receipts and outlays. From this broad perspective, the effort focuses on the *source* of cash capability, the *use* of cash capability, and the interrelationship of the two. The basic objective of cash resource management is to use cash capability to reflect the characteristics of each source.

Cash Resource Analysis

Cash resource analysis concentrates on the changes that occur in a firm's financial structure between two time periods. Properly categorized, the changes represent the source and disposition of the net cash capability gained by the business over that period.

To illustrate, we use two consecutive fiscal year end balance sheets of the Parker Company, a small valve manufacturer. The first step in the analysis, summarized in Table 28-1, isolates the increase or decrease in each balance sheet account (except cash) from one year to the next.

Table 28-1
Comparative Fiscal Year End Balance Sheets
The Parker Company

	12/31/89	12/31/90	Changes
Cash	$100,000	$ 75,000	
Accounts Receivable	110,000	170,000	$ 60,000
Inventory	160,000	195,000	35,000
Fixed Assets (net)	60,000	250,000	190,000
Prepaid Expenses	20,000	10,000	(10,000)
Total Assets	$450,000	$700,000	
Accounts Payable	$100,000	$220,000	$120,000
Other Liabilities	30,000	20,000	(10,000)
Long-Term Debt	100,000	200,000	100,000
Total Liabilities	$230,000	$440,000	
Stockholders' Equity	$220,000	$260,000	$ 40,000
Liabilities and Equity	$450,000	$700,000	

The next step places the net change in each account into one of two categories. Each change translates into either a source or a use of cash capability in the business.

A business gains an increase in its cash capability from:

1. A decrease in assets (other than cash)
2. An increase in liabilities
3. An increase in stockholders' equity

Alternatively, a business employs cash capability to:

1. Increase assets
2. Decrease liabilities
3. Decrease stockholders' equity

Table 28-2 illustrates a format that facilitates this phase of the analysis and provides a concise picture of the disposition of the net cash capability available to the business.

Table 28-2
Cash Resource Analysis
The Parker Company

Beginning Cash Reserves (12/31/89)	$100,000
Sources of Cash Capability:	
1. Reduction in prepaid expenses	$ 10,000
2. Increase in accounts payable	120,000
3. Increase in long-term debt	100,000
4. Increase in stockholders' equity	40,000
Total Sources of Cash Capability	$370,000
Uses of Cash Capability:	
1. Increase in accounts receivable	$ 60,000
2. Increase in inventory	35,000
3. Increase in net fixed assets	190,000
4. Decrease in other liabilities	10,000
Total Uses	($295,000)
Ending Cash Reserves (12/31/90)	$ 75,000

The Parker Company ended 12/31/89 with $100,000 in cash reserves. Changes in its financial structure during 1990 produced an additional $270,000 in cash capability. An increase in credit consideration in the form of accounts payable and long term debt provided $220,000 of that added capability. Also, Parker enjoyed another $40,000 contribution from an increase in stockholders' equity, presumably from profitable operations during the year (although a part of that increase might have come from the sale of common stock).

Finally, a net reduction in prepaid expenses translated into a $10,000 increase in total cash capability. A reduction in prepaid expenses as a source of cash capability may appear questionable. Yet conceptually, the liquidation of any asset (except cash) becomes additional cash capability for the business. Here the liquidation of the prepaid expenses lowers the actual cash expended for operations during the year ending 2/31/90. The business is merely regaining the cash capability used in the previous period to pay the expenses in advance.

The $10,000 reduction in prepaid expenses raises the total cash capability available to the company to $370,000. Had the company held all other elements in its financial structure constant, the 12/31/90 balance sheet would have included $370,000 in cash reserves. Instead, the company decided to employ the bulk of that capability for other purposes. In fact, other changes in the financial structure absorbed $295,000 of the $370,000 total.

The major part of the cash capability contributed to a $190,000 increase in net fixed assets. An additional $95,000 supported an increase in Parker's investment in accounts receivable and inventory. Finally, it managed a $10,000 reduction in other liabilities, ending 12/31/90 with $75,000 in cash reserves. Table 28-2 summarizes the net cash capability that flowed from changes in the company's financial structure, as well as the ultimate disposition of that capability. This disposition also is reflected directly in the financial structure.

The final step in cash resource analysis is less precise than the first two. In fact, it requires no direct calculation. Instead, you complete the analysis with a critical assessment of the relationship between the sources and uses of cash capability represented by the changes in the financial structure. This assessment compares the source of the cash capability to the disposition of that capability, and it operates according to two fundamental principles:

1. The cash capability devoted to permanent assets should come from an increase in stockholders' equity or long term debt.
2. The cash capability devoted to current assets may come from an increase in accounts payable or other short term liabilities.

Thus a business should not use trade credit as the source of cash capability to finance the purchase of fixed assets. The business that makes that mistake invites a cash flow problem, since the trade credit comes due almost immediately. Indeed, permanent assets should have the support of a permanent source of capability.

Alternatively, so long as the business maintains prompt payment habits, trade credit may be the appropriate source of cash capability to finance an increase in receivables or inventory. Again, cash resource management seeks the proper match between the sources and uses of cash capability in the business. A business also may use fixed sources—long term debt and equity—to support its permanent, minimum investment in current assets, but this also represents a proper match.

Finally, the business must recognize the ultimate effect of the interrelationships on its cash reserves. If other sources are exhausted, the decision to use cash capability for any purpose naturally absorbs some of these reserves. This can be summarized in:

Concept 65: **Positive cash flow management properly matches the source and use of any cash capability used in a business.**

Referring to Table 28-2, note that the Parker Company has some cause for concern. It increases its net investment in fixed assets between 12/31/89 and 12/31/90 by $190,000. Yet stockholders' equity and long term debt registered an increase of only $140,000. Thus $50,000 out of the cash capability devoted to the fixed assets had to come from other sources. In this instance, accounts payable increased by $120,000, while Parker's investment in receivables and inventory rose by only $95,000. Consequently, Parker used $25,000 in supplier credit consideration as a source of cash for the increase in fixed assets. Another $25,000 came from a reduction in cash reserves.

The Parker Company remains in a relatively healthy financial position, but improperly matching the sources and the uses of cash capability has reduced its financial flexibility. Another increase in current assets may impose an additional drain on cash reserves that will reduce that flexibility even further.

Use the Parker Company's case as a reminder of the need to interrelate periodically the sources and uses of cash capability.

Chapter 29

The Cash Flow Budget

The cash flow budget provides the signals that spur the positive management actions necessary to fill any impending gaps in the cash flow cycle. Indeed, it becomes the focal point of your cash flow management effort. This chapter reviews the basic concepts for developing a cash flow budget.

Financial and Cash Transactions

A manufacturer or wholesaler seldom generates a sale directly in exchange for cash. Instead, he trades his product for his customer's promise to pay for the purchase in accordance with his designated selling terms. A business typically purchases inventory on the same basis. Cash payment usually follows the actual purchase by thirty days.

Unfortunately, the basic accounting process does not distinguish between financial and cash transactions. On the seller's side, a financial transaction requires a record of the sale on the day it occurs, even though no cash actually changes hands. The buyer's side similarly records a purchase (although not necessarily an expense), and at the same time records an increase in inventory and accounts payable. But the financial transaction has no immediate effect on either business's cash reserves.

The process often appears more confusing because the accrual accounting process also requires balance sheet entries reflecting the exchange of cash that completes a financial transaction. The business incurs no expense at the time of the transaction, even though cash flows out of the business.

Financial accounting enables a business to measure its financial performance by properly matching its revenues and expenses as they occur. But accrual accounting does not provide a proper picture of a firm's actual cash flow. This picture comes from the record of cash receipts and payments that register the actual exchange of cash.

The exchange of cash completes a business transaction. It represents either a customer's payment for a purchase or a business's final fulfillment of its own obligations. The record of cash receipts and disbursements reflects the actual cash flow into and out of a business. That record provides the proper picture of the cash flow whether or not the financial transactions coincide with the cash transactions. Positive cash flow management clearly distinguishes between financial and cash transactions.

The Cash Flow Budgeting Process

A cash flow budget projects the cash receipts and disbursements anticipated in the normal course of business. But the budget proceeds beyond the simple summation of the year's upcoming activity to project the actual time that cash will flow in and out. Our illustration projects that flow on a monthly basis, but you could also project a weekly or even a daily cash flow.

The precision of the budget depends on the characteristics of the business coupled with a reasonable estimate of its cash capability. The larger that capability, the more cushion the business has to absorb an unforeseen fluctuation in cash collections. This will become more apparent as we review the procedures that make up the basic budgeting process.

Many business managers shy away from cash flow budgeting because they think it is too esoteric or complex. However, the process can easily be broken down into five straightforward steps:

1. Forecasting sales,
2 Projecting cash receipts,
3. Projecting cash disbursements,
4. Interrelating cash receipts and cash disbursements, and
5. Filling the gaps.

In the discussion of each step, concentrate on the fundamental simplicity of the process. You will find that even a haphazard effort can provide important benefits for your business.

The Sales Forecast

Any financial plan must begin with a sales forecast. Of course, every projection contains some uncertainty. Actual sales rarely equate exactly with the forecast. Variables in the economy, the industry, and the company preclude absolute predictability. Nevertheless, this does not eliminate the need or value of the forecast. Even an intuitive effort, such as using the previous year's volume, adjusted for inflation, provides an adequate basis for the development of a cash flow budget. This effort will enable you to anticipate most major cash flow problems. Of course, the more accurate your forecast, the better your cash flow budget. The value of this forecast can be summed up in:

Concept 66: The sales forecast is the cornerstone of the cash flow budget.

To illustrate, we will use the sales forecast developed by the Prudent Company, a specialty paper wholesaler with a history of sound financial planning. For the first six months of its upcoming fiscal year, the company projects the following monthly sales volume (in $1,000s):

January	February	March	April	May	June
$200	$250	$400	$500	$300	$200

This forecast provides the basis for the next two steps in the budgeting process.

Projecting Cash Receipts

The cash flow budget recognizes that the primary source of cash flow into a business comes not from sales (unless the sales are for cash), but from the collection of accounts receivable. Consequently, this step of the process does not look beyond the anticipated flow from collections.

The Prudent Company relies on historical experience to project the cash flow into the business over the first six months of the upcoming year. This history indicates that the company collects its receivables according to the following pattern:

Table 29-1
Float Management
(in $1,000s)

	October	November	December	January	February	March	April	May	June
Sales (actual for first three months; the rest are forcasted)	200	200	200	200	250	400	500	300	200
Collections:									
First Month at 70%	—	—	—	140	140	175	280	350	210
Second Month at 20%	—	—	—	40	40	40	50	80	100
Third Month at 10%	—	—	—	20	20	20	20	25	40
Total Cash Inflow from receipts			200	200	235	350	455	350	

1. 70% in the month immediately following the sale
2. 20% in the second month following the sale
3. 10% in the third month following the sale

Anticipating that the historical collection pattern will extend into the future, the Prudent Company projects its cash flow for the next six months, as shown in Table 29-1. (The company's actual sales for the three months immediately preceding the projection totaled $200,000 in each month.)

From this pattern, the company anticipates $200,000 in collections in January. These collections represent 70% of December's sales, 20% of November's sales, and 10% of October's sales. Of course, collections equal to monthly sales are not usual for the company. A look at the projections for March indicates sales of $400,000 for the month, but collections from previous sales of only $235,000. This shows that collections come from prior sales, not the current month's.

If your sales *and* average collection period remain constant from month to month, the cash flow into your business will match your sales volume. A business with $1,000 in daily sales and a consistent forty day average collection period generates sales of $30,000 per month and matches that with collections from previous sales. That simplifies the cash flow budgeting process.

Projecting Cash Disbursements

Most cash disbursements by a business fall into one of three basic categories: (1) to pay for purchases, (2) to pay operating expenses, and (3) to retire debts. Usually a business can project the expenditures required in each category with reasonable accuracy.

Of course, the repayment of any scheduled debt obligation stands as a certain cash expenditure. However, using its sales forecast, a business makes purchase and operating expense commitments that also become relatively certain cash expenditure requirements. Indeed, it usually must expend the cash appropriate for those purposes, even though actual sales in a month fall below the level forecasted.

Note that depreciation does not appear in a firm's projected cash disbursements. It is a noncash expense, so it is not part of the cash flow budget.

To demonstrate the elements that enter into a projection of monthly cash expenditures, let's note additional characteristics about Prudent's business:

1. Cost of goods sold averages 60% of sales.
2. Prudent purchases the inventory for each month's forecasted sales volume one month in advance.

3. Suppliers allow Prudent thirty days to pay for its purchases; consequently, the firm pays for all inventory in the month following the actual purchase.
4. Monthly cash operating expenses average 30% of sales.
5. Prudent has $10,000 in monthly debt-service requirements.

Using the sales forecast as a starting point, Table 29-2 projects the Prudent Company's cash expenditures for the six month period.

In January, Prudent must pay $120,000 for inventory purchased in December. The company purchased that amount based on the January sales forecast. Cash operating expenses (30% of sales) in January will total $60,000. That, coupled with the $10,000 fixed debt payment, increases the company's total cash needs for the month to $190,000.

Repeating the projection process for the next six months, we find that Prudent's monthly cash expenditures peak at $460,000 in April, then drop back to $190,000 in June. This fluctuation reflects a seasonal demand for Prudent's products in the spring.

Table 29-2
Projecting Cash Expenditures
The Prudent Company
(in $1,000s)

	January	February	March	April	May	June
Sales	$200	$250	$400	$500	$300	$200
Payments: Purchases (60% of sales)	120	150	240	300	180	120
Operating Expenses (30% of sales)	60	75	120	150	90	60
Debt Service	10	10	10	10	10	10
Total Cash Payments	$190	$235	$370	$460	$280	$190

The next step interrelates the two cash flow projections and measures the net effect those flows will have on the company's cash reserves each month.

Interrelating the Cash Flows

Table 29-3 interrelates the two cash flow projections and isolates the resulting net effect on the Prudent Company's cash reserves. This identifies the specific months in which the company can expect a net increase or decrease in cash.

A $10,000 net increase in cash is projected in January. However, over the next three months, cash expenditures exceed anticipated cash collections by a cumulative total of $280,000. Alternatively, in the final two months of the forecast period, Prudent generates healthy cash surpluses. This follows naturally from the collection of receivables due from the seasonal peak in sales.

Table 29-3
Interrelating Cash Collections with Cash Expenditures
The Prudent Company
(in $1,000s)

	January	February	March	April	May	June
Projected Cash Collections	$200	$200	$235	$350	$455	$350
Projected Cash Expenditures	(190)	(235)	(370)	(460)	(280)	(190)
Net Effect on Cash Reserves	+10	(35)	(135)	(110)	+175	+160

Now we will use the information in Table 29-3 to project the company's need for external financing to offset the impending imbalance in its cash flow.

Filling the Gaps in the Cash Flow Budget

The final step in the cash flow budgeting process interrelates the Prudent Company's cash reserves with the monthly net inflow or outflow of cash. There is little cause for concern so long as the net cash outflow in any month doesn't indicate a drain of the company's cash reserves below some practical minimum. But if any monthly drain drops operating reserves below the minimum, the company must seek external financing to fill the gap. Or, alternatively, it can execute the positive management action necessary to avoid the gap by reducing the investment in receivables or inventory or by using some other cash flow action tool.

Note three additional facts about the company's circumstances:

1. Prudent will open the six month period with a $100,000 cash reserve.
2. It has a $300,000 revolving line of credit.
3. Company policy requires $100,000 in cash as the minimum operating balance necessary to begin any month.

Table 29-4 interrelates these facts with the previous projections to identify the potential gaps in Prudent's cash flow over the forecast period. The projection also specifies the extent to which Prudent must use its line of credit to satisfy its cash operating constraints.

Prudent has no cash flow problem projected in January. In fact, the net $10,000 gain enables the company to enter February with $110,000 in cash reserves. In February, however, Prudent feels the first effects of the seasonal increase in sales on its cash reserves. While the $35,000 net cash drain in that month doesn't create a problem, it does mean that the company must use $25,000 of its revolving line to satisfy its minimum cash operating constraint.

Table 29-4
Filling the Gaps in the Cash Flow Budget
The Prudent Company
(in $1,000s)

	January	February	March	April	May	June
Beginning Cash	$100	$110	$100	$100	$100	$100
Net Change	+10	(35)	(135)	(110)	+175	+160
Ending Cash (without borrowing)	110	75	(35)	(10)	275	260
Borrowing	—	25	135	110	(175)	(95)
Ending Cash	110	100	100	100	100	165
Cumulative Borrowing	—	25	160	270	95	—

The $135,000 net cash drain projected in March emphasizes the critical justification for the cash flow budgeting process. Failure to foresee that deficit in the absence of a cash flow budget would have left Prudent with a severe cash flow problem. Instead, Prudent will anticipate the problem and use an additional $135,000 of its credit line to maintain the $100,000 minimum operating balance.

Prudent borrows another $110,000 in April to reach a peak usage of its external financing of $270,000. The positive cash flow in the following two months of the projection enables the company to repay its debt and end June with a comfortable $165,000 in cash reserves. The importance of the cash flow budget rates recognition in:

Concept 67: **A cash flow budget is the single, indispensable tool for positive cash flow management.**

Although many businesses enjoy a more regular cash flow than is apparent in Prudent's seasonal business, the cash flow budget remains valid and, indeed, indispensable.

Cash Flow Action Tools

The Prudent Company fills the gap in its projected cash flow with the aid of external financing. This remains the obvious answer to any cash flow problem. However, the cash flow budget may serve as the signal to initiate other positive actions that will eliminate a problem without the aid of external financing. For example, you might fill the gap with the cash that flows from a reduction in your investment in accounts receivable. A more restrictive credit policy may generate cash that eliminates the need for external financing.

Similar logic applies to an investment in inventory. Item analysis may indicate that the business can achieve its projected volume with less inventory. Lowering that investment again frees funds that fill the gap in the cash flow budget.

In the extreme circumstance, the solution to a projected deficit cash flow might come from less desirable, although nonetheless necessary, management decisions. For example, a business might use trade credit as the source of external financing. This means that the business decides to defer payment to suppliers beyond their designated terms. This solves the cash flow problem, but it risks the business's credit rating.

Alternatively, the solution might come from a lower sales volume. In other words, the business might find that it can avoid a deficit cash flow only by lowering its expectations. Holding expansion in check often becomes a rational alternative to a cash flow problem. In any circumstance, whatever management actions you take, you must first identify the potential problem. This is the critical contribution that comes from the cash flow budget.

Cash Safety Stock

Since we have often drawn assumptions that set the minimum level of cash a business needs for normal operations, let's review a basic approach that helps identify that minimum level of operating cash.

From one perspective, you can view cash reserves as you view your investment in inventory. In other words, your cash reserves should be sufficient to meet daily cash expenditure. To that basic inventory, you should add some cash safety stock to absorb any unforeseen expenditure requirements. You might also carry an additional investment in cash sufficient to take advantage of profitable opportunities that require cash.

Here we focus on the method that determines the practical minimum cash balance necessary for normal operations including the appropriate safety stock. You identify that balance from a straightforward analysis of your own historical experience. You merely calculate your *average daily cash expenditures* over recent months. Then, recognizing the special characteristics of your business, you estimate the appropriate cash reserves as a specific number of days' average cash outflow.

For example, assume that your business made $180,000 in cash expenditures in each of the last three months. Using a thirty day month as the basis for analysis, your average daily outflow comes from the calculation:

$$\frac{\text{Average Daily}}{\text{Cash Expenditure}} = \frac{\text{Monthly Cash Expenditure}}{30} = \frac{\$180,000}{30} = \$6,000$$

The business expends an average of $6,000 in cash per day. However, unless you are certain that daily cash collections will equal or exceed daily cash expenditures, you must carry some cash safety stock—cash equivalent to several days' expenditures—to reduce the risk of not meeting all obligations on time.

You can identify that balance with another simple calculation. Relying on the example above, a business might determine that cash sufficient to meet six days' average expenditures is sufficient for normal operations. In that event, the minimum required balance is found as:

$$\frac{\text{Average Daily}}{\text{Expenditure}} \times \frac{\text{Days Cash}}{\text{Required}} = \frac{\text{Minimum Operating}}{\text{Balance}}$$

$$\$6,000 \quad \times \quad 6 \quad = \quad \$36,000$$

In this instance, whenever the balance drops below $36,000, the manager should use an action tool appropriate to regain that minimum level.

Unfortunately, the number of days' cash safety stock required varies with the circumstance. You must identify that number by considering (1) the predictability of cash inflows, (2) the flexibility of cash expenditures, and (3) the availability of external financing.

First, the certainty associated with your cash collections exerts a direct influence on the days of cash expenditures required for your reserves. The more certain the collection rate, the fewer days' expenditures that are required as a minimum balance. Alternatively, an erratic collection rate calls for a large cash reserve. Without the larger reserve, the business with unpredictable collections increases the risk of a cash flow problem—the inability to meet all obligations promptly.

The flexibility of projected cash expenditures also influences the size of a business's necessary cash reserves. If you can defer supplier payments without losing discounts or impairing future credit consideration, you can reduce your minimum operating balance. If you lack that flexibility, a larger minimum balance may be necessary to preserve your financial integrity.

Finally, the pivotal factor that affects the size of a minimum operating cash balance is a firm's immediate access to additional external financing. If you have immediate access to additional financing, you can absorb the risk normally associated with lower operating balances. In such instances, the failure to receive anticipated collections is offset easily with perhaps no more than a phone call that draws on a line of credit.

The business that lacks the ability to obtain an immediate cash advance from some external financing source must employ larger minimum cash balances. In any event, the prudent business manager recognizes the need to carry the appropriate safety stock to avoid an unforeseen disruption in his cash flow. Safety stock reduces the risk of a cash flow problem.

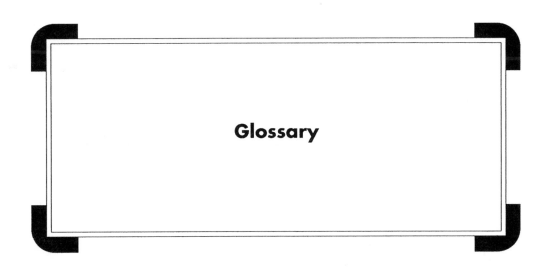

Glossary

Accounts Payable: Amounts due for purchases made on credit.

Accounts Receivable: A claim against a debtor for merchandise sold or services rendered in exchange for the customer's promise to pay.

Accounts Receivable Revolving Loan (ARRL): A unique borrowing method that employs the firm's accounts receivable as collateral for a continuous revolving loan arrangement.

Accounts Receivable Turnover: The net credit sales during a specific period divided by the average accounts receivable due from trade debtors; evaluates the quality of the accounts by relating the average total outstanding to the volume of credit sales.

Accrual Accounting: An accounting method that recognizes sales when made and expenses when incurred, regardless of when the cash transactions actually occur.

Acquisition Cost: The cost a business incurs from purchasing inventory, distinct from actual product costs, such as ordering costs.

Advance Rate: A percentage measure of the loan value relative to the accounting value of an asset pledged as collateral for credit consideration.

Aged Analysis of Accounts Receivable: A report showing how long accounts receivable have been outstanding; it identifies the receivables not past due and those past due by, for example, one month, two months.

Cash Flow Problem Solver

Annual Cash Flow: The total of a firm's net income plus depreciation; the total measures the net incremental cash generated by operations over the course of a year.

Asset Turnover: The ratio of total sales to total assets; a measure of the efficiency of asset utilization.

Average Collection Period: The average number of days each credit sales dollar remains outstanding; a qualitative indicator of the collectibility of a firm's accounts receivable.

Average Investment Period: The length of time each dollar remains in inventory before a sale converts it into cash or accounts receivable.

Average Payable Period: The average length of time a business employs each dollar of trade credit consideration.

Bad-Debt Write-Off: The loss incurred when an open account sale proves to be uncollectible.

Balance Sheet: A financial statement that indicates what the firm owns and how those assets are financed in the form of liabilities and ownership interest.

Break-Even Analysis: An analytic technique for studying the relationships among fixed costs, variable costs, and profits.

Break-Even Cash Flow: The level of operations where total cash expenses equal total cash revenue.

Break-Even Point: The volume of sales in a business where total costs equal total revenue.

Carrying Costs: Financial or operational expenses incurred from a firm's investment in assets.

Cash Accounting: An accounting method that recognizes sales and expenses only when the cash transactions actually occur.

Cash Capability: The total that comes from adding the firm's cash reserves to any available but unemployed credit consideration.

Cash Conversion Period: The time lapse between the customer's decision to purchase a product and the date the payment for the purchase becomes cash available for reinvestment.

Cash Flow Cycle: The natural flow of cash through the operations in a business: cash to inventory to accounts receivable to cash.

Cash Insurance: See Credit Insurance.

Collection Period: See Average Collection Period.

Common Stock: A document that represents ownership in a corporation.

Compensating Balance: A required minimum checking account balance that a firm must maintain as partial consideration for a loan from a commercial bank.

Component Management: The management effort that concentrates on control of the firm's investment in assets.

Contribution Margin: Excess of sales price over variable expenses; an important element in break-even analysis.

Cost of Goods Sold: The cost associated with units sold during a specific time period.

Credit Insurance: A unique form of insurance that indemnifies the firm for material losses because of accounts receivable that become uncollectible.

Credit Policy: The guidelines used in the decision process that approves or disapproves of an open account sale.

Current Ratio: Current assets divided by current liabilities; a measure of a firm's liquidity.

Days' Sales in Inventory: See Average Investment Period.

Debt/Equity Ratio: The ratio of the total debt to the total equity employed in a business.

Depreciation: A deduction of part of the cost of an asset from income in each year of the asset's useful life.

EBIT: Earnings before interest and taxes.

Economic Ordering Quantity (EOQ): The optimum (least cost) quantity of inventory that should be ordered.

Equity: See Stockholders' Equity.

Factoring: Selling accounts receivable to a finance company or bank.

FIFO Accounting: A system of writing off inventory into cost of goods sold; items purchased first are written off first; referred to as first in, first out.

Financial Structure: The firm's balance sheet.

Fixed Assets: Relatively permanent assets used in the operation of a business.

Cash Flow Problem Solver

Fixed Asset Turnover: The result obtained by dividing the firm's sales volume by its investment in fixed assets; a measure of the efficiency in employing those assets.

Fixed Costs: Operating costs that remain constant regardless of the firm's sales volume; an important element in break-even analysis.

Float: The amount of funds represented in checks that have been written but are still in process and have not yet been collected.

FYE: Fiscal year-end.

Gross Profit Margin: Total sales minus total cost of goods sold.

Growth Stock: That portion of the firm's investment in inventory designed to satisfy an anticipated increase in sales.

Income Statement: A financial statement that measures the profitability of the firm over a period of time; all expenses are subtracted from sales to arrive at net income.

Indemnification: The principle of insurance that compensates a policyholder for incurred losses.

Inventory: Goods, purchased or manufactured, held by a business for sale.

Inventory/Sales Ratio: The proportional relationship between a firm's investment in inventory and its monthly sales volume; a criterion for controlling the firm's investment in inventory.

Inventory Turnover Rate: The cost of goods sold for a period divided by the firm's average investment in inventory; a measure of inventory management efficiency.

Investment: The funds a business invests in accounts receivable, inventory, and fixed assets.

Invoice: A detailed list of goods shipped or services rendered, with an account of all charges due from the customer; the bill that evidences a sale.

Item Analysis: the technique that isolates the turnover rate associated with the specific items that make up the inventory in a business.

Leverage: The ratio between the total debt and the total assets employed in a business.

LIFO Accounting: A system of writing off inventory into cost of goods sold; items purchased last are written off first; referred to as last-in, first-out.

Line of Credit: An arrangement whereby a financial institution commits itself to lend up to a specified amount of funds during a specified period.

Liquidity: The ability of a business to meet obligations in a timely manner.

Nonnotification: Part of a lending arrangement whereby a business obtains a loan secured by accounts receivable; however, the lender does not notify debtors that receivables are pledged to secure the loan.

Notification: A procedure often employed when a borrower pledges accounts receivable to secure a loan; the lender advises the debtors that their promises to pay secure the credit consideration.

Open Account Sale: A sale made in exchange for the purchaser's promise to pay on a later date; however, no promissory note is involved.

Opportunity Costs: Earnings that might have been obtained if a productive asset, service, or capacity had been applied to some alternative use.

Overinvestment: Any cash committed to excess investment in accounts receivable, inventory, or fixed assets; or, extra assets unnecessary for the firm's level of operations.

Physical Count: The actual count of the items held in the firm's inventory.

Preferred Stock: A hybrid security combining some of the characteristics of both common stock and debt.

Purchase Order: The document or advice that enters an order for the purchase of merchandise or services.

Quantity Discounts: Price reductions obtained by purchasing goods in larger lots.

Receivable/Sales Ratio: The proportional relationship between a firm's investment in accounts receivable and its monthly sales volume; a criterion for controlling the firm's investment in accounts receivable.

Return on Assets (ROA): Earnings divided by average total assets; a profitability ratio.

Return on Investment (ROI): Earnings divided by average total assets; same as return on assets. A measure of the firm's operating efficiency.

Safety Stock: Inventory held by a firm in excess of anticipated requirements to protect against unforeseen shortages.

Sales/Fixed Assets Ratio: See Fixed Asset Turnover.

Selling Terms: The length of time a seller allows for payment of purchases made on credit; often includes discounts allowed for early payment.

Stockholders' Equity: The total of common stock and all retained earnings.

Stock-Out Cost: The opportunity cost that results from the inability to satisfy customer demand because of insufficient inventory; the firm loses the profit from a potential sale.

Straight Line Depreciation: A method of depreciation that takes the depreciable cost of an asset and divides it by its useful life to determine the annual depreciation expense; straight line depreciation creates a uniform expense every year an asset is depreciated.

Structural Management: The management perspective that seeks to maintain the proper balance among the elements that make up the financial structure in a business.

Tangible Net Worth: The book value of a business less any intangible assets; the value of the corporeal assets.

Trade Credit: Interbusiness debt that arises from credit sales; recorded as an account receivable by the seller and as an account payable by the buyer.

Trade Discount: A deduction in the list price of goods allowed by a seller in return for payment within a specified time; for example, 2% 10, net30 day terms allows a 2% discount from the list price if paid within ten days.

Variable Cost: A cost that is uniform per unit, but that fluctuates in total in direct proportion to changes in the related total activity or volume; an important element in break-even analysis.

Wire Transfer: Transfer of funds through the electronic network that unites the banking system.

About Sourcebooks Trade

In 1990, Sourcebooks Inc., started its trade division, Sourcebooks Trade. Our goal was to provide easy-to-understand, empowering how-to books for today's consumers. We began by developing practical business and finance books. Offering a wide range of expertise, we now also include titles in the areas of marketing, current affairs, self-help and reference designed to make consumers' lives easier. **Our Sourcebooks Trade Titles include:**

The Basics of Finance: Financial Tools for Non-Financial Managers
by Bryan E. Milling

Ideal for every businessperson without a financial background who now aspires to management responsibility. Written in readable language, *The Basics of Finance* offers tools to help non-financial managers master financial information including understanding annual reports, interacting with financial personnel and using financial analysis to better understand the business world. It features 31 fundamental principles of financial management clearly and concisely explained, and includes simplified case histories illustrating each principle.

The Basics of Finance is an essential desk companion for any manager with direct or indirect financial responsibility ... and a key tool for professionals aspiring to the corner office.

210 pages ISBN 0-942061-18-7 (paperback) $14.95
ISBN 0-942061-25-X (hardcover) $24.95

Cash Flow Problem Solver: Common Problems and Practical Solutions
by Bryan E. Milling

Thousands of business owners have discovered that the *Cash Flow Problem Solver: Common Problems and Practical Solutions* is a tool of surpassing value in the day-to-day management of a firm's cash flow. Now in its third edition, *Cash Flow Problem Solver* is a proven bestseller and has helped over 20,000 business owners **improve their cash flow and benefit from effective cash flow management.**

Cited as one of the three books on the "Smart CEO's Reading List" in INC Magazine. Selected as an alternate of both the **Business Week Book Club** and the **Fortune Book Club.** *Cash Flow Problem Solver: Common Problems and Practical Solutions* is a profits-oriented approach to cash flow management. In addition, *Cash Flow Problem Solver* **provides a results-oriented, step-by-step guide with tools and specific tactics to assure positive cash flow and to help boost a firm's profits.**

296 pages ISBN 0-942061-27-6 (paperback) $19.95
0-942061-28-4 (hardcover) $32.95

Creating Your Own Future: A Woman's Guide to Retirement Planning
by Judith A. Martindale, CFP and Mary J. Moses

Planning your future can be a wonderful and trying experience all at the same time. As authors, Judith Martindale and Mary Moses found, creating a simple, more relaxed and enjoyable retirement takes patience and hard work. "Critical decisions must be made well in advance to turn a dream into a comfortable reality," say Martindale and Moses.

The authors argue that although retirement planning is important to everyone, factors unique to women, such as, shorter work lives due to child rearing, longer life expectancy, differing health needs than men, among others, make appropriate preparations essential.

256 pages ISBN 0-942061-09-8 (paperback) $14.95
0-942061-08-X (hardcover) $28.95

Finding Time: Breathing Space For Women Who Do Too Much
by Paula Peisner

Finding Time: Breathing Space For Women Who Do Too Much is a terrific book for today's women who always seem to be doing more than they have time to do. Balancing careers, families, homes, and outside interests, women are feeling out of control and stressed.

This book is for all women who want to take control of their own time and make more of it. The book shows women how to identify and eliminate actions by themselves and others that rob them of their most precious asset... time.

"Comprehensive and insightful - easy tips to understand.
Taking even a few of these tips to heart should allow some breathing space."
— Sandra N. Bane, Partner, KPMG Peat Marwick.

"Provides a wonderful insight into a working woman's management of time.
A very practical primer. I found it very useful."
— Anita R. Gershman, President and CEO, World International Network

256 pages   ISBN 0-942061-33-0 (paperback) $7.95

Future Vision: The 189 Most Important Trends of the 1990s
From the Editors of Research Alert

"**. . . the ultimate guide to the new decade.**"—*American Demographics*

". . . a valuable tool and a bargain."—*Media Industry Newsletter*

". . . a stunningly complete summary."—*Executive Trend Watch*

". . . especially useful."—Robert Tuefel, President, Rodale Press

Future Vision gives substance to the dynamically changing forces that are reshaping the American marketplace. Its unique presentation of both the facts and the fictions presents readers with an evenhanded perspective of what will happen next. . . with enough detail for them to see the implications of their own work.

Presented in a usable, readable format, this guide examines key trends in areas including: Money, Media, Home, Leisure, Food, Environmentalism and the Workplace. No outdated trends or thinking. . . just the cutting-edge numbers drawn from hundreds of sources.

256 pages ISBN 0-942061-16-0 (paperback) $12.95
0-942061-17-9 (hardcover) $21.95

The Lifestyle Odyssey: The Facts Behind the Social, Personal and Cultural Changes Touching Each of Our Lives. . . From the Way We Eat Our Cookies to Our Desire for a Better World
by Eric Miller and the Editors of Research Alert

The Lifestyle Odyssey touches all social and cultural changes affecting our American lifestyle it takes us on a journey — a pathway describing a new American lifestyle. Beyond the obvious demographic shifts, American society is changing the way it chooses to live. The cumulative effect of those choices will give way to a "new" American lifestyle. All of us have experienced these changes to some extent. *The Lifestyle Odyssey* crystallizes the loose feelings that these changes have engendered in many Americans and outlines what else we may expect.

"Whatever your profession or personal investment program, somewhere in this remarkable new book lurks a fact or a trend that will change what you do. **If you have but one life to live, read this book**," says John Mack Carter, editor-in-chief of *Good Housekeeping* Magazine.

304 pages ISBN 0-942061-36-5 (paperback) $15.95
0-942061-31-4 (hardcover) $32.95

Outsmarting the Competition:
Practical Approaches to Finding and Using Competitive Information
by John J. McGonagle Jr. and Carolyn M. Vella

Competitive intelligence can help you understand where your product or your company stands with respect to your competition, and can give you some advance warning of the stirrings in your competitor's offices—without doing anything illegal or unethical. The first book to show both what information you need and how to get it.

". . . competitive intelligence is essential for any business. . . **Now you can develop this important business skill with the help of *Outsmarting the Competition*."**
— *Adweek's Marketing Week*

"Please measure your CI (Competitive Intelligence) index right now. You may be courting disaster." — *The Wall Street Journal*

"(John) McGonagle and (Carolyn) Vella. . . have written another excellent business book; this one will help any businessperson understand the marketplace and the competition."
— *Library Journal*

"**. . .provides sound advice on how to obtain inside knowledge.**" — *Entrepreneur*

"The book is so comprehensive that few marketing managers will be able to take advantage of all its suggestions." — *Business Marketing*

A must for any businessperson's library

388 pages ISBN 0-942061-06-3 (hardcover) $29.95
ISBN 0-942061-04-7 (paperback) $17.95

The Small Business Survival Guide: How To Manage Your Cash, Profits and Taxes
by Robert E. Fleury

The Small Business Survival Guide includes discussions on: planning for and filing taxes • cash flow analysis and management • understanding and developing financial statements • methods of taking and valuing inventory • how to value a business for buying and selling • managing your payroll & recordkeeping • PLUS...**NO-ENTRY ACCOUNTING...a means of doing and understanding your own accounting, without double-entry bookkeeping**

With two full case studies, lots of examples and forms, this book takes the mystery out of managing the financial side of a business.

> **"Innovative**, this book can help you gain control of your cash flow."
> —Jane Applegate, Syndicated Small Business Columnist, *Los Angeles Times*

256 pages ISBN 0-942061-11-X (hardcover) $29.95
ISBN 0-942061-12-8 (paperback) $17.95

Small Claims Court Without A Lawyer
by W. Kelsea Wilber, Attorney-at-Law

Small Claims Court Without A Lawyer is an invaluable guide to understanding the small claims system. It allows you to file a claim and get a judgement quickly and ecomomically, without an attorney's assistance or fee. Written in clear, uncomplicated language, this useful new book includes details about each state's small claims court system, so that wherever you live you can use it to successfully file a claim and see that claim through to a judgement.

> "An excellent primer for individuals or small businesses attempting to collect their own debts." — Arthur G. Sartorius, III, Attorney-at-Law.

> "The easy-to-read format is comprehensive but offers the basics necessary for the non-lawyer to proceed and succeed!" —Drew W. Prusiecki, Attorney-at-Law

224 pages   ISBN 0-942061-32-2 (paperback) $18.95

To order these books or any of our numerous other publications, **please contact your local bookseller,** or call Sourcebooks at 1-800-798-2475.

You can also obtain a copy of our catalog by writing or FAXing:
Sourcebooks Trade
A Div. of Sourcebooks, Inc.
P.O. Box 372
Naperville, IL 60566
(708) 961-2161
FAX: 708-961-2168

Thank you for your interest in our publications.